T0329950

A Research Agenda for the Social Impacts of Tourism

Elgar Research Agendas outline the future of research in a given area. Leading scholars are given the space to explore their subject in provocative ways, and map out the potential directions of travel. They are relevant but also visionary.

Forward-looking and innovative, Elgar Research Agendas are an essential resource for PhD students, scholars and anybody who wants to be at the forefront of research.

For a full list of Edward Elgar published titles, including the titles in this series, visit our website at www.e-elgar.com.

A Research Agenda for the Social Impacts of Tourism

Edited by

ROBIN NUNKOO

*Professor of Sustainable Tourism and Research Methods,
Department of Management, University of Mauritius, Mauritius*

THANIKA DEVI JUWAHEER

*Professor of Services Marketing, Department of Management,
University of Mauritius, Mauritius*

SIAMAK SEYFI

*Assistant Professor in Tourism Geography, Geography Research
Unit, University of Oulu, Finland*

Elgar Research Agendas

Edward Elgar
PUBLISHING

Cheltenham, UK • Northampton, MA, USA

Published by
Edward Elgar Publishing Limited
The Lypiatts
15 Lansdown Road
Cheltenham
Glos GL50 2JA
UK

Edward Elgar Publishing, Inc.
William Pratt House
9 Dewey Court
Northampton
Massachusetts 01060
USA

A catalogue record for this book
is available from the British Library

Library of Congress Control Number: 2024930581

This book is available electronically in the **Elgar**online
Geography, Planning and Tourism subject collection
http://dx.doi.org/10.4337/9781789908305

ISBN 978 1 78990 829 9 (cased)
ISBN 978 1 78990 830 5 (eBook)

Printed and bound in Great Britain by
TJ Books Limited, Padstow, Cornwall

Contents

Contributors

Zaheer Allam, Live+Smart Research Lab, School of Architecture and Built Environment, Deakin University, Australia.

Tim Coles, Department of Management, University of Exeter Business School, UK.

César Y. Cancán Estares, Universidad ESAN, Lima, Peru.

Galen Godbey, Moravian College in Bethlehem, Pennsylvania, USA.

Geoffrey Godbey, Penn State University, Department of Recreation Park and Tourism Management, USA.

Manuela Guerreiro, Research Centre for Tourism, Sustainability and Well-being (CinTurs) and Faculdade de Economia, Universidade do Algarve, Portugal.

Irene Huertas-Valdivia, University Rey Juan Carlos, Spain.

David S. Jones, Monash Indigenous Studies Centre, Monash University, Australia.

Thanika Devi Juwaheer, Department of Management, University of Mauritius, Mauritius.

Jeroen Klijs, Breda University of Applied Sciences, Breda, the Netherlands.

Hio Kuan Lai, Research Centre for Tourism, Sustainability and Well-being (CinTurs), Universidade do Algarve, Portugal.

Milene Lança, Research Centre for Tourism, Sustainability and Well-being (CinTurs) and Faculdade de Economia, Universidade do Algarve, Portugal.

João Filipe Marques, Research Centre for Tourism, Sustainability and Well-being (CinTurs) and Faculdade de Economia, Universidade do Algarve, Portugal.

Miguela M. Mena, Asian Institute of Tourism, Philippines.

Ondrej Mitas, Breda University of Applied Sciences, Breda, the Netherlands.

Jeroen Nawijn, Breda University of Applied Sciences, Breda, the Netherlands.

Marta G. Nel·lo-Andreu, Department of Geography, Rovira i Virgili University, Vila-seca, Spain.

Robin Nunkoo, Department of Management, University of Mauritius, Mauritius.

Luís Nobre Pereira, Research Centre for Tourism, Sustainability and Well-being (CinTurs) and Escola Superior de Gestão, Hotelaria e Turismo, Universidade do Algarve, Portugal.

Patrícia Pinto, Research Centre for Tourism, Sustainability and Well-being (CinTurs) and Faculdade de Economia, Universidade do Algarve, Portugal.

Célia Ramos, Research Centre for Tourism, Sustainability and Well-being (CinTurs) and Escola Superior de Gestão, Hotelaria e Turismo, Universidade do Algarve, Portugal.

Otto Regalado-Pezúa, ESAN Graduate School of Business, Lima, Peru.

Ana Renda, Centre for Tourism Research, Development and Innovation (CITUR) and Escola Superior de Gestão, Hotelaria e Turismo, Universidade do Algarve, Portugal.

Siamak Seyfi, Geography Research Unit, University of Oulu, Finland.

Gaunette Sinclair-Maragh, College of Business and Management, University of Technology, Jamaica.

Eirini Strataki, School of Business Department of Tourism, Economics and Management, University of the Aegean.

George Triantafyllou, Department of Sociology, School of Social Sciences, University of Crete.

Alba Viana-Lora, Department of Geography, Rovira i Virgili University, Vila-seca, Spain.

Maria Fe Villamejor-Mendoza, University of the Philippines, Philippines.

Thanakarn Bella Vongvisitsin, Lee Shau Kee School of Business and Administration, Hong Kong Metropolitan University, Hong Kong.

Antony King Fung Wong, School of Hotel and Tourism Management, The Hong Kong Polytechnic University, Hong Kong.

About the editors

Robin Nunkoo is a Professor of Sustainable Tourism and Research Methods at the University of Mauritius; a Senior Research Fellow at the University of Johannesburg; an Adjunct Professor at Griffith University; a Visiting Researcher at the Copenhagen Business School; and an Eminent Scholar at Kyung Hee University, South Korea. He holds a PhD (Political Economy) from the University of Waterloo, Canada. He is the Managing Editor for *Journal of Hospitality Marketing & Management* and an editorial board member of several leading journals. Robin is recognized as a highly cited researcher by Clarivate and has published in several leading journals.

Thanika Devi Juwaheer, PhD, is a Professor of Services Management and Marketing at the University of Mauritius and currently serves as Adjunct Professor at the Okavango Research Institute of the University of Botswana. Dr Juwaheer has extensive teaching, industrial and consulting experience in the marketing, hospitality and tourism fields. She has published various articles in reputed academic journals, conference proceedings and trade journals in the field of tourism and hospitality management and on the impact of green marketing, customer relationship management and the environmental management strategies of hotels and other companies of Mauritius. Dr Juwaheer serves on the editorial board of several international refereed academic journals. Her research interests include ecotourism, rural tourism, service quality, customer satisfaction, Digital Marketing and eCRM and health care management.

Siamak Seyfi is an Assistant Professor at the Geography Research Unit of the University of Oulu, Finland. He is also an Adjunct Professor at the Department of Tourism Marketing of the University of Eastern Finland, and a Visiting Associate Professor at the School of Hospitality, Tourism and Events, Taylor's University, Malaysia. Using a multi-/interdisciplinary approach and informed by diverse disciplinary perspectives, his research focuses on tourism mobilities, tourist behavior, resilience, sustainability and politics of tourism and peace through tourism. Siamak has published in leading tourism journals and serves on the editorial boards of several leading journals in the field of tourism.

Acknowledgements

The editors would like to gratefully thank our authors who participated in this book project, overcoming the challenges posed by the COVID-19 pandemic. Their dedication and commitment to delivering their contributions despite these difficulties have played a pivotal role in the successful completion of this book. The editors would also like to extend special appreciation to Stephanie and Katy and the entire team at Edward Elgar for continuing to support this project despite the stresses of the last few years.

1 Rethinking research on social impacts of tourism

Siamak Seyfi, Robin Nunkoo and Thanika Devi Juwaheer

1 Background

Tourism is a global phenomenon that has experienced tremendous growth and transformation over the decades. The number of international tourist arrivals has been on a consistent upward trajectory, with projections estimating a significant increase to 1.8 billion international tourists by 2030 (UNWTO, 2020). However, this prediction may need to be re-evaluated in the light of the ongoing COVID-19 pandemic. The pandemic has had a profound and negative impact on the tourism industry worldwide. The disruptions caused by the pandemic have resulted in significant declines in international tourist arrivals, as well as disruptions to domestic tourism. Travel restrictions, lockdown measures, and concerns about health and safety have led to a sharp decline in tourism activities (Gössling et al., 2020; Seyfi et al., 2022, 2023). While international tourism often garners the most attention, the majority of tourism activities actually take place domestically, accounting for nearly 85 percent of global travel (Hall, 2015). People traveling within their own countries for leisure, business, or other purposes make up a substantial portion of the tourism industry. Prior to the pandemic, the annual number of tourist trips exceeded the global population, underscoring the immense scale and impact of the tourism industry. It has become a significant contributor to the global economy, generating substantial revenue and employment opportunities. In 2022, for instance, the tourism sector contributed approximately 7.6 percent of the world's GDP, amounting to an estimated US$8.6 trillion (WTTC, 2023).

Due to its significant economic importance and sustained growth, the impacts of tourism at various levels have been extensively examined in academic research (e.g., Mathieson & Wall, 1982; Pizam & Milman, 1986; King et al., 1993; Archer & Cooper, 1998; Easterling, 2005; Nunkoo & Ramkissoon, 2007, 2011; Deery et al., 2012; Sharpley, 2014; Gursoy & Nunkoo, 2019; Gursoy et al., 2019; Woosnam & Ribeiro, 2023; Ramkissoon, 2023). This stream of research has been prompted by the recognition that tourism can exert both positive and negative effects on the social, cultural, economic, and environmental aspects of a destination. Tourism holds the potential to significantly contribute to the economic development of a country or region through the creation of income and employment opportunities. This not only stimulates the local economy but also yields positive effects on the environment, culture, and heritage of the visited destination. By supporting local businesses and promoting cultural and natural preservation, tourism can help diversify the local economy and support sustainable development of a tourism destination. However, tourism development can also have adverse effects on local communities. Despite potential economic benefits, the influx of tourists can disrupt local customs and social dynamics, leading to overcrowding, congestion, and a loss of privacy. Additionally, the exploitation of local labor within the tourism industry, characterized by low wages and poor working conditions, can exacerbate social inequalities and negatively impact the local community (Pizam & Milman, 1986; Gursoy & Nunkoo, 2019; Gursoy et al., 2019).

While most of the early studies of the impacts of tourism primarily focused upon the economic aspects of tourism, it is imperative to recognize and comprehend the social impacts of tourism. This is because tourism, at its core, is a "social phenomenon" that revolves around interactions between tourists and local residents. These interactions can deeply influence the social fabric of the host community, shaping the way individuals engage with one another and their sense of identity and culture (Gursoy & Nunkoo, 2019; Gursoy et al., 2019). Hence, understanding the social impacts of tourism is vital to ensure that tourism is managed in a way that maximizes the positive outcomes and mitigates any adverse consequences for the local community.

Against this backdrop, this introductory chapter aims to offer an initial glimpse into the realm of social impacts research in tourism. It encompasses an exploration of the theoretical foundations that have shaped this field, an examination of the methodological approaches that have been employed in previous studies, and an overview of the contemporary and future aspects of social impacts research. Furthermore, the chapter outlines key interconnected issues that are pertinent to tourism social impacts research, drawing links to the respective chapters in the book. These issues and their respective implications for the tourism industry will set the context for the book. The chapter ends with a brief overview of the organization of the book.

2 The theoretical and methodological evolution of research into the social impacts of tourism

The significance of studying the social impacts of tourism is widely acknowledged among academics, industry practitioners, NGOs and government tourism agencies. It is important to understand how local individuals and communities perceive the benefits and drawbacks of tourism, as failure to strike a balance could lead to negative reactions towards tourists and the tourism industry as a whole (Gursoy et al., 2019). Although there has been a wide array of reviews on the social impacts of tourism (e.g., Harrill, 2004; Easterling, 2005; García et al., 2015; Sharpley, 2014; Gursoy et al., 2019; Rasoolimanesh & Seyfi, 2021; Woosnam & Ribeiro, 2023; see also Chapters 2 and 3 in this book), as noted by Deery et al. (2012, p. 65), research on the social impacts of tourism "appears to be in a state of 'arrested development' – in other words, there is a sense that the advances in understanding the impacts of tourists on host communities is incremental at best or potentially circular".

The evolution of social impact research in tourism can be delineated into five key stages, each characterized by distinct attributes and research focuses. In their comprehensive analysis of research on social impacts of tourism, Deery et al. (2012) proposed a classification comprising four primary stages. In the initial stage, studies were primarily exploratory and descriptive, and focused on defining concepts and typologies (e.g., Mathieson & Wall, 1982; Liu et al., 1987; Pizam & Milman, 1986). These studies laid the groundwork for understanding the intricate social dynamics between tourists and local communities.

The second stage of research was characterized by the development of theoretical models and focused on constructing frameworks to analyze social impacts. Notable models, such as Doxey's Irridex Model (1975) and Butler's Life Cycle Model (1980), emerged during this period and have since been widely utilized in social impact research. The emergence of case study-based empirical research during this stage further contributed to identifying the diverse perspectives of residents towards tourism development.

The third and fourth stages of social impact research in tourism were dedicated to the design, development, testing, and refinement of measures to assess residents' attitudes. These stages also witnessed an increased emphasis on sustainability and the application of theoretical frameworks such as social exchange theory. More recently, Woosnam and Ribeiro (2023) proposed the existence of a fifth phase in the study of social impacts of tourism. This new phase reflects the ongoing evolution of research in this field and is characterized by a focus on developing and testing theoretical models using advanced quantitative methods (e.g., structural equation modeling and other statistical analyses). In this phase, social impacts of tourism are often examined as antecedents of outcome variables, such as emotional solidarity, receptiveness towards tourists during the COVID-19 pandemic, and pro-tourism behavioral support (Woosnam & Ribeiro, 2023). The introduction of this fifth phase highlights the continued refinement and advancement of social impact research in tourism.

The study of social impacts in tourism has undergone significant evolution, with the development of new theories and methodologies aimed at better understanding the intricate relationships between tourists and host communities. However, despite these advancements, there has been a dominant presence of a positivist paradigm in research on the social impacts of tourism, as highlighted by Deery et al. (2012) and echoed by other researchers such as Hadinejad et al. (2019), Rasoolimanesh and Seyfi (2021), and Woosnam and Ribeiro (2023). The positivist approach, while valuable in many aspects, has its limitations in providing a comprehensive understanding of social impacts of tourism. Often, research has focused on generating lists of impacts without delving into the underlying processes that shape perceptions or exploring potential ways to alter such perceptions if necessary (Deery et al., 2012). This realization emphasizes the importance of tracing the evolution of research on social impacts of tourism over the past few decades.

By examining the historical trajectory of this research, we can identify the gaps and limitations of previous approaches, paving the way for more holistic and nuanced investigations. Exploring alternative paradigms and methodologies can offer fresh perspectives and shed light on the complex dynamics involved in tourism social impacts. This deeper understanding is crucial for designing effective strategies to mitigate negative impacts, enhance positive outcomes, and promote sustainable tourism practices that benefit both host communities and tourists.

2.1   Past perspectives

While extensive research has been conducted on the environmental and economic impacts of tourism, the conceptual and empirical aspects of social impacts have not received as much attention. As noted earlier, social impact research is essential because the support of host communities is considered to be a critical factor in ensuring a sustainable tourism industry (Harrill, 2004; Saarinen & Rogerson, 2014; Higgins-Desbiolles, 2006; Higgins-Desbiolles & Bigby, 2023). However, the current global context, exacerbated by the COVID-19 pandemic and global issues of justice, war, and climate change, has shifted the focus of tourism studies from solely economic gains to other impacts such as social-cultural, environmental, and political impacts (Woosnam & Ribeiro, 2023). This broadened perspective recognizes that tourism's influence extends beyond financial considerations and acknowledges the importance of understanding and managing the multifaceted impacts on communities and society as a whole.

Most social impact studies have primarily focused on understanding the attitudes and perceptions of resident/host communities towards the impacts of tourism development. This approach has been commonly used throughout social impact research, particularly in the early stages of establishing definitions and key terms such as "host residents," "social impacts," "perceptions," and "attitudes" to lay the groundwork for research (Deery et al., 2012; Rasoolimanesh & Seyfi, 2021).

The perceptions of local residents towards the social impacts of tourism are a key aspect of tourism research. This is because residents have a significant impact on the tourism experience, as they are directly affected by the presence of tourists in their communities. The study of residents' perceptions of the social impacts of tourism is important for promoting sustainable tourism practices that benefit both visitors and local communities, and for creating positive relationships between residents and tourists in tourism destinations.

Research on residents' perceptions of the sociocultural impacts of tourism has shown mixed results. While some studies indicate that residents perceive negative sociocultural impacts (Andereck et al., 2005; Mody et al., 2023), others highlight the diverse benefits they associate with tourism (Sirakaya et al., 2002). Positive attitudes towards sociocultural impacts are often associated with support for tourism; other studies indicate that tourism can bring both benefits and social costs to host communities. Overall, the impact of tourism on sociocultural aspects is context-dependent and varies based on the specific circumstances of tourism development. Research on the antecedents of residents' perceptions of social impacts of tourism is often accompanied by studies on their consequences. Many studies have investigated the impact of residents' attitudes and perceptions on various factors such as their support for tourism development, satisfaction with tourism, participation in tourism activities, and overall quality of life.

Since the 1970s, extensive research has been conducted on resident attitudes towards tourism development. Numerous studies have attempted to identify the factors that can influence residents' perceptions of tourism impacts. Rasoolimanesh and Seyfi (2021) classified the factors that influence residents' perception of social impacts of tourism into two main categories: intrinsic and extrinsic factors. Intrinsic factors encompass variables such as economic and employment dependence on tourism, community attachment, spatial factors, host–guest interactions, personal values, environmental awareness, and demographic variables (e.g., age, gender, and education). Extrinsic factors, on the other hand, include the level and type of tourism development, the tourist market, the seasonality of tourism, and the national stage of development. In a similar vein, Woosnam and Ribeiro (2023) classified predictors of residents' perceptions of social impacts of tourism into three categories: internal, interactive, and external variables. Internal variables are unique to the residents and often assessed through psychological and socio-demographic measures (e.g., community attachment, economic dependence, empowerment, knowledge of tourism, perceived benefits and costs of tourism, personal values, place attachment, socio-demographics, and trust). Interactive variables involve relationship aspects with tourists (e.g., emotional solidarity, degree of interaction, and social distance). External variables are specific to the destination and include measures such as the density of tourists and tourism development, destination stage of tourism development, distance from the tourism zone, nature and type of tourists and tourism, and seasonality.

From theoretical perspectives, theories originating from sociology, psychology, and anthropology have been applied to study residents' perceptions and attitudes towards social impacts of tourism. These include social exchange theory (SET), social representation theory, stakeholder theory, growth machine theory, community attachment theory, emotional solidarity, and Weber's theory of substantial and formal rationality, among others. While SET has been the most commonly used theory (Sharpley, 2014; Rasoolimanesh & Seyfi, 2021), it has been criticized for its limitations in conceptualizing and operationalizing the effects of antecedents on residents' perceptions and attitudes towards tourism development. Recent studies have attempted to address these limitations by combining SET with other theories such as Weber's theory (Andereck et al., 2005; Boley et al., 2014), or revising the framework of SET (Rasoolimanesh et al., 2015). Despite some progress in the application of theoretical frameworks, research on the social impacts of tourism is still largely hindered by a lack of development and testing of theoretical models which was highlighted by the review of research on social impacts of tourism (e.g., Nunkoo & Gursoy, 2012; Nunkoo et al., 2013; Gursoy & Nunkoo, 2019; Hadinejad et al., 2019; Rasoolimanesh & Seyfi, 2021; Woosnam and Ribeiro, 2023).

From a methodological perspective, studies have primarily used quantitative methods to examine residents' perceptions and attitudes towards the social impacts of tourism, resulting in a dearth of literature on qualitative and mixed-methods research. This gap in the literature has been highlighted by scholars who suggest that mixed-methods research can provide a more comprehensive understanding of residents' attitudes by combining subjective and objective analyses (Hadinejad et al., 2019; Rasoolimanesh & Seyfi, 2021; Woosnam & Ribeiro, 2023). Moreover, the majority of quantitative studies have tended to measure economic, sociocultural, and environmental perceptions as distinct concepts or by combining them into positive and negative perceptions. This has resulted in a limited understanding of how these perceptions interact to influence residents' attitudes towards tourism development (Rasoolimanesh & Seyfi, 2021). Therefore, there is a need for more diversified research methods to provide a comprehensive understanding of residents' perceptions towards tourism development.

3   A new research agenda: rethinking the theoretical and methodological foundations of research on the social impacts of tourism

Among the first issues that should be addressed in future research is the adoption of rigorous theoretical foundations to provide thorough understandings of social impacts of tourism development on destination communities. Previous studies on residents' attitudes and perception of social impacts of tourism have revealed the limitations of the current dominant theory, SET, in the literature on residents' perceptions. Emerging issues such as over-tourism and rapid technological advancements have highlighted the need for new theories and frameworks. As most of the dominant theories in this field come from other disciplines, advancements in this area would influence future research directions on residents' attitudes. For instance, within the field of psychology, sub-fields like social and cognitive psychology have potential for new research streams (Rasoolimanesh & Seyfi, 2021). Additionally, research on alternative theoretical perspectives at different stages in the tourism development cycle would also be beneficial. Future research should focus on developing integrated models based on the possible integration of extant theories.

Additionally, social impacts of tourism research should concentrate on addressing the United Nations' Sustainable Development Goals (SDGs), such as reducing poverty, promoting good health, ensuring sustainable urbanization, encouraging responsible consumption and production, and combating climate change. The COVID-19 pandemic has emphasized the importance of these goals, and researchers should undertake studies that can aid in achieving them. The outcomes of such research can lead to the development of sustainable tourism businesses, enhance the wellbeing of disadvantaged individuals and communities, and preserve the environment and cultural heritage.

From a methodological viewpoint, the lack of agreement on how to measure residents' positive and negative perceptions of tourism's social impacts is a major obstacle to comparing and generalizing results across contexts (Rasoolimanesh & Seyfi, 2021; Woosnam & Ribeiro, 2023). To address this, future studies in the quantitative research stream need to establish a consensus on the indicators to measure residents' perceptions and the nature of these indicators. It is also advisable to explore the possibility of measuring residents' perception and attitude as a multidimensional formative construct rather than a reflective one. Moreover, future studies should identify new antecedents and outcomes of residents' perceptions towards tourism development, particularly in the era of technology (Nunkoo et al., 2023), climate change (Van Riper et al., 2013), social inequality and social justice (Higgins-Desbiolles & Bigby, 2023), and over-tourism and peer-to-peer accommodations (Yeager et al., 2023; see also Chapter 9 in this book), taking into account the dissatisfaction and irritation of local residents with tourism impacts in overcrowded destinations alongside over-tourism factors (Hadinejad et al., 2019; Woosnam & Ribeiro, 2023). Moreover, it is anticipated that innovative methods, similar to those used to explore tourists' perceptions and emotions, that enable real-time measurement of residents' perceptions and emotions will become increasingly popular in future which could provide a new approach to studying this popular topic. To provide a more profound comprehension of residents' perceptions and attitudes, qualitative approaches such as ethnography, phenomenology, focus groups, participant observation, and longitudinal studies could be employed, while mixed-methods research can establish new or confirm existing items and dimensions for measuring residents' perceptions. This aligns with Deery et al.'s (2012) perspective that an overemphasis on quantitative methods could restrict a thorough understanding of tourism's effects on both the local community and visitors. Thus, new qualitative approaches offer more comprehensive insights into the "layers" of social impact perceptions. Moreover, a recent call for measuring actual behavior through incorporating experimental or quasi-experimental research methods (Viglia & Dolnicar, 2020; Demeter et al., 2023) could be a promising approach for measuring the behavior of local communities regarding tourism impacts and support for tourism. This methodological approach can provide a more accurate representation of local attitudes and behaviors towards tourism, rather than relying solely on self-reported surveys. This approach could further enhance the methodological underpinnings of social impacts of tourism research and help to generate more robust findings.

4   Conclusion

Tourism can significantly influence the sociocultural fabric of a destination by impacting the customs, social life, habits, beliefs, and values of local residents. While tourism brings forth new opportunities, it can also generate pressure and overcrowding, which can potentially erode the cultural identity and social reality of communities. Therefore, it is essential to evaluate tourism's impacts beyond economic assessments, given its ubiquitous presence in daily life (Stoffelen & Ioannides, 2022) and take into account interdisciplinary perspectives and critical theories such as post-structuralism and feminist perspectives. These perspectives can help analyze power relations, inequality, social justice, ethics, and social sustainability in tourism contexts. Applying these perspectives helps unravel the complex social dynamics at play and sheds light on the potential consequences of tourism. Future research should continue to foster interdisciplinary collaboration, encouraging the exchange of ideas, methodologies, and best practices across disciplines, to capture the full complexity of social impacts of tourism and develop comprehensive strategies for their management.

The significance of examining social impacts of tourism becomes even more apparent in light of the COVID-19 pandemic. The crisis has profoundly affected the well-being and quality of life of residents in tourism destinations (see Chapters 11 and 12 of this book). In light of this crisis, it has become evident that resilience and coping strategies within host communities are crucial for effectively managing such situations and mitigating negative social impacts. Empowering local communities becomes imperative as they play a vital role in managing the crisis and its aftermath.

To attain a comprehensive and context-specific understanding of how tourism influences societies, it is essential to rethink the research on the social impacts of tourism. This rethinking should consider various dimensions of social impacts, such as economic, cultural, environmental, and psychological aspects. By doing so, research can contribute to the development of comprehensive strategies and policies that aim to promote sustainable tourism practices, minimize negative impacts, protect local cultures and the environment, and enhance the overall well-being and quality of life for both host communities and the broader society. Additionally, there is a need to focus on global issues and align tourism research with the SDGs. The SDGs provide a framework for addressing global challenges, including poverty alleviation, sustainable development, and environmental protection (see also Chapter 14 of this book).

In conclusion, the social impacts of tourism are a vital area of research with wide-ranging implications for local communities, cultures, and societies. By understanding these impacts and identifying effective strategies for managing them, we can foster sustainable tourism practices that benefit both visitors and host communities. In doing so, we lay the foundation for a future wherein tourism contributes positively to the social fabric of destinations while preserving their unique cultural heritage and fostering inclusive development.

Our collective hope is that the knowledge shared within the chapters of this book serves as a catalyst for a transformative shift – an awakening that propels tourism to become a powerful force for positive change and sustainable growth in destinations across the globe.

5   Outline of the book

Chapter 1 reviews social impacts of tourism, outlines its major stages of development, and presents past and future perspectives on its theoretical and methodological advancements. The chapter concludes by discussing the key issues in relation to research on social impacts of tourism in the context of pressing global issues such as the COVID-19 pandemic, SDGs, over-tourism, social justice, technological advancements and climate change. Chapter 2 presents a bibliometric analysis of the research on the social impact of tourism and sustainable tourism. Based on the findings of the bibliometric analysis, the chapter suggests several directions for future research on this topic. Similarly, Chapter 3 presents a bibliometric analysis of the research on residents' attitudes towards the impacts of tourism, which is one of the widely researched areas in the social impacts of tourism. The analysis focuses on papers published in journals indexed in Web of Science (WOS) and provides insights into the trends, patterns, and gaps in this area of research. Chapter 4 provides an overview of the existing literature on social impact assessment (SIA) in the context of tourism, using three evaluation tools: the Research Excellence Framework (REF), the Engagement and Impact Assessment (EIA), and the Social Impact Open Repository (SIOR). The chapter outlines an agenda for the theoretical and practical applications of SIA as an indicator in the field of tourism.

Chapter 5 highlights the need for the development of social life-cycle assessment (S-LCA) in the field of tourism. The chapter focuses on the application of this tool for supporting more socially sustainable solutions in tourism businesses. Chapter 6 examines citizenship as a lens through which to view the social impact of tourism. The chapter selectively examines some of the central ideas underpinning the concept of citizenship and discusses its relevance to travel and tourism. It also explores the current and future research agenda on citizenship and tourism, particularly in the context of COVID-19 and the UK's experiences and contexts. By discussing well-established theories related to attitudes towards tourism and tourism development and connecting these to more recent empirical work on the management of impacts of tourism, Chapter 7 identifies possible synergies between the right to travel and the right to live from the perspectives of both local residents and visitors/tourists by proposing two related pathways that address the interaction between these two groups. The chapter concludes by offering implications for implementing these pathways in destination management and marketing practices.

Chapter 8 delivers a breakthrough in existing community-based tourism (CBT) knowledge by extending the potential of the concept to other types of communities, including urban communities in Bangkok Metropolis and LGBTQ+ communities in Hong Kong. The chapter proposes CBT as a universal approach by illustrating how both cases applied the concept to enhance community participation and inclusiveness in tourism development. Chapter 9 focuses on residents' sociocultural perceptions of tourism in Algarve, Portugal and explores how the existence or ownership of local lodging influences the residents' attitudes, perceptions, and behaviors towards tourism. Chapter 10 presents an overview of the current understanding of governance for sustainable tourism and explores the difficulties faced by Maribojoc, a small municipality in the Philippines, in creating a roadmap for local tourism planning and development after experiencing a catastrophic earthquake in 2013 and subsequent political elections in 2016. The chapter delves into the challenges encountered by the local government in implementing sustainable tourism practices while balancing the needs of the community and the industry.

Chapters 11, 12, and 13 center on the COVID-19 pandemic and its impact on tourism. Chapter 11 discusses the social implications of COVID-19 on the tourism industry. Specifically, the chapter examines three areas of social impact: the heightened vulnerability of women working in tourism, the increased marginalization of rural tourism communities, and the unique psychosocial challenges faced by tourism stakeholders. The chapter concludes by providing recommendations regarding the social adaptation theory as a means of mitigating and driving subsequent changes. Chapter 12 examines the perceptions of residents in the 16 municipalities of the Algarve region in Portugal regarding the sociocultural impacts of tourism. The chapter compares the perception of residents before and during the COVID-19 pandemic. Chapter 13 examines the negative consequences of promoting tourism based on colonial historical narratives and ignoring the unique cultures and legacies of Indigenous peoples and "transported" peoples. In this regard, the chapter provides recommendations that focus on the classification of culture as an evolving and dynamic feature of nature. Chapter 14 offers a theoretical discussion regarding the concept of a "new tourism paradigm." This concept is being explored in light of the significant environmental and health-related changes that are currently affecting the tourism industry. The chapter delves into a prospective analysis of how the industry can adapt to these changes and evolve into a new paradigm that is more sustainable and resilient.

References

Andereck, K. L., Valentine, K. M., Knopf, R. C., & Vogt, C. A. (2005). Residents' perceptions of community tourism impacts. *Annals of Tourism Research, 32*(4), 1056–1076.

Archer, B., & Cooper, C. (1998). The positive and negative impacts of tourism. In W. F. Theobald (Ed.), *Global Tourism* (pp. 63–81). Oxford: Butterworth-Heinemann.

Boley, B. B., McGehee, N. G., Perdue, R. R., & Long, P. (2014). Empowerment and resident attitudes toward tourism: Strengthening the theoretical foundation through a Weberian lens. *Annals of Tourism Research, 49*, 33–50.

Butler, R. (1980). The concept of the tourist area cycle of evolution: Implications for the management of resources. *Canadian Geographer, 24*, 5–12.

Deery, M., Jago, L., & Fredline, L. (2012). Rethinking social impacts of tourism research: A new research agenda. *Tourism Management, 33*(1), 64–73.

Demeter, C., Fechner, D., & Dolnicar, S. (2023). Progress in field experimentation for environmentally sustainable tourism: A knowledge map and research agenda. *Tourism Management, 94*, 104633.

Doxey, G. (1975). A causation theory of visitor–resident irritants: Methodology and research inferences. *Proceedings of the Sixth Annual Conference of the Travel and Tourism Research Association* (pp. 195–198). San Diego: The Travel Research Association.

Easterling, D. S. (2005). The residents' perspective in tourism research: A review and synthesis. *Journal of Travel & Tourism Marketing, 17*(4), 45–62.

García, F. A., Vázquez, A. B., & Macías, R. C. (2015). Resident's attitudes towards the impacts of tourism. *Tourism Management Perspectives, 13*, 33–40.

Gössling, S., Scott, D., & Hall, C. M. (2020). Pandemics, tourism and global change: A rapid assessment of COVID-19. *Journal of Sustainable Tourism, 29*(1), 1–20.

Gursoy, D., & Nunkoo, R. (Eds.). (2019). *The Routledge Handbook of Tourism Impacts: Theoretical and Applied Perspectives.* Abingdon: Routledge.

Gursoy, D., Ouyang, Z., Nunkoo, R., & Wei, W. (2019). Residents' impact perceptions of and attitudes towards tourism development: A meta-analysis. *Journal of Hospitality Marketing & Management, 28*(3), 306–333.

Hadinejad, A., Moyle, B. D., Scott, N., Kralj, A., & Nunkoo, R. (2019). Residents' attitudes to tourism: A review. *Tourism Review, 74*(2), 150–165.

Hall, C. M. (2015). On the mobility of tourism mobilities. *Current Issues in Tourism, 18*(1), 7–10.

Harrill, R. (2004). Residents' attitudes toward tourism development: A literature review with implications for tourism planning. *Journal of Planning Literature, 18*(3), 251–266.

Higgins-Desbiolles, F. (2006). More than an "industry": The forgotten power of tourism as a social force. *Tourism Management, 27*(6), 1192–1208.

Higgins-Desbiolles, F., & Bigby, B. C. (Eds.). (2023). *The Local Turn in Tourism: Empowering Communities.* Bristol: Multilingual Matters.

King, B., Pizam, A., & Milman, A. (1993). Social impacts of tourism: Host perceptions. *Annals of Tourism Research, 20*(4), 650–665.

Liu, J. C., Sheldon, P. J., & Var, T. (1987). Resident perception of the environmental impacts of tourism. *Annals of Tourism Research, 14*, 17–37.

Mathieson, A., & Wall, G. (1982). *Tourism: Economic, Physical and Social Impacts.* Harlow: Longman.

Mody, M., Woosnam, K. M., Suess, C., & Dogru, T. (2023). Hapless victims or empowered citizens? Understanding residents' attitudes towards Airbnb using Weber's Theory of Rationality and Foucauldian concepts. *Journal of Sustainable Tourism, 31*(2), 284–306.

Nunkoo, R., & Gursoy, D. (2012). Residents' support for tourism: An identity perspective. *Annals of Tourism Research, 39*(1), 243–268.

Nunkoo, R., Gursoy, D., & Dwivedi, Y. K. (2023). Effects of social media on residents' attitudes to tourism: Conceptual framework and research propositions. *Journal of Sustainable Tourism, 31*(2), 350–366.

Nunkoo, R., & Ramkissoon, H. (2007). Residents' perceptions of the socio-cultural impact of tourism in Mauritius. *Anatolia, 18*(1), 138–145.

Nunkoo, R., & Ramkissoon, H. (2011). Residents' satisfaction with community attributes and support for tourism. *Journal of Hospitality & Tourism Research, 35*(2), 171–190.

Nunkoo, R., Smith, S. L., & Ramkissoon, H. (2013). Residents' attitudes to tourism: A longitudinal study of 140 articles from 1984 to 2010. *Journal of Sustainable Tourism, 21*(1), 5–25.

Pizam, A., & Milman, A. (1986). The social impacts of tourism. *Tourism Recreation Research, 11*(1), 29–33.

Ramkissoon, H. (2023). Perceived social impacts of tourism and quality-of-life: A new conceptual model. *Journal of Sustainable Tourism, 31*(2), 442–459.

Rasoolimanesh, S. M., Jaafar, M., Kock, N., & Ramayah, T. (2015). A revised framework of social exchange theory to investigate the factors influencing residents' perceptions. *Tourism Management Perspectives, 16*, 335–345.

Rasoolimanesh, S. M., & Seyfi, S. (2021). Residents' perceptions and attitudes towards tourism development: A perspective article. *Tourism Review, 76*(1), 51–57.

Saarinen, J., & Rogerson, C. M. (2014). Tourism and the millennium development goals: Perspectives beyond 2015. *Tourism Geographies, 16*(1), 23–30.

Seyfi, S., Hall, C. M., & Saarinen, J. (2022). Rethinking sustainable substitution between domestic and international tourism: A policy thought experiment. *Journal of Policy Research in Tourism, Leisure and Events.* https://doi.org/10.1080/19407963.2022.2100410.

Seyfi, S., Hall, C. M., & Shabani, B. (2023). COVID-19 and international travel restrictions: The geopolitics of health and tourism. *Tourism Geographies, 25*(1), 357–373.

Sharpley, R. (2014). Host perceptions of tourism: A review of the research. *Tourism Management, 42*, 37–49.

Sirakaya, E., Teye, V., & Sonmez, S. (2002). Understanding residents' support for tourism development in the central region of Ghana. *Journal of Travel Research, 41*, 57–67.

Stoffelen, A., & Ioannides, D. (2022). Introduction to the Handbook of Tourism Impacts: Social and environmental perspectives. In A. Stoffelen & D. Ioannides (Eds.), *Handbook of Tourism Impacts: Social and Environmental Perspectives* (pp. 2–19). Cheltenham, UK and Northampton, MA, USA: Edward Elgar Publishing.

United Nations World Tourism Organization (2020). *UNWTO World Tourism Barometer (English version)*. https://www.e-unwto.org/loi/wtobarometereng.

Van Riper, C. J., Kyle, G. T., Sutton, S. G., Yoon, J. I., & Tobin, R. C. (2013). Australian residents' attitudes toward pro-environmental behaviour and climate change impacts on the Great Barrier Reef. *Journal of Environmental Planning and Management, 56*(4), 494–511.

Viglia, G., & Dolnicar, S. (2020). A review of experiments in tourism and hospitality. *Annals of Tourism Research, 80*, 102858.

Woosnam, K. M., & Ribeiro, M. A. (2023). Methodological and theoretical advancements in social impacts of tourism research. *Journal of Sustainable Tourism, 31*(2), 187–203.

WTTC (2023). *Economic Impact Reports*. https://wttc.org/research/economic-impact.

Yeager, E., Boley, B. B., & Goetcheus, C. (2023). Conceptualizing peer-to-peer accommodations as disruptions in the urban tourism system. *Journal of Sustainable Tourism, 31*(2), 504–519.

2   A bibliometric analysis and visualization of social impact of tourism and sustainability

Otto Regalado-Pezúa and César Y. Cancán Estares

Introduction

The noteworthy growth in tourism in the last few decades has been important for the development of many countries; this rapid expansion has led to a greater diversification in touristic destinations and, consequently, to a concurrent geographic expansion. Quintero Santos (2004) mentions that in 1950, the 15 main touristic destinations (all located in Europe) attracted 97 percent of global arrivals, while in 2000, that figure had dropped to 62 percent, increasing the participation of developing countries. At the same time, he mentions that tourism activities have to be planned, managed, and supervised through a sustainable development proposal; otherwise, future development in the touristic regions could be compromised due to an imbalance between economic growth and finite natural resources. Lozano (2008), on the other hand, states that recent, unprecedented advances in development and industrialization have resulted in an increase in life expectancy in developed countries, a 50 percent decrease in infant mortality, an increase in literacy, and a rapid increase in the production and consumption of food that had surpassed the population growth rate. However, these activities have had negative economic, environmental, and social effects, too, generating fear that the environment and future generations' quality of life could be harmed, as reductionist, cause-and-effect relations have been unable to fully explain the dynamic, complex relationships between economic, environmental, and social issues. Geissdoerfer et al. (2017) indicate that tourism has caused environmental problems, such as loss of biodiversity; water, air, and soil pollution; the depletion of resources; and the excessive use of land. Societal expectations have not been met due to problems such as high unemployment, poor work conditions, social vulnerability, the poverty trap, intergenerational inequity, and an increase in inequality. Economic challenges, such as supply risk, problematic ownership structures, unregulated markets, and defective incentive structures, lead to more and more frequent financial and economic instability for individual companies and entire economies. These issues are of vital importance for the correct, sustainable development of humanity and even for humanity's very survival.

Debates about sustainability no longer consider sustainability to only be about environmental concerns and now incorporate economic and social dimensions as well. Economic sustainability seeks the efficient use of resources to achieve long-term profitability. Social sustainability includes social justice, social capital, community development, and social responsibility (Dempsey et al., 2011). Finally, environmental sustainability seeks to improve human welfare, protecting sources of raw materials used to meet human needs and ensuring that human waste disposal does not overwhelm the system, so that no people are harmed (Goodland, 1995). Geissdoerfer et al. (2017) add that sustainability is the balanced integration of economic performance, social inclusion, and environmental resiliency in order to benefit current and future generations.

Mensah (2019) indicates that, for scientific progress to occur, it is important to take into account the concept of sustainability, highlighting what Porter and Linde (1995) voiced: that the best options will probably continue to be those that satisfy societal needs and that are environmentally and economically viable. Quintero Santos (2004) adds that sustainable tourism development must be biologically acceptable, economically viable, socially admissible, and culturally sustainable. Any sustainable tourism development proposal should be supported by the government and by other stakeholders in the tourism industry, in order to guarantee its effectiveness. Wanamaker (2020) indicates that there are three interconnected "spheres" of sustainability: environmental, economic, and social. These spheres are a set of related concepts that, when taken together, can form a solid foundation from which decisions can be made and important actions can be taken. Everyone wins when the concepts contained in the three spheres of sustainability are applied to real-world situations. By preserving natural resources and protecting the environment, the economy is not impaired, and people's quality of life either improves or is maintained. This interconnection is depicted in Figure 2.1, clarifying that almost all we do or plan has an effect on overall sustainability.

It is important to review and evaluate the progress in tourism research, as this sector has a positive impact on economic growth and development. Frechtling (2013) declares that tourism generates more work and income for the local population, leading to an improved quality of life for them. Webster and Ivanov (2014) add that well-administered, responsible tourism leads to visitors who spend more money at the visited destination, which will lead

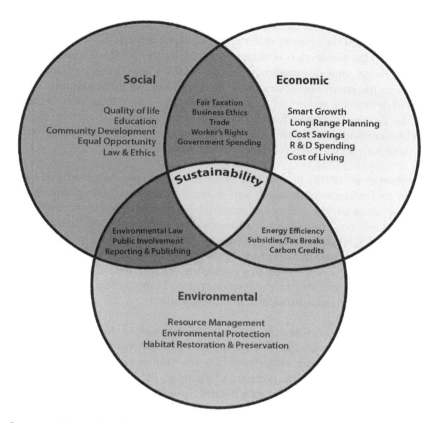

Source: Wanamaker (2020)

Figure 2.1   Relationships among social, environmental, and economic sustainability

to an increase in the GDP and economic growth at the destination, which means increased economic well-being among the local population. Dale and Robinson (2001) think that the rapid expansion of tourism as an industry contributes significantly to local and national economies, which encourages researchers to carry out more studies on tourism. However, tourism activities can also be harmful. Wearing and McGehee (2013) have stated that tourism, in a free-market economy, represents the commercialization of the human need to travel, exploiting at the same time natural and cultural resources as a means to accumulate profit. They believe that demand for these experiences is what drives the market, often leaving the destination community out of the process. Buckley (2012) argues that tourism produces direct local impacts on the air, water, soil, and biota of a place, as well as the indirect impacts of the production and transport of material goods. These impacts cause atmospheric emissions; the production of solid and liquid waste; and the consumption of water, energy, and raw materials. Quintero Santos (2004) explains that pressures on the environment can cause the appearance of environmental stress due to destructive action and the overexploitation of the natural environment, as the economic, sociocultural, and environmental impacts of tourism are ambivalent and are related to the carrying capacity, which determines what costs or benefits different tourism activities have.

Ranjbari et al. (2019) believe that in recent years, more attention has been given to environmental, social, and economic concerns, stating that in the last two decades, the concept of sustainability has attracted more and more scholars and professionals from all around the world. However, years earlier, Butler (1999) argued that merely claiming that sustainable tourism is the path to the future because there is growing interest in the concept will not ensure its adoption or success, stressing that evaluating the real impacts of tourism and the level of sustainability reached would require a longitudinal, in-depth study and an environmental, economic, and social audit.

The importance of researching the social impacts of tourism cannot be overestimated; it is crucial that the industry and governmental agencies and departments of tourism understand how the individuals within a host community, as well as the host community in general, perceive the advantages and disadvantages of tourism due to a possible hostile response toward tourists if a balance is not reached. Although research on the social impacts of tourism is substantial and ongoing, a level of maturity has been reached that means that there are periodic updates on the work carried out and on the findings uncovered (Deery et al., 2012). Higgins-Desbiolles (2006) adds that it is fundamental for tourism scholars, planners, and leaders to have a broader perspective of the role of tourism in societies and the global community, if they want tourism to avoid growing opposition and critique in a probable future characterized by insecurity and scarcity.

Deery et al. (2012) indicate that the success of tourism in many regions depends to a large degree on the support of the local community. It is necessary to understand, control, and manage the impact of tourism on the host community. Ferreira et al. (2021) suggest that the interactions between visitors and the host community can lead to short-term and long-term positive and negative impacts on the sociocultural, economic, and environmental fabric of touristic destinations. Buckley (2012) describes the relationship between tourism, prosperity, and sustainability as complex and large-scale, also mentioning that prosperity increases the environmental impact. Casagrandi and Rinaldi (2002) feel that sustainable tourism can be achieved as long as stakeholders are cautious to reinvest their profits and are willing to protect the environment; sustainability is often hanging by a thread, since accidental clashes between stakeholders can easily unleash a change from profitable and environmentally friendly behavior to behavior that is neither profitable nor good for the environment.

This chapter seeks to present an evaluation of the research on the social impact of tourism and sustainable tourism. The techniques used to analyze the research contributions, topics, and trends of a specific field run the gamut from qualitative (often subjective) evaluations to objective, quantitative measures of research contributions (Benckendorff, 2009). Bibliometrics offers a powerful set of methods and measures to study the structure and process of academic communication (Borgman and Furner, 2005). Bibliometric methods use a quantitative focus to describe, evaluate, and follow up on published research. These methods have the potential to provide a systematic, transparent, reproducible review process and thus improve the quality of reviews (Zupic and Čater, 2015).

1   Data and methodology

1.1   Data source and research process

One important part of research is information gathering through databases, which provide basic bibliographic information, like the author's name and the journal's name, volume number, and page numbers. Jiang et al. (2019) mention that bibliographic databases have increased the coverage of tourism journals and have allowed for more complete access to their citations. For this study, the Scopus database was selected to gather information from. Scopus was preferred due to its advantages in terms of its ease of use and the wide range of scientific articles it contains in comparison to other databases. Falagas et al. (2008) mention that Scopus offers approximately 20 percent greater coverage than Web of Science (WOS), including a wider range of journals limited to recent articles only (published after 1995). Joshi (2016) adds that a comparison between WOS and Scopus finds that Scopus contains a greater number of indexed journals, albeit ones with lesser impact, limited to recent articles; both databases allow users to search the results and classify them according to parameters, such as author, citation, and the institution, based on the impact factor and the index.

1.2   Analytical tool and method

Briner and Denyer (2012) argue that the number of research-oriented publications has rapidly increased, making it difficult to keep updated regarding the most recent publications. López et al. (2009) add that one cause of this growth in information is the development of information technology. Buckley (2012) indicates that there is a large quantity of literature in the tourism field and that research studies on science, the environment, resource management, global change, human health, economics, and development politics are also relevant to sustainable tourism. Tranfield et al. (2003) emphasize the importance of the literature review in any project and highlight that the researcher is in charge of evaluating relevant content to outline the research question in order to broaden the knowledge in the field. Pritchard (2006) recommends that the reflective, dedicated researcher be conscious of the nature of their own academic collectives in order to be aware of the epistemological traditions and power structures that have shaped the production of knowledge in their disciplines.

Bibliometric analysis is an established method for evaluating the production of research in a specific field during a period of time using indicators and, in spite of its shortcomings, it does provide a useful indicator of the development of tourism research, as the bibliometric data are used as a means to "grade" individual researchers and influence the opportunities of those researchers to obtain jobs or promotions (van Raan, 2005; Diem and Wolter, 2013). Palmer et al. (2005) add that bibliometric analysis provides a general vision of the methodological directions tourism research has taken, shedding additional light into the use of statistical methodology in the articles, and measures the statistical sophistication of the field well. The term "bibliometric" refers to the application of quantitative procedures to written communication, considering elements like the authors, the title of the publication, the type of document, language, abstract, and keywords. Using bibliometrics to objectivize the quality and quantity of scientific production makes it tangible and measurable (López et al., 2009; Rodríguez et al., 2009).

1.2.1   Definition of the keywords

The importance of using the correct keywords is the key to bibliometric analysis: omitting or mistyping a single word changes the whole search and, thus, the results. That is why a combination of several different keywords was used for the search in the Scopus database. To effectively cover the field of the social impact of tourism and sustainable tourism, the following keywords were used: "social impact," "sustainability," "sustainable," and "tourism," using the search criteria "title, abstract, keyword," and in this initial search, articles, books, book chapters, conference papers, and even uncited articles came up in the results. With the correct keywords, the research was focused, avoiding the potential problem of the study's going off track and becoming meaningless. Past research, which primarily used "sustainability" and "tourism" as keywords, was taken into account as a reference (Garrigos-Simon et al., 2018; Seguí-Amortegui et al., 2019; Yoopetch and Nimsai, 2019).

1.2.2   Initial results of the search and the filtering process

The keyword search in the Scopus database brought to light many articles on the studied topics; as can be observed in Table 2.1, the initial number was 5,588 documents. Even from the beginning, it can be observed that the number of studies on sustainability in the tourism field is greater than the number of studies on the social impact of tourism, validating the claim of Higgins-Desbiolles (2006), who stressed the extreme difficulty of finding references on social tourism initiatives in the tourism literature.

Table 2.1   Initial search in Scopus

Keyword search result	Total number of documents
"tourism sustainability" OR "sustainable tourism"	4966
"tourism social impact" OR "social impacts of tourism"	622
Total	5588

1.2.3   Filtering of the results

The filtering of the initial search was carried out in order to eliminate duplicate documents and discard whatever documents were not articles; in other words, papers presented at conferences, books, and book chapters were discarded. It is important to emphasize the number of indexed articles in the Scopus database, as one limitation of the database is that it can only store up to 2,000 documents on a single list, and therefore it was decided that selected articles must be cited by at least 10 other articles.

As can be observed in Table 2.2, the total number of documents was reduced through the filtering of the articles, and the bibliometric analysis was carried out using this filtered information. The filtering process was able to reduce the initial number of analyzed documents from 5,588 to 1,620 articles that had been cited at least 10 times by other articles indexed in Scopus.

Table 2.2   Initial search results after filtering

Keyword search result	Total number of documents
"tourism sustainability" OR "sustainable tourism"	1415
"tourism social impact" OR "social impacts of tourism"	231
Total, duplicates removed	1620

The information gathered was downloaded from the Scopus database in the CSV format and contained the following data: citation information, bibliographic information, abstract, keywords, finance details, and other relevant information. With that information, it was possible to carry out a follow-up analysis.

1.2.4   Initial statistics

As can be seen in Figure 2.2, the number of publications in the field of the social impact of tourism and sustainable tourism has grown considerably in recent years, indicating that the research in this field has become more and more relevant as the years have gone by. The publication dates of the articles evaluated indicate an upward trend in recent decades, 2016 and 2017 being the years with the most articles published that have been cited by a minimum of 10 other articles. However, in recent years, a fall in the number of Scopus indexed articles that have been cited by at least 10 other articles can be observed. This fall could be explained through the fact that new articles are not yet being recognized by researchers in the field, but it can be expected that new articles on sustainable tourism will be of vital importance to the development of tourism that is economically and environmentally sustainable and socially viable.

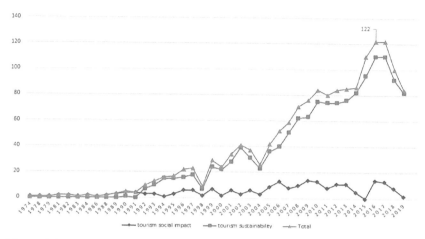

Figure 2.2   Articles published on the social impact of tourism and sustainable tourism

2   Bibliometric analysis of the literature: results and discussion

There are many reasons to analyze the contributions to research and productivity in the field of the social impact of tourism and sustainability. Jogaratnam et al. (2005) believe that it is beneficial for academic administrators to use the information in their decisions regarding pay, promotion, and resource assignation, keeping in mind that a general knowledge of research productivity can help academic institutions evaluate and establish standards for academic production. They add that documentation of research productivity also provides evidence of the changes in research contributions over time. Sharpley (2014) describes how for a long time, academic attention has been paid to the social impacts of tourism in general but how despite the significant volume and ever-greater reach of the research, it is uncertain to what extent it has improved our understanding of tourism. In Table 2.3, it can be observed that the *Journal of Sustainable Tourism* has the greatest number of articles on the social impact of tourism and sustainable tourism. Another important point is that more than 50 percent of the articles are concentrated in the top two journals of the top 10. The CiteScore calculation is based on the number of citations of documents by a journal over the course of three years, divided by the number of the same types of documents indexed in Scopus and published in those same three years. This metric is a simple way of measuring sources' impact. However, it is not

Table 2.3   Top 10 journals publishing papers on the social impact of tourism and sustainable tourism

Journals	Papers	Percentage	Accumulated percentage	CiteScore 2019
Journal of Sustainable Tourism	379	43.87%	43.87%	6.4
Tourism Management	113	13.08%	56.94%	12.8
Sustainability Switzerland	81	9.38%	66.32%	3.2
Annals of Tourism Research	72	8.33%	74.65%	6.8
Tourism Geographies	50	5.79%	80.44%	5.0
Current Issues in Tourism	40	4.63%	85.07%	7.5
Journal of Cleaner Production	40	4.63%	89.70%	10.9
Tourism Management Perspectives	34	3.94%	93.63%	5.5
Journal of Travel Research	30	3.47%	97.11%	10.9
Asia Pacific Journal of Tourism Research	25	2.89%	100.00%	3.3
Total of the top 10	864			

possible to compare between fields using CiteSource, since the metric is not normalized by field.

The large amount of literature on the social impact of tourism and sustainable tourism makes the selection of the articles pertinent to this study difficult. Table 2.4 shows the top 10 most-referenced articles in the field. The quantity of references reflects the impact that each article has had on the community, being an important reference to help select the literature to incorporate into

Table 2.4   Top 10 most-referenced articles on the social impact of tourism and sustainable tourism

Title	Year	Authors	Journal	Scopus citations
Global environmental consequences of tourism	2002	Gössling, S.	*Global Environmental Change*	560
Food, place and authenticity: Local food and the sustainable tourism experience	2009	Sims, R.	*Journal of Sustainable Tourism*	508
Sustainable tourism as an adaptive paradigm	1997	Hunter, C.	*Annals of Tourism Research*	492
Sustainability indicators for managing community tourism	2006	Choi, H. C., Sirakaya, E.	*Tourism Management*	472
Sustainable tourism development: A critique	2003	Liu, Z.	*Journal of Sustainable Tourism*	465
Tourism and sustainable development: Exploring the theoretical divide	2000	Sharpley, R.	*Journal of Sustainable Tourism*	458
Traditions of sustainability in tourism studies	2006	Saarinen, J.	*Annals of Tourism Research*	451
Determinants of market competitiveness in an environmentally sustainable tourism industry	2000	Hassan, S. S.	*Journal of Travel Research*	406
Mindful visitors: Heritage and tourism	1996	Moscardo, G.	*Annals of Tourism Research*	367
Influence analysis of community resident support for sustainable tourism development	2013	Lee, T. H.	*Tourism Management*	359

other studies. However, it is possible that older articles can have more citations than recently published articles. In this context, newer articles are at a disadvantage solely due to their age. Table 2.4 shows that the article with the highest number of citations is "Global environmental consequences of tourism" by Stefan Gössling, with a total of 560. It is important to mention that the articles mentioned in the top 10 were published between 1996 and 2013, confirming that the articles with the greatest number of references are those that were published longer ago.

Table 2.5 presents the top 10 authors with the most publications on the social impact of tourism and sustainable tourism. This table quantifies the articles published by author in the fields mentioned and indicates the h-index of each author and the cumulative percentage of the 10 authors who have published the greatest number of articles on the topic in question. The number of articles published and the h-index of the authors were compiled by Scopus. The h-index tries to measure both productivity and the impact of the work published by a scientist or scholar. For the database, the h-index is not a static value but rather is constantly being updated. Hirsch (2005) states that this indicator allows researchers' scientific activity to be evaluated, which allows productivity to be measured. Some limitations of this index are that it does not allow for the interdisciplinary comparison of researchers, that it does not take into account the quality of the journals where documents are published, and that it does not take into account authors who publish less frequently. A researcher possesses index "h" if the "h" number of that researcher's papers have at least "h" citations each, and that researcher's other papers possess "h" citations each, at most. As shown in Table 2.5, at present, the author Stefan Gössling possesses the greatest number of articles published on the topic of the social impact of tourism and sustainable tourism, with a total of 25 articles; it is also important to highlight that he has an h-index of 52, indicating that he is a popular author to follow and cite.

As for the analysis of the countries that have the highest productivity on the topic of the social impact of tourism and sustainable tourism, Table 2.6 lists them in descending order based on the countries that have the most articles published on the topic. As Table 2.6 illustrates, the greatest percentage of the top 10 is concentrated in the top three countries (60.56 percent): the United States is the country with the greatest number of articles published in the field in question.

Table 2.5 Top 10 authors with the most publications on the social impact of tourism and tourism sustainability

Author	Number of articles published in the studied field	h-index of the author	Cumulative percentage
Gössling, Stefan	25	52	16.89%
Hall, Colin Michael	21	62	31.08%
Bynum Boley, B.	19	18	43.92%
Weaver, David	18	31	56.08%
Dolnicar, Sara	15	50	66.22%
Bramwell, Bill	11	35	73.65%
Jamal, Tazim	11	29	81.08%
Woosnam, Kyle Maurice	10	26	87.84%
Coghlan, Alexandra	9	22	93.92%
Dodds, Rachel	9	18	100.00%

Table 2.6 Top 10 countries with the most articles on the social impact of tourism and sustainable tourism

Country	Number of published documents	Cumulative percentage
United States	295	20.70%
United Kingdom	289	40.98%
Australia	279	60.56%
Spain	105	67.93%
Canada	104	75.23%
Italy	85	81.19%
New Zealand	78	86.67%
China	72	91.72%
Sweden	61	96.00%
South Africa	57	100.00%

2.1   Science mapping analysis

Bibliometric analysis is often combined with scientific mapping techniques to detect and visualize conceptual subdomains (Cobo et al., 2011). Jiang et al. (2019) add that the use of new bibliometric visualization techniques makes a methodological contribution to mapping and the presentation of bibliometric data on tourism research. The use of these techniques provides new knowledge on research patterns (van Eck and Waltman, 2014). The most commonly studied relationships are citation relations, keyword co-occurrence relations, and co-authorship relations. With citation relations, an additional distinction can be made between direct citation relations, co-citation relations, and bibliographic coupling relations.

This study has used the VOSviewer to visualize the existing relations indicated. The main motive for which this program was chosen is the ease with which it makes bibliometric maps, as well as its ability to use data that have been downloaded from the Scopus database, which contain citation information, bibliographic information, keywords, etc. VOSviewer is used to construct maps according to the type of analysis required by the author, including co-authorship, co-occurrence, citation, bibliographic coupling, and, finally, co-citation. The program is freely available for the bibliometric research community through the following link: www.vosviewer.com. The VOSviewer program was used to view existing relationships.

2.2   Co-occurrence analysis

Boeris (2010) explains that this type of analysis has the goal of identifying the relationships that exist between the concepts of a determined linked group. The words extracted from the analyzed documents make it possible to identify the topics dealt with by the authors and the existing relationships among those topics. The keyword co-occurrence analysis that was applied in the field of the social impact of tourism and sustainable tourism identified the topics studied by the researchers. Through co-occurrence analysis in which all of the keywords adhered to the restriction that the minimum number of occurrences of the keyword needed to be greater than or equal to 5, it was observed that, of a total of 5,791 keywords, only 550 met this threshold. Table 2.7 shows the most frequently occurring keywords and the total link strength. This value indicates the number of links an element has to other elements and the total strength of the links between one element and another.

Table 2.7   Keywords used in the social impact of tourism and sustainable tourism

Keyword	Occurrences	Total link strength
ecotourism	710	5708
sustainable tourism	579	3836
tourism development	508	3968
sustainability	382	2873
sustainable development	382	2969
tourism management	326	2593
tourism	260	1900
tourist destination	234	2170
perception	118	1045
stakeholder	118	1118
social impact	111	753
tourism market	103	894
environmental impact	93	801
tourist behavior	90	769
tourism economics	88	847

3   Conclusions and directions for future research

The rapid expansion of tourism has brought diversification to new destinations and new tourism activities, and increased negative impacts (changes in communities' lifestyles, increases in transport's carbon footprint, environmental damage due to increased human waste). Many studies propose solutions to contribute to the development of sustainable tourism. However, the massive number of documents related to this topic make the rapid identification of information relevant to the researcher impossible. Using bibliometric analysis of publications indexed in Scopus, this chapter transmits an updated image of the research trends in the scientific production on tourism and sustainable tourism. A significant growth in the number of publications can be observed, which demonstrates the relevance of these topics, and it can be recognized that the *Journal of Sustainable Tourism* has published the greatest number of relevant articles, as it is a journal that encourages research on tourism and sustainable development. The most-cited article was "Global environmental consequences of tourism" by Stefan Gössling, with a total of 560 citations; it has been recognized by the community as an influential and important article on the sustainable development of tourism. In an analysis on author productivity, Gössling was identified as the scholar with the greatest number of articles published on the topic of the social impact of tourism and sustainable tourism: these articles have been recognized by the community, given the number of times these articles have been cited. Finally, on the country level, the United States has been the most prolific and productive source of documents, which indicates that there is a greater preference there for research into the field of the social impact of tourism and sustainable tourism; the United Kingdom and Australia have also published a considerable number of articles on this topic. The keyword co-occurrence analysis on the social impact of tourism and sustainable tourism highlights "ecotourism," "sustainable tourism," "tourism development," "sustainability," and "sustainable development" as the most frequent keywords, corroborating the main themes in the literature on sustainable tourism.

Some limitations of this study can be mentioned: first, although the Scopus database includes one of the most complete collections of knowledge in the social sciences, articles were only selected if they were cited at least 10 times, which left potentially relevant documents (book chapters, conference papers, reviews) out of the study. This selection decision could be a weakness when evaluating the significant research contributions of some researchers. However, the present analysis was able to provide a point of reference for future bibliometric studies, serving as a starting point for those researchers who wish to contextualize the trajectory of the social impact of tourism and sustainable tourism. Especially important to note is the fact that previous studies dealt with sustainable tourism, but before now, there has been no bibliometric analysis on the social impact of tourism, as the latter is a lesser-studied field.

These results contribute to the wider discourse on the epistemology of tourism research and, consequently, to possible trends. This chapter can help researchers suggest future research lines, as it clarifies that, in general, there is a tendency toward research on sustainable tourism, and, demonstrated by the number of publications in Scopus, it emphasizes that there are fewer studies on the social impact of tourism, which indicates that researchers require deeper knowledge on this topic. A complementary keyword analysis emphasizes the need to include new fields of knowledge, such as ecotourism, demonstrating environmental concerns and the need to address problems with strategies and adequate management in order to guarantee companies' and organizations' success in a sustainable way. This finding highlights that tourism research integrates the distinctive components of other disciplines as it creates new knowledge.

Government organizations and researchers should take the findings of research literature into account, as the literature reinforces the benefits of being sustainable. With the information presented in this chapter, it is possible to encourage tourism competitiveness through collaborations that bring together authors, journals, and countries, creating invisible networks that encourage the creation of knowledge and the development of the tourism field.

For future research, a similar bibliometric analysis of the WOS database is recommended, with the goal of evaluating the most important journals, authors, and publications that this database contains, adding a keyword co-occurrence analysis to determine whether the topics uncovered by this recommended analysis are the same as those found in Scopus, as this would enrich the analysis of the most relevant literature and suggest which database should be used to publish or search for information on the field of social impacts and sustainable tourism.

References

Benckendorff, P. (2009). Themes and trends in Australian and New Zealand tourism research: A social network analysis of citations in two leading journals (1994–2007). *Journal of Hospitality and Tourism Management, 16*(1), 1–15.

Boeris, C. (2010). Aplicación de métodos bibliométricos a la evaluación de colecciones: El caso de la Biblioteca del Instituto Argentino de Radioastronomía. *II Jornadas del Doctorado en Geografía.* http://sedici.unlp.edu.ar/handle/10915/17179.

Borgman, C. L. and Furner, J. (2005). Scholarly communication and bibliometrics. *Annual Review of Information Science and Technology, 36*(1), 2–72.

Briner, R. B. and Denyer, D. (2012). Systematic review and evidence synthesis as a practice and scholarship tool. In D. M. Rousseau (Ed.), *The Oxford Handbook of Evidence-Based Management.* doi:10.1093/oxfordhb/9780199763986.013.0007.

Buckley, R. (2012). Sustainable tourism: Research and reality. *Annals of Tourism Research, 39*(2), 528–546.

Butler, R. W. (1999). Sustainable tourism: A state-of-the-art review. *Tourism Geographies, 1*(1), 7–25.

Casagrandi, R. and Rinaldi, S. (2002). A theoretical approach to tourism sustainability. *Ecology and Society, 6*(1). http://www.consecol.org/vol6/iss1/art13/.

Cobo, M. J., López-Herrera, A. G., Herrera-Viedma, E. and Herrera, F. (2011). An approach for detecting, quantifying, and visualizing the evolution of a research field: A practical application to the fuzzy sets theory field. *Journal of Informetrics, 5*(1), 146–166.

Dale, C. and Robinson, N. (2001). The theming of tourism education: A three-domain approach. *International Journal of Contemporary Hospitality Management*, *13*(1), 30–35.

Deery, M., Jago, L. and Fredline, L. (2012). Rethinking social impacts of tourism research: A new research agenda. *Tourism Management*, *33*(1), 64–73.

Dempsey, N., Bramley, G., Power, S., and Brown, C. (2011). The social dimension of sustainable development: Defining urban social sustainability. *Sustainable Development*, *19*(5), 289–300.

Diem, A. and Wolter, S. C. (2013). The use of bibliometrics to measure research performance in education sciences. *Research in Higher Education*, *54*(1), 86–114.

Falagas, M. E., Pitsouni, E. I., Malietzis, G. A., and Pappas, G. (2008). Comparison of PubMed, Scopus, Web of Science, and Google Scholar: Strengths and weaknesses. *The FASEB Journal*, *22*(2), 338–342.

Ferreira, F. A., Castro, C., and Gomes, A. S. (2021). Positive and negative social-cultural, economic and environmental impacts of tourism on residents. In J. V. de Carvalho et al. (Eds.), *Advances in Tourism, Technology and Systems* (pp. 288–298). Dordrecht: Springer.

Frechtling, D. (2013). The economic impact of tourism: Overview and examples of macroeconomic analysis. UNWTO Statistics and TSA Issue Paper Series STSA/IP/2013/03 (Online), UNWTO, Madrid. https://doi.org/10.18111/9789284415625.

Garrigos-Simon, F. J., Narangajavana-Kaosiri, Y., and Lengua-Lengua, I. (2018). Tourism and sustainability: A bibliometric and visualization analysis. *Sustainability (Switzerland)*, *10*(6), 1–23.

Geissdoerfer, M., Savaget, P., Bocken, N. M. P., and Hultink, E. J. (2017). The circular economy: A new sustainability paradigm? *Journal of Cleaner Production*, *143*, 757–768.

Goodland, R. (1995). The concept of environmental sustainability. *Annual Review of Ecology and Systematics*, *26*, 1–24.

Higgins-Desbiolles, F. (2006). More than an "industry": The forgotten power of tourism as a social force. *Tourism Management*, *27*(6), 1192–1208.

Hirsch, J. E. (2005). An index to quantify an individual's scientific research output. *Proceedings of the National Academy of Sciences of the United States of America*, *102*(46), 16569–16572.

Jiang, Y., Ritchie, B. W., and Benckendorff, P. (2019). Bibliometric visualisation: An application in tourism crisis and disaster management research. *Current Issues in Tourism*, *22*(16), 1925–1957.

Jogaratnam, G., Chon, K., McCleary, K. W., and Mena, M. (2005). An analysis of institutional contributors to three major academic tourism journals: 1992–2001. *Tourism Management*, *26*(5), 641–648.

Joshi, A. (2016). Comparison between Scopus & ISI Web of Science. *Journal Global Values*, *7*(1), 1–11.

López, E. S., Castellanos Quintero, S. J., Rodríguez del Rey, M. M. L., and Hernández Fernández, J. I. (2009). La bibliometría: Una herramienta eficaz para evaluar la actividad científica postgraduada. *MediSur*, *7*(4), 59–62. http://scielo.sld.cu/scielo.php?script=sci_arttext&pid=S1727-897X2009000400011&lng=en&tlng=en.

Lozano, R. (2008). Envisioning sustainability three-dimensionally. *Journal of Cleaner Production*, *16*(17), 1838–1846.

Mensah, J. (2019). Sustainable development: Meaning, history, principles, pillars, and implications for human action: Literature review. *Cogent Social Sciences*, *5*(1), 1–21.

Palmer, A. L., Sesé, A., and Montano, J. J. (2005). Tourism and statistics. Bibliometric study 1998–2002. *Annals of Tourism Research*, *32*(1), 167–178.

Porter, M. E. and Linde, C. van der (1995). Toward a new conception of the environment-competitiveness relationship. *Journal of Economic Perspectives*, *9*(4), 97–118.

Pritchard, A. (2006). Guest editorial. Listening to leisure voices: Getting engaged in dialogues, conversations and entanglements. *Leisure Studies*, *25*(4), 373–377.

Quintero Santos, J. (2004). Los impactos económicos, socioculturales y medioambientales del turismo y sus vínculos con el turismo sostenible. *Anales del Museo de América*, *12*, 263–274.

Ranjbari, M., Morales, G., Esfandabadi, Z. S., and Carrasco-Gallego, R. (2019). Sustainability and the sharing economy: Modelling the interconnections. *Dirección y Organización*, *68*, 33–40.

Rodríguez, M. D., Sáenz, R. G., Arroyo, H. M., Herera, D. P., Barranco, D., and Caballero-Uribe, C. V. (2009). Bibliometría, conceptos y utilidades para el estudio médico y la formación profesional/Bibliometrics: Concepts and utility to study and medical training. *Salud Uninorte*, Barranquilla (Col.), *25*(2), 319–330.

Seguí-Amortegui, L., Clemente-Almendros, J. A., Medina-Mijangos, R., and Gala, M. G. (2019). Sustainability and competitiveness in the tourism industry and tourist destinations: A bibliometric study. *Sustainability (Switzerland)*, *11*(22), 6351. https://doi.org/10.3390/su11226351.

Sharpley, R. (2014). Host perceptions of tourism: A review of the research. *Tourism Management*, *42*, 37–49.

Tranfield, D., Denyer, D., and Smart, P. (2003). Towards a methodology for developing evidence-informed management knowledge by means of systematic review. *British Journal of Management*, *14*(3), 207–222.

van Eck, N. J. and Waltman, L. (2014). Visualizing bibliometric networks. In Y. Ding, R. Rousseau, and D. Wolfram (Eds.), *Measuring Scholarly Impact* (pp. 285–320). Cham: Springer International Publishing.

van Raan, A. F. J. (2005). For your citations only? Hot topics in bibliometric analysis. *Measurement: Interdisciplinary Research & Perspective*, *3*(1), 50–62.

Wanamaker, C. (2020). *The Environmental, Economic, and Social Components of Sustainability*. https://soapboxie.com/social-issues/The-Environmental-Economic-and-Social-Components-of-Sustainability.

Wearing, S. and McGehee, N. G. (2013). Volunteer tourism: A review. *Tourism Management*, *38*, 120–130.

Webster, C. and Ivanov, S. (2014). Transforming competitiveness into economic benefits: Does tourism stimulate economic growth in more competitive destinations? *Tourism Management*, *40*, 137–140.

Yoopetch, C. and Nimsai, S. (2019). Science mapping the knowledge base on sustainable tourism development, 1990–2018. *Sustainability (Switzerland)*, *11*(13), 3631. https://doi.org/10.3390/su11133631.

Zupic, I. and Čater, T. (2015). Bibliometric methods in management and organization. *Organizational Research Methods*, *18*(3), 429–472.

3   Residents' attitudes for tourism: research, linkages and future research themes

George Triantafyllou and Eirini Strataki

1   Introduction

Why bibliometric analysis?

Science in general is always cumulative. New researches always build on preceding works, and therefore, extend knowledge in the particular field. The process of review consists of "identifying, obtaining and consulting the literature and other materials, which are useful for the purposes of our study" (Hernández et al., 2007).

The past two decades have seen a good number of innovative practices in research. Scientific production has witnessed the growth and its collection in bibliographic databases. This phenomenon has led to the use of "bibliometric" tools as a useful resource to measure scientific activities based on the statistical analysis of scientific literature (Sancho, 1990). Pritchard (1969) was one of the first authors to define the term bibliometric as the "application of statistical and mathematical methods set out to define the processes of written communication and the nature and development of scientific disciplines by using recounting techniques and analysis of such communication".

The term "bibliometric analysis" is defined as a statistical evaluation of published journal papers, books, or other scientific articles, and it is an effective way to measure the influence of publications, scholars, or institutions in the scientific community.

Based on the bibliometric analysis and from the perspective of macro development, this chapter systematically aims to:

- Summarize the latest research outcomes on industrial heritage in China and Western countries;

- Describe the development process of the industrial heritage discipline scientifically and quantitatively;
- Compare the outcomes and dynamic evolution laws of industrial heritage protection research in China and Western countries under two different development states horizontally, providing a valuable reference base for subsequent heritage conservation research.

Bibliometric analysis is now being used to evaluate academic outcomes quantitatively, which is beginning to challenge practice-based research. The process of bibliometric analysis includes four modules: data acquisition, data preprocessing, statistical calculation, and application analysis. Data sources are divided into database data and web data, and the acquisition methods are divided into a manual acquisition and automatic acquisition. Data preprocessing is mainly format conversion, splitting and extraction, and filtering the data that does not meet the requirements. A statistical calculation can be divided into Top N statistics, singular value statistics, quantity distribution statistics, annual growth statistics, and other related statistics.

Bibliometric analysis has become an important branch of information science and philology. At the same time, it also shows its methodological value as a special research method of information science. In the internal logical structure of information science, bibliometric analysis has gradually occupied the core position and is an academic practice closely related to science communication and basic theory.

From a historical point of view, bibliometric analysis has been used to track the relationship between citations in academic journals. Citation analysis, that is, examining the references of a project, is used to find materials and analyze its advantages. Citation indexes, such as the science network of the Institute for Scientific Information, allow users to search for the latest publications with reference to projects from articles in a timely manner.

Research on quantitative literature analysis can be traced back to the early twentieth century. Some important milestones are:

- In 1917, F. J. Cole and N. B. Eales first studied the literature of comparative anatomy published from 1543 to 1860 by using quantitative analysis. The relevant books and journal articles were counted and classified by country.
- In 1923, E. W. Hulme used the term "documentary statistics" and explained that: "through the statistics of written communication and the analysis of other aspects, we can observe the process of written communication and nature and development direction of a certain discipline".

- In 1969, A. Pritchard, a philologist, proposed to replace documentary statistics with bibliometric methods. He expanded the research object of literature statistics from journals to all books and periodicals.

According to this scientific analysis, researchers can carry out research including but not limited to:

- Quantitatively evaluating the academic quality of a certain domain of journals, authors, or institutions by statistical methods such as citation rates.
- A quantitative analysis of academic literature of a certain domain based on metrics such as citations. It consists of a review of the literature, indicating the number, evaluation, and main trends of publications concerning the domain.
- Analysis of a series of publications in a certain domain based on quantitative indicators, such as its evolution over time, number of citations, most prolific authors, etc.
- A quantitative method used to examine the knowledge structure and development of a certain domain based on the analysis of related publications, such as research status, hotspots, development forecast, etc.

A literature review, referred to as a review, is a kind of academic paper that collects a large number of relevant materials on a certain field, a certain specialty or a certain aspect of a topic, problem or research topic, and reveals the latest progress, academic opinions or suggestions of the current problem or research topic through analysis, reading, sorting and summarizing.

Both literature review papers and bibliometric papers emphasize the collation of previous studies in order to find out the current situation and shortcomings of the research. They differ in the following respects:

- The literature review emphasizes the theoretical and empirical content, that is, what aspects of the existing research include and what are the deficiencies. In terms of the number of search papers and references that can be included, representative papers should be extracted from the existing literature and written according to a predetermined research context.
- Bibliometric analysis is mainly to collect papers from different sources as far as possible in a general research direction. The number of search papers should be more than that of a literature review. It is not necessary to analyze the research content of each article in detail but to summarize the number of published papers, research hotspots, research methods, and distribution of authors. Most of the references cited are highly cited papers. We can use CiteSpace, histiocytes, and other professional software to analyze the data.

2   Methodology

About the database

For over 40 years, the database Web of Science of Thomson Reuters (hereinafter WoS) was the only one that allowed this type of bibliometric study. Its multidisciplinary character and availability of references, among other features, made it continue at the forefront for decades.

Articles published in leading scientific journals are accepted as "certified knowledge" (Ramos-Rodríguez & Ruiz-Navarro, 2004). Therefore, leading tourism journals were selected as a sample for this current study. Articles related to bibliometric studies were obtained from leading hospitality and tourism journals ranked by the Social Sciences Citation Index (SSCI) in 2014. In particular, nine hospitality and tourism journals with high impact factors were selected. Five of these nine journals were tourism-focused journals, and four of them were more hospitality-focused. These journals are also recognized as leading journals in bibliometric studies in the tourism field (Ottenbacher & Harrington, 2010; Kietzmann et al., 2011; Köseoglu et al., 2015; Morasan et al., 2014; Racherla & Hu, 2010). The five leading tourism journals selected for this study were the *Annals of Tourism Research* (ATR), the *Journal of Sustainable Tourism* (JST), *Tourism Management* (TM), the *Journal of Travel Research* (JTR) and the *International Journal of Tourism Research* (IJTR). The four leading hospitality journals selected for this study were the *International Journal of Hospitality Management* (IJHM), *Cornell Hospitality Quarterly* (CHQ), the *International Journal of Contemporary Hospitality Management* (IJCHM) and the *Journal of Hospitality and Tourism Research* (JHTR).

We describe here how the data was prepared for the bibliometric analysis. This study identified the papers from the scientific literature through keyword searches for "residents attitudes" and "tourism". The papers extracted were available in multidisciplinary databases of WoS. The following exact syntax was used to perform the search of papers:

- TOPIC ("residents attitudes" AND "tourism")
- Refined by LANGUAGES (ENGLISH)
- Timespan 1992–2020
- Indexes SCI-EXPANDED, SSCI, A&HCI, CPCI-S, CPCI-SSH, ESCI

The syntax indicates that only English language papers were downloaded. All the good indexes from the WoS were utilized for these purposes.

The objective was to create a descriptive-quantitative analysis of the presence of the concept of residents' attitude and the tourism related facilities, over the last twenty-eight years, i.e., 1992–2020. Web of Science is a platform based on web technology created in 1960 and owned by Thomson Reuters. It has collected a wide range of bibliographic databases, citations and references of scientific publications in any discipline of knowledge – scientific, technological, humanistic and sociological – since 1945 (see Table 3.1 for details).

Table 3.1   Key details of extracted documents by WOS

Description	Results
MAIN INFORMATION ABOUT DATA	
Timespan	1992:2020
Sources (journals, books, etc.)	162
Documents	437
Average years from publication	6.69
Average citations per documents	25.84
Average citations per year per doc	2.788
References	15817
DOCUMENT TYPES	
Article	363
Article; early access	19
Article; proceedings paper	3
Editorial material	2
Letter	1
Proceedings paper	35
Review	13
Review; early access	1
DOCUMENT CONTENTS	
Keywords Plus (ID)	659
Author's Keywords (DE)	1241
AUTHORS	
Authors	952
Author Appearances	1215

Description	Results
Authors of single-authored documents	48
Authors of multi-authored documents	904
AUTHOR COLLABORATION	
Single-authored documents	60
Documents per author	0.459
Authors per document	2.18
Co-authors per documents	2.78
Collaboration Index	2.4

The important thing to note is the biggest number of documents are journal articles, i.e., 363. Conference proceedings are not available in large numbers, i.e., 38. In other themes, *Learning one*, the conferences need a good presentation from the papers on residents' attitude and tourism related themes. Academic events are omitted from this discussion.

As per the records of WoS extracted data, the total number of authors who worked on the theme is 952. Single-authored documents were 60, which is a small number. The collaboration index is quite low on this research theme, i.e., 2.4. *Learning two*, if the authors collaborate on the theme probably more documents could be produced.

3   Analysis

Documents and sources

There have been a considerable number of factors identified as influencing residents' attitudes towards tourism. The demographic characteristic of the residents is one of the determining factors that generally influence the attitude towards emerging impacts. Notable works in this direction include Iroegbu and Chen (2001); Cavus and Tanrisevdi (2003); Harrill and Potts (2003); McGehee and Andereck (2004); Andereck et al. (2005); Petrzelka et al. (2005); Anthony and Govindarajan (2007); Rastegar (2010); and Snyman (2014) who have examined the relationship between perceived impact of tourism development and demographic characteristics of local people. Bearing these issues in mind, the present study examines the influence of demographic factors of local residents on their perceived impacts of tourism development.

The literature offers some research using bibliometric techniques in order to identify pioneering scholars and seminal works in tourism research, recent subject areas and citation patterns of tourism research, the quality of tourism journals, and to analyze special questions in tourism such as psychological research on tourism, trends in medical tourism research, research on human resources developed in tourism and hospitality management literature, and literature about tourism and sustainability. Nevertheless, no bibliometric or visualization analyses about research on quality in tourism were found. However, despite the lack of bibliometric analyses of tourism quality (TQ), this analysis is useful and important both for authors and for practitioners. For authors it is essential in order to understand the problems, new trends, and emerging areas, and this study can offer an overview of the research about quality in the tourism field and visualize the structure, development, and main trends and impacts of this research. This information is essential as it can offer key points to plan future research. For practitioners and policy makers it is also important, as they need to be more informed in order to lead their actions regarding the kind of tourism developments that are more likely to enhance the competitiveness of firms and destinations, the preservation of the environment and the patrimony for other generations, and also the enhancement of residents' quality of economic and social life. Focusing on this last aspect, the analysis of quality in tourism, together with cooperation among all the actors that participate in the provision of quality products and services, is essential to meet tourist expectations, which will further ensure sustainability and long term competitiveness of destinations and tourism firms. Due to the lack of bibliometric analysis of the literature about quality issues in tourism, and also due to its importance, this work intends to provide an in depth bibliometric analysis of the evolution of TQ literature. As mentioned earlier, we consider works, drawing on data from the Web of Science (WoS) and we used VOSviewer software (version 1.6.9, Leiden University, the Netherlands) to graphically map the data.

During the initial years, there were 1–3 articles being published on the theme of residents' attitude for tourism. For the last five years, this number has grown significantly. On average over the last five years the theme has generated more than ~50 papers each year. It is clear that as the number of publications increases, concurrently the number of citations increases also. Academia now demonstrates a keen interest in the social impact of tourism. Figure 3.1 shows that over the last five years academic researchers have published a significant number of studies. This is the natural result that we should expect due to the huge growth of researchers and scientists worldwide (Merigo et al., 2017).

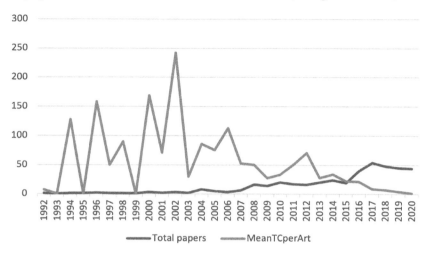

Figure 3.1   Cumulative figure on annual number of documents on the theme "Most important journals"

Table 3.2   Most important journals

Sources	Articles
Tourism Management	42
Journal of Sustainable Tourism	25
Annals of Tourism Research	24
Journal of Travel Research	24
Sustainability	22
International Journal of Tourism Research	15
Journal of Tourism and Cultural Change	15
Current Issues in Tourism	14
Tourism Planning & Development	12
Tourism Geographies	11

We asked the question, which journals are publishing most of the papers? Which journals should prospective authors target for their future publications? For this question we used the criterion that the journal should have published a minimum of 10 articles (see Table 3.2 for details). In total there were 10 journals which have published more than ten documents, as minimum (Table 3.2).

It is very interesting to note that out of top ten there are three journals which are not published in English. This indicates that there is a good scope for non-native English speakers and writers too.

Growth of sources/journal

In fact the *International Journal of Wine Business Research* (IJWBR) has contributed the highest number of articles on our topic, which means that most of the publications on the theme "residents' attitude for tourism" are published by the this journal. The growth of the top five sources was recorded and we found that IJWBR has published a significant number of papers on the same theme and continues to do so. During 2008–2012 *Tourism Management* and *PASOS* published the highest number of papers on the theme, although there was a decline in the number of publications on residents' attitude for tourism and related themes thereafter. The rest of the journals have contributed significantly but their publications are far fewer than these top three sources (see Figure 3.2 for details).

After the sources, an important discussion remains about the significant contributing authors on the theme "residents' attitude for tourism". We set criteria that we will take into account only the authors who have produced more than five documents at least and the authors must carry an *h*-index more than three. The *h*-index is an author-level metric that attempts to measure both the productivity and citation impact of the publications of a scientist or scholar. The *h*-index is defined as the maximum value of h such that the given author/journal has published h papers that have each been cited at least h times. The index is designed to improve upon simpler measures such as the total number of citations or publications. The index works properly only for comparing scientists working in the same field; citation conventions differ widely among different fields (Bornmann & Daniel, 2007).

$$h\text{-index } (f) = \max_{i} \min \left(f(i), i \right)$$

The *g*-index is an author-level metric suggested in 2006 by Leo Egghe. The index is calculated based on the distribution of citations received by a given researcher's publications, such that given a set of articles ranked in decreasing

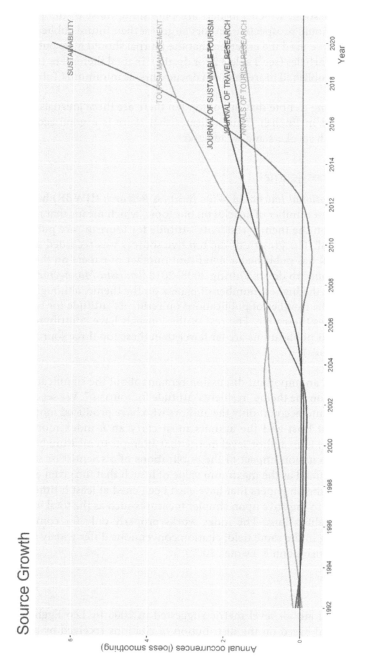

Figure 3.2   Cumulative figure on the most relevant sources and the pattern in their growth, based on documents on the theme "Most contributing authors to the domain"

order of the number of citations that they received, the g-index is the unique largest number such that the top g articles received together at least g² citations.

It can be equivalently defined as the largest number n of highly cited articles for which the average number of citations is at least n (Egghe, 2006). This is in fact a rewriting of the definition

$$g^2 \leq \sum_{i \leq g} ci$$

as

$$g \leq \frac{1}{g} \sum_{i \leq g} ci$$

The *m*-index is simply one's *h*-index divided by the number of years one has been publishing. While this acts as a sort of age correction, it is still unsatisfactory, essentially because it tends to penalize early career researchers in particular.

Table 3.3   Most contributing authors and different index

Author	*h*-index	*g*-index	*m*-index	TC	NP	PY_start
WOOSNAM KM	9	21		441	24	2010
NUNKOO R	13	14	1	1090	14	2009
RAMKISSOON H	7	8	0.538	862	8	2009
RIBEIRO MA	5	8		125	8	2013
ERUL E	3	7		55	7	2016
PAVLIC I	2	3	0.286	13	6	2015
PUH B	2	3	0.286	13	6	2015
GURSOY D	5	5	0.278	781	5	2004
MARUYAMA NU	2	5	0.4	43	5	2017
PORTOLAN A	2	3	0.286	13	5	2015

Note: TC = total citations, PY_start = production year of first document

Table 3.3 shows that the author WOOSNAM KM has got most of the papers. Whereas, while having a lower number of papers, NUNKOO R has got the highest *h*-index, because this author has got a large number of citations also. Table 3.4 supports the endeavor and shows that the top contributing author has got sixth rank, if local citations are removed.

Table 3.4   Most cited authors

Author	TC
WOOSNAM KM	441
NUNKOO R	1090
RAMKISSOON H	862
RIBEIRO MA	125
ERUL E	55
PAVLIC I	13
PUH B	13
GURSOY D	781
MARUYAMA NU	43
PORTOLAN A	13

Note: Global citations = total citations – local citations

Collaborations and country of authors

Collaboration between countries is presented as a percentage of single country publication (SCP) and percentage of multiple country publication (MCP). SCP represents intra-country collaboration while MCP represents inter country collaboration (Sweileh et al., 2016).

Table 3.5 has much significant information hidden in it. The USA is with first rank, whereas Spain has got the highest number of papers as single country papers. Figure 3.3 and Table 3.5 combined indicate that Australia has got the highest ratio of MCP/SCP.

In terms of frequency, Table 3.6 lists the countries with the total number of papers and their rankings. It is interesting to note that the USA and China have got a higher ratio of MCP. These countries work more collaboratively or maybe they have more funding opportunities to attract the papers and other research activity in collaborations.

Figure 3.4 represents the country wise analysis. The darkest shading indicates highly productive and the lightest is least productive. The Western side of the map is more productive on the theme "residents' attitude and tourism" and seems to be more engaged in the total production of research articles on this theme.

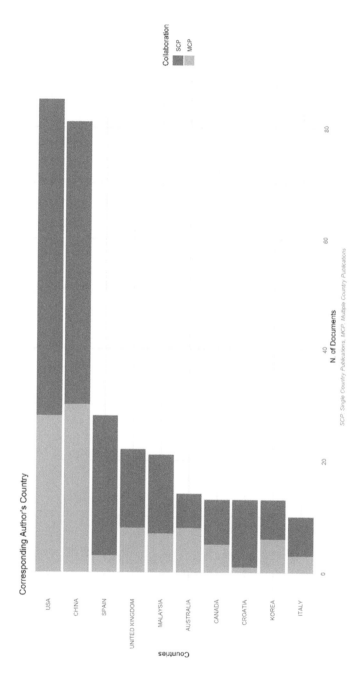

Figure 3.3   Visual representation of countries and collaboration index

Table 3.5   Countries and collaboration index

Country	Articles	Freq	SCP	MCP	MCP_Ratio
USA	85	0.20047	57	28	0.3294
China	81	0.19104	51	30	0.3704
Spain	28	0.06604	25	3	0.1071
UK	22	0.05189	14	8	0.3636
Malaysia	21	0.04953	14	7	0.3333
Australia	14	0.03302	6	8	0.5714
Canada	13	0.03066	8	5	0.3846
Croatia	13	0.03066	12	1	0.0769
Korea	13	0.03066	7	6	0.4615
Italy	10	0.02358	7	3	0.3

Note: MCP = multiple country publication; SCP = single country publication

Table 3.6   Countries and total production

Region	Frequencies
USA	187
China	154
UK	61
Spain	55
Malaysia	43
Australia	38
South Korea	28
Serbia	23
Turkey	23
South Africa	22

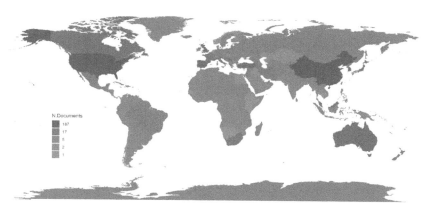

Figure 3.4   Country scientific production

Keywords analysis

The keywords used to identify previous works in our area of study are very useful information when searching for documents in any database. This information also enables future researchers to identify over researched topics, under researched keywords, and trending keywords also. This study employs the authors' keywords for the analysis. In this sense, "residents' attitude for tourism" is the most used term in the databases. These are followed by tourism, tourism development and wine and others also. With the help of VOSviewer, the keywords cluster analysis was done and seven clusters were found (Figure 3.5).

These findings offer very important and significant information for future researchers. Table 3.7 and Figure 3.5 indicate that there are seven clusters in all the keywords. In all, 1142 keywords have been identified through 472 papers. The minimum number of occurrences of a keyword was set as five and the top 55 keywords were considered eligible for analysis. The map showed some names of countries as keywords; these were removed and finally a table was prepared to aid future researchers.

In all the clusters, "development" is a prominent word. Cluster 1 seeks to be related with market strategies. Cluster 2 is wine tourism specific; Cluster 3 includes inhabiting some sense of rurality and sustainability; Cluster 4 includes consumer behavior and their experience too; Cluster 5 is more inclined towards market and management; Cluster 6 is involved with gastronomy and motivations; Cluster 7 utilizes an altogether different approach based on ecotourism, heritage and vineyards.

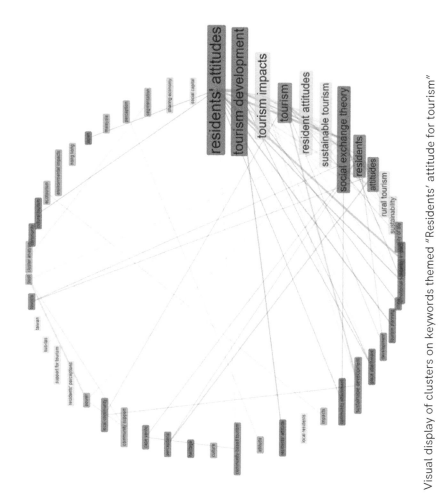

Figure 3.5   Visual display of clusters on keywords themed "Residents' attitude for tourism"

Table 3.7   Clusters of keywords on "Residents' attitude for tourism"

Cluster 1	Cluster 2	Cluster 3	Cluster 4	Cluster 5	Cluster 6	Cluster 7
Marketing strategy	Innovation	Culinary tourism	Consumer behavior	Consumer perception	Gastronomy	Ecotourism
Tourism development	Regional development	Development	Destination image	Content analysis	Marketing	Heritage
Wine business	Rural development	Experience economy	Loyalty	Market segmentation	Motivations	Landscape
Culture	Wine industry	Rural areas	Satisfaction	Survey research	Social impact	Vineyards
Impact	Attitude	Rural tourism	Sustainable tourism	Tourism management	Rural	Resident attitude
	Wine sector	Sustainability	Tourism experience			
	Sharing economy	Sustainable development	Festival			
	Sustainability	Territory	Local tourist			
		Heritage				

4   Discussion

The purpose of this chapter was to analyze how tourism and quality combines with the attitude of the residents for tourism. This issue was studied and defined theoretically, observing the relevance of quality on destinations, organizations, hosts, and also on tourists. Therefore, the chapter analyzed the topic of tourism and quality, observing the diverse advances in the literature and considering it as a multidimensional area that encompasses the well-being (physical, material, ecological, social, or even emotional) of those destinations and the diverse stakeholders involved in the production or consumption of tourism goods and services, and also the features of performance of the tourism product or service as it was expected, perceived, or experienced by the tourist. The chapter also concentrated on the search for previous analysis of the structure of the field of tourism and quality, focusing on the existence of previous bibliometric studies. However, no bibliometric study or visualization analysis about research on quality in tourism was found. Observing this lack, and also the relevance of the bibliometric approach, our work developed a bibliometric and visualization analysis of the related documents. The results of our analysis examined the need to observe the field from an interdisciplinary perspective that could integrate environmental, social, economic, and essentially managerial and marketing perspective dimensions of TQ. The research shows that after several conceptual and also methodological papers, essentially related to structural equation models, the question could be developed by focusing on other perspectives and trends, by focusing on other methodological instruments, and more applied and empirical research to analyze diverse specific questions related to the topic. Research about tourism and quality has been developing regularly since 1989; however, it has experienced a huge growth recently, especially in the last decade, with almost 800 documents annually in the last two years, whereas until 2008 they did not exceed 100 published papers a year. However, the literature is still scarce, compared to other topics, and this study has been pioneering in analyzing the structure and trends in the research. The increasing importance of TQ combined with the residents' attitude for tourism was reflected in the number of citations. Hence, the most cited paper in the tourism field, the one by Buhalis (2000), had almost 2500 citations in the WoS. Moreover, there were another three papers that also received more than 500 citations, although they were relatively recent papers, as they were published in the twenty-first century, but a fourth one was published in 1999. These results emphasize the recent relevance of TQ in terms of the attitude of the locals. Examination of the sources indicated that the top journals in the area were *Tourism Management, Journal of Travel Research, Journal of Travel and Tourism Marketing*, and *Sustainability*. Moreover, the results indicate that the main categories of publications were hospitality, leisure sport and tourism, management, and environmental sciences, although this is expanding across multiple academic disciplines. The keywords co-occurrence revealed that "tourism", "satisfaction", "service quality", "medical tourism", "quality of life", and "sustainability" were the most frequent keywords. This indicated the relevance of "service quality" and "quality of life" as the main factors observed, and also the relevance of managerial, marketing, medical, and environmental perspectives. A review of the keywords revealed the relevance of managerial and destination management issues ("service quality", "quality of life", "quality", and "rural tourism"), marketing perspectives ("satisfaction", "service quality", "customer satisfaction", "perceived value", and "loyalty"), also medical ("medical tourism") and environmental issues ("impact", and "environmental change"), and especially the relevance of sustainability ("sustainability", "sustainable tourism", and "sustainable development"). These results stress the relevance of quality as an important topic in the tourism management literature and as one of the core topics of sustainability and environmental sciences, such as has been previously explained in the literature review. This co-occurrence analysis also included some of the most important places of research ("China" and "Spain") and the emerging areas ("nature based tourism", and "social media"). Co-citation analysis indicated that the article by Fornell and Larcker (1981) and another two articles by Parasuraman et al. (1985, 1988), led the rank of the top cited papers of the documents in the database. They were methodological papers, the first was about structural equation models, and the other two were about service quality in general, its conceptualization and measurement with a marketing focus. This study revealed the relevance of diverse clusters, with the same perspectives observed previously (management, marketing, and environmental), observing also one cluster about information technology and social media. The journal co-citation network illustrated four clusters of journals: the main one, led by *Journal of Marketing* and most of the journals of the selected list including journals oriented to management and marketing; the second one, led by *Tourism Management* and other relevant sources in tourism research.

In the literature that observed mainly a tourism centered perspective, the third cluster, led by *Thesis* (outside the main journals) mainly observed an environmental-ecological orientation; and the fourth reduced cluster led by *Tourism Economics* was associated with an economic perspective. The author co-citation study indicated seven clusters. The clusters included research in the area of marketing in general, and also the use of methodological instruments. The second cluster, led by Hall (2011), included important authors in tourism and hospitality management and planning, including diverse areas such as service quality, ecological, and environmental impacts, and topics related to sustainability. Other clusters essentially dealt with marketing issues in tourism (Chen & Uysal, 2002), the impact of tourism on residents' quality of life (Gursoy et al., 2019), the strategic use of information technologies and social media (Buhalis, 2000), socio-cultural perspectives, and differences between people (Wedgwood, 2009). The bibliographic coupling of authors indicated the existence of ten clusters of authors. The main one did not include any of the 20 top authors, the main perspective being a managerial focus on tourism. The second cluster, led by Law (2014) was focused on the analysis of information technologies in tourism. The third cluster also observed a technological perspective, mainly associated with customers' attitudes. Other clusters included medical tourism and health sciences, quality of life and residents' well-being, environmental quality of coasts and products and economic demand, quality certifications and environmental management, and tourism marketing perspectives. The co-authorship analysis of TQ showed the prevalence of the USA, Spain, China, Australia, and the UK, leading three of the main clusters. The analysis observed a main cluster of east European countries led by Germany; another group of north European countries, which included and was led by Canada; and another group of South American countries, led by Spain. Other clusters showed Muslim countries from Asia, countries from Europe and Africa, a dispersed cluster, and another two clusters, one related to the UK and China, and the other to the USA and Australia. The study indicated that the top institutions analyzing the tourism field were Hong Kong Polytechnic University, Griffith University, and Kyung Hee University. The analysis also observed a big dispersion of relationships, showing 14 clusters. The main results only showed the relevant collaboration among European universities, US universities, and Spanish universities.

5   Conclusions

The main objective of this work was to perform a bibliometric analysis of the scientific literature published specifically on wine tourism. The study also aimed at identifying which of the themes respond better to how much, who, what, where and how research in wine is carried out. In view of the results, and the extensive bibliography, the study is in a position to present the main conclusions:

- The article published in scientific journals is the type of document most used by authors to present the results of their research. This has been the case for the last five years when more than 60 percent of the present papers have been published in the databases.

- A majority of authors have only written one article with a low average productivity. The co-authorship analysis reveals that the articles are signed primarily by two or three authors, which makes the co-authorship index 2.1.
- Almost 90 percent of the centers to which the authors are affiliated are universities in Australia, USA, Spain, Italy and similar countries.
- The results are in agreement with Bradford's (1934) law, whereby a small number of journals publish most articles on a particular subject.
- The keywords that most helped us to locate previous existing papers in our research area in WoS are residents' attitude for tourism followed, but by far, by tourism, tourism development and attitude.

This study on the related documents indicated that this area is very broad and varied which should integrate and reconcile diverse perspectives. These perspectives essentially come from managerial, but also from environmental areas, observing sustainability issues as a core relevance. In this vein, the work indicated the different lines of research in TQ, their relative importance, and some interesting trends in the literature. These results are important for practitioners when considering different policies, and especially important to researchers, as the study observes connections and differences between the diverse areas studying TQ, and some topics that can open new areas of research. Focusing on policy makers and practitioners, the diverse perspectives cannot be avoided during the planning and management of organizations and destinations. Hence, they should include, comprise, and integrate the complexity of the area. In particular, social (e.g., quality of life and tourist satisfaction), environmental–ecological (e.g., water quality and climate change), managerial, economic, and marketing (e.g., service quality and destination image) perspectives should be incorporated, and also medical ones, differences of cultures, and the relevance of information technologies and social media, as was highlighted in this bibliometric analysis of the literature about TQ. Our results also indicated that some of these perspectives were shared with some of the main areas of the sustainability literature in the tourism sector as it was illustrated in a recent bibliometric study. In addition, new starting themes such as perspectives related to new technologies and social media impacts should be included in the development of organizational and destination management improvements

Observing the theoretical relevance of this chapter, our bibliometric analysis could help researchers advance in their investigations about TQ. Following Lai et al. (2015, p. 31) "Knowing more about tourism problems can enhance the understanding of factors that affect tourism knowledge production". Moreover, according to these authors, the understanding of tourism problems has a relevant impact on which tourism problems to solve, influencing the initial or early stage of tourism research. In this respect this chapter identifies new trends in research, and will help authors discover new possible areas or areas where the research on TQ is still scarce. Following Garrigos-Simon et al. (2018), these aspects could be addressed by three questions: questions related to trends in TQ in the classical areas of research, the development of new areas where TQ has not been developed yet, and the expansion of fashionable questions that can be considered related to TQ. Focusing on these aspects, first of all the development of TQ research observed in this study showed that TQ had developed in some classical areas such as management and marketing, and it was also developing in areas such as medicine, economics, and environmental sciences, showing a close relationship with sustainability issues (actually, sustainability, sustainable tourism, and sustainable development were some of the main topics of research in the TQ field according to the results of this chapter).

In addition, the study observed that there was a lack of diverse classical fields related to sciences or social sciences, which were not relevant in the current literature. Hence they need more research. In particular, there is a lack in fields such as physics, mathematics, biology, sociology, and geography. Secondly, new areas for research, expanding now in academia, were not observed in a relevant way in TQ, which offer new opportunities, especially in questions related to information technologies, engineering, social media, or open innovation (which are offering new relevant trends). This is a fact that can help researchers to focus on these questions (in this vein, TQ should evolve towards the most popular areas in general academia). This study could also add areas within management or marketing fields such as innovation or entrepreneurship or ethics. Thirdly, the analysis of the works with most influence or with most citations by the TQ papers, or the ones that receive more citations among our sample, or the more relevant keywords (or the keywords that are increasing) can help researchers to see the most fashionable research questions, with more possibilities to be accepted by the diverse journals. Hence, the most cited papers could provoke the development of more papers on topics related to TQ that can be accepted as they can have more impact or citations in the future. In addition, of these three questions, the study has to add, especially, the need for more empirical and methodological articles, related to new indicators of TQ and more methodological papers that use new techniques especially apart from structural equation models.

Apart from these conclusions, this chapter obviously has a number of limitations that can help to prompt further research. In this respect, our methodology of using bibliometric and visualization analysis has limitations as it was based on the objective treatment of keywords that could provoke confusing results if they are not complemented with more qualitative and focused studies. We have to add the limitations of our sample, as it only considered the works used in the WoS collection, and also only considered articles, reviews, letters, and notes. In this respect, the study did not include some works like proceedings, professional documents, or theses, or documents from other databases (for instance in other languages apart from English, which although secondary in the "fashionable" worldwide literature, could offer us interesting and pioneering trends). Hence, the extent of this research to include these databases and documents can also offer further new, interesting analyses. Future studies should also focus on some of the trends observed in the different analyses developed in this work. In addition, they could concentrate on some of them, by developing them with a deeper focus. For instance, they could observe the evolution of the diverse keywords in the literature, or concentrate on a deep analysis of some of the clusters or themes of research detected in our studies. Moreover, new papers could also consider new methodologies (inside or outside bibliometric analyses) to structure and study the literature about TQ. Furthermore, they can use other software to study bibliometrics, or develop other possibilities that the VOSviewer also permits (e.g., more bibliographic coupling, co-citations, or co-authorship analyses). All these works should extend, enrich, and complement the present work.

6   Politics and future of bibliometric research

Since bibliometric studies generate new research agendas and directions for disciplines and/or fields, researchers can identify gaps in literature and practice. The findings of the bibliometric analysis in tourism can highlight the relationship between tourism and other disciplines or fields. Thus, new politics may be developed to enrich these relationships. Additionally, these studies are useful for policy makers and senior administrators who work at universities, government agencies, and research funding organizations when making policy decisions and allocating resources. Therefore, bibliometric studies are always needed at any maturity level of fields or disciplines.

7   Limitations and future research

As mentioned, this study has limitations. First, the sample included only certain leading tourism journals. It is possible that there may be more bibliometric studies published in other tourism related journals or in journals in other fields. It is suggested that future studies should include a larger sample of journals. Second, as Hall (2011) stated, bibliometric analysis can be applied to any bibliometric unit, and it is not limited to studies of journal citations. However, in this current study, the sample included only articles published in nine tourism journals. Future studies may consider conference proceedings, books, and doctoral dissertations. Finally, bias might appear when the review studies are classified, since some papers cover two or more groups. In future studies, multiple authors may collectively classify these studies. There are several other avenues for future studies. First, future studies can focus on a systematic review to identify contributors, such as authors, institutions, and countries. Second, the quality of bibliometric studies may be investigated by developing scales measuring the quality of research. Third, the performance of the bibliometric studies by using citation and/or co-citation impacts can be measured to gain more understanding in the field. Fourth, collaboration and the social network in bibliometric studies should be mapped and/or visualized. Fifth, the growth of the studies and productivity of researchers working in these fields of studies should be discussed in relation to research morals, values, economics, well-being, etc. Sixth, bibliometric analysis of bibliometric studies in tourism in developed and developing countries should be sought. Seventh, future studies should look at how methodological processes have been utilized in bibliometric studies. Finally, future studies may compare bibliometric studies in the tourism field with bibliometric studies in other fields or disciplines.

References

Andereck, K., Valentine, K., Knopf, R., & Vogt, C. (2005). Residents' perceptions of community tourism impacts. *Annals of Tourism Research, 32*, 1056–1076.

Anthony, R. N. & Govindarajan, V. (2007). *Management Control Systems.* New York: McGraw-Hill.

Bornmann, L. & Daniel, H. (2007). What do we know about the h-index? *Journal of the American Society for Information Science and Technology, 58*(9), 1381–1385.

Bradford, S. C. (1934). Sources of information on specific subjects. *Engineering, 137*, 85–86.

Buhalis, D. (2000). Marketing the competitive destination of the future. *Tourism Management, 21*, 97–116.

Cavus, S. & Tanrisevdi, A. (2003). Residents' attitudes toward tourism development: A case study in Kusadasi, Turkey. *Tourism Analysis, 7*, 259–269.

Chen, J. S. & Uysal, M. (2002). Market positioning analysis: A hybrid approach. *Annals of Tourism Research, 29*, 987–1003.

Cole, F. J. & Eales, N. B. (1917). The history of comparative anatomy: Part I. A statistical analysis of the literature. *Science Progress, 11*(44), 578–596.

Egghe, L. (2006). Theory and practice of the g-index. *Scientometrics, 69*(1), 131–152.

Fornell, C. & Larcker, D. F. (1981). Evaluating structural equation models with unobservable variables and measurement error. *Journal of Marketing Research, 18*(1), 39–50.

Garrigos-Simon, F. J., Narangajavana, Y. K. & Lengua, I. L. (2018). Tourism and sustainability: A bibliometric and visualization analysis. *Sustainability, 10*(6), 1976.

Gursoy, D., Ouyang, Z., Nunkoo, R., & Wei, W. (2019). Residents' impact perceptions of and attitudes towards tourism development: A meta-analysis. *Journal of Hospitality Marketing & Management, 28*(3), 306–333.

Hall, C. M. (2011). Publish and perish? Bibliometric analysis, journal ranking and the assessment of research quality in tourism. *Tourism Management, 32*, 16–27.

Harrill, R. & Potts, T. (2003). Tourism planning in historic districts: Attitudes toward tourism development in Charleston. *Journal of the American Planning Association, 69*, 233–244.

Hernández, R., Fernández, C., & Baptista, P. (2007). *Metodología de la Investigación.* Mexico City: McGraw-Hill.

Hulme, E. W. (1923). *Statistical Bibliography in Relation to the Growth of Modern Civilization: Two Lectures Delivered in the University of Cambridge in May, 1922.* London: Grafton & Co.

Iroegbu, H. & Chen, J. (2001). Urban residents' reaction toward tourism development: Do subgroups exist? *Tourism Analysis, 6*, 155–161.

Kietzmann, J. H., Hermkens, K., McCarthy, I. P., & Silvestre, B. S. (2011). Social media? Get serious! Understanding the functional building blocks of social media. *Business Horizons, 54*, 241–251.

Köseoglu, M. A., Sehitoglu, Y., & Craft, J. (2015). Academic foundations of hospitality management research with an emerging country focus: A citation and co-citation analysis. *International Journal of Hospitality Management, 45*, 130–144.

Lai, K., Li, J., & Scott, N. (2015). Tourism problemology: Reflexivity of knowledge making. *Annals of Tourism Research, 51*, 17–33.

Law, R., Buhalis, D., & Cobanoglu, C. (2014). Progress on information and communication technologies in hospitality and tourism. *International Journal of Contemporary Hospitality Management, 26*(5), 727–750.

McGehee, N. & Anderek, K. (2004). Factors predicting rural residents' support of tourism. *Journal of Travel Research, 43*, 131–140.

Merigo, J. M., Blanco-Mesa, F., Gil-Lafuente, A. M., & Yager, R. R. (2017). Thirty years of the *International Journal of Intelligent Systems*: A bibliometric review. *International Journal of Intelligent Systems, 32*(5), 526–554.

Morasan, P., Behrens, A., Alessi, M., & Janus, H. (2014). *Millenium Development Goals and beyond 2015: A Strong EU Engagement.* Luxembourg: Publications Office of the EU.

Ottenbacher, M. C. & Harrington, R. J. (2010). Strategies for achieving success for innovative versus incremental new service. *Journal of Services Marketing, 24*, 3–15.

Parasuraman, A., Zeithaml, V. A., & Berry, L. L. (1985). A conceptual model of service quality and its implications for future research. *Journal of Marketing, 49*, 41–50.

Parasuraman, A., Zeithaml, V. A., & Berry, L. L. (1988). SERVQUAL: A multiple-item scale for measuring consumer perceptions of service quality. *Journal of Retailing, 64*, 12–40.

Petrzelka, P., Krannich, R., & Brehm, J. (2005). Identification with resource-based occupations and desire for tourism: Are the two necessarily inconsistent? *Society & Natural Resources, 19,* 693–707.

Pritchard, A. (1969). Statistical bibliography or bibliometrics. *Journal of Documentation, 25,* 348–349.

Racherla, P. & Hu, C. (2010). A social network perspective of tourism research collaborations. *Annals of Tourism Research, 37*(4), 1012–1034.

Ramos-Rodríguez, A. & Ruiz-Navarro, J. (2004). Changes in the intellectual structure of strategic management research. *Strategic Management Journal, 25,* 981–1004.

Rastegar, R. (2010). Tourism development and residents' attitude: A case study of Yazd, Iran. *Tourismos, 5*(2), 203–211.

Sancho, F. (1990). Distribución de la renta en un modelo SAM de la economía española. *Estadística Española, 32*(125), 537–567.

Snyman, S. (2014). Assessment of the main factors impacting community attitudes towards tourism and protected areas in six southern African countries. *Koedoe – African Protected Area Conservation and Science, 56*(2), 1–12.

Sweileh, W. M., Sawalha, A. F., Al-Jabi, S. W., et al. (2016). A bibliometric analysis of literature on malaria vector resistance: 1996–2015. *Global Health, 12,* 76.

Wedgwood, N. (2009). Connell's theory of masculinity: Its origins and influences on the study of gender. *Journal of Gender Studies, 18,* 329–339.

4   Evaluation of the social impact of tourism research

Alba Viana-Lora and Marta G. Nel·lo-Andreu

1   Introduction

The concern over guaranteeing sustainability and identifying the intended or non-intended effects that cause planned interventions, led to the development of the National Environmental Policy Act (NEPA) in the United States in 1969 (Burdge and Robertson, 1990). This Act demands an environmental assessment of all federal projects and programmes, and was the turning point for the Environmental Impact Assessment (EIA) to gain momentum. After the introduction of EIA legislation in various countries, international bodies, such as the World Bank and the European Union, have started to promote EIA within their policies, and in 1985 the EU's EIA Directive was introduced (Glasson et al., 2013).

Social impact assessment (SIA) was developed in the late 1970s because EIA was seen to have a strong social presence (Dendena and Corsi, 2015), emerging as a section within EIA (Freudenburg, 1986). In a project developed in 1973, on creating an oil pipeline to transport petrol in Alaska, the "social impact assessment" appeared in the EIA documents. This is because the project required numerous US workers who could provoke impacts on the culture of the Inuits, the local population in that area of Alaska (Momtaz and Kabir, 2013). EIA seeks to minimize uncertainty in planning processes and SIA adds social science aspects such as social change management, public participation and social research (Bakar et al., 2015). Social impact measurement is more complex than environmental impact measurement, because they are not simple relationships with a single effect, they can occur as a result of rumours or false expectations (Esteves et al., 2017).

Originally SIA was not created to make the best policy decision or to detect projects with negative consequences, but to emphasize public disclosure and discussion of potential impacts (Harvey, 2011), through public participation and public consultation (Burdge, 2002). Public participation becomes a fundamental component of SIA (Tang et al., 2008). The key to the participatory approach lies in the impact assessment that can be carried out by citizens directly affected by an action or project (Becker et al., 2003). Therefore, as SIA evolved, it became a transparency tool that ensured decision-making in project selection, thanks to this participatory process and the assessment of potential impact (Vanclay, 1999). For this reason, there are countries that have integrated SIA into the planning process (Tang et al., 2008), going from being an optional tool to a mandatory one in countries such as Australia and New Zealand (Antonson and Levin, 2018).

This chapter aims to theoretically contextualize SIA for conducting an assessment in the field of tourism. Therefore, following this introductory section , this chapter is structured as follows: section 2 shows the definition, objectives and main principles gathered within SIA; section 3 sets out different aspects of SIA classification; section 4 performs an analysis of the social impact of tourism research using three evaluation tools – the Research Excellence Framework (REF), the Engagement and Impact Assessment (EI) and Social Impact Open Repository (SIOR); section 5 shows the main problems encountered in measuring social impact; section 6 sets out the conclusion of the analysis; and finally, section 7 develops an agenda for future research.

2   Definition, objectives and principles of social impact assessment

Research is considered to have a social impact when knowledge has been produced, published and transferred to society with a positive effect on society (Flecha, 2018). SIA, therefore, "is a tool of assessing and managing the consequences of development projects on people" (Ahmadvand and Karami, 2017). For Vanclay et al. (2015) it "is an analytical and research process that aims to influence decision-making and management of social issues". This analytical process will also monitor and manage the social consequences of planned interventions and any social changes it brings about (Vanclay, 2003). Becker (2001) defines SIA as "the process of identifying the future consequences of a current or proposed actions, which are related to individuals, organisations and social macro-systems".

SIA has gained visibility with the rise of social specialists and the importance of social problems (Esteves et al., 2012). It should be a learning process in which problems are understood, potential impact pathways are analysed and assessed, strategies are developed, and a monitoring programme is designed and implemented (McCombes et al., 2015).

SIA enables research organizations to monitor and manage their performance, justifies the expenditure of public money on research, develops criteria for allocating future funding and facilitates understanding of the most effective methods for delivering impact (Penfield et al., 2014), while providing guidance to practitioners on the appropriate approach to select.

The objectives of SIA are several, for Finsterbusch (1977) to assess the benefits and costs of each action or project in order to choose the best alternative and to assist in policy design and management. For Kolotzek et al. (2018) the aim is to assess humans in a broader context, e.g. capturing community interests, cultural perspectives and gender equality concepts.

The need for guidelines for applying SIA in project development led the Interorganizational Committee on Guidelines and Principles (1995) to create a framework for social impact assessment consisting of 10 steps: public involvement, identification of alternatives, baseline conditions, scoping, projection of estimated effects, predicting responses to impacts, indirect and cumulative impacts, changes in alternatives, mitigation and monitoring.

Different authors have modified this framework, extending the participatory approach to different stages, creating a final stage of management and evaluation (Arce-Gomez et al., 2015) or adding a baseline indicator selection stage (Esteves et al., 2017).

3   Classification of social impact assessment

Measuring the social impact of research is a complex phenomenon; knowledge is an intangible resource and difficult to measure in the social context (Lima and Wood, 2014). Its outcome does not show a single homogeneous impact but a set of social effects. For this reason, the methods used to assess impact change according to the objectives and the target audience (Permanyer-Miralda et al., 2016); it is not possible to standardize metrics since qualitative indicators will hardly be comparable as when trying to equate the creation of a new hospital with that of a theatre (Penfield et al., 2014).

The most successful models for assessing impact are those that combine quantitative and qualitative indicators, as it helps to better understand the multidimensional and contextual nature of society (Reale et al., 2017). Bornmann (2013) accepts three different ways of measuring the social impact of research: econometric studies, surveys and case studies.

Spaapen and Van Drooge (2011) propose to focus the evaluation of the social impact of research on an approach of productive interactions, in which all stakeholders are taken into account, being a more real and closer process. This process makes it possible to steer the social problems of the community to the right recipients thanks to the participation of stakeholders (Aucamp and Lombard, 2018).

This approach was developed within the SIAMPI project, which sought to measure the social impact of research projects through qualitative indicators, such as face-to-face communication with user communities, and quantitative indicators, such as the number of presentations with audiences pigeonholed into three categories of productive interactions: direct, indirect and financial (Spaapen and Van Drooge, 2011).

Penfield et al. (2014) introduced the term Social Return on Investment (SROI) in the evaluation of research impact. SROI is used to demonstrate the value of the investment by identifying the social, environmental and economic impact it has produced. It is a way of describing in monetary terms the social impact of an organization in relation to the investment employed (Penfield et al., 2014; Lingane and Olsen, 2004). It is calculated by dividing the net present value of the benefits by the net present value of the investment (Millar and Hall, 2013). It is a term more commonly used in business based on cost-benefit analysis; it is true that its attribution to science would allow to detect which research is applied, but the problem lies in the complexity of monetizing social benefits.

Social impact assessment can be classified according to the size of the project into three types. On a smaller scale we find micro-social impact assessment, focusing on people and their behaviour. In between, we find meso-social impact assessment, focusing on organizations and social networks (including communities). At a larger size is the macro-social impact assessment, based on national and international social systems (Becker, 2001).

SIA can also be classified according to the timing of the assessment into ex ante, in itinere and ex post, as it is not a one-off assessment, but a process that lasts for the life of the project (Aucamp and Lombard, 2018). The ex ante evaluation of the social impact of the research is collected in the project preparation phase. It is a preliminary stage that marks the baseline of the project, collecting all baseline data, delimiting the scope of the social issues relevant to the research and detecting existing information gaps (Vanclay et al., 2015). This is the time to conduct field visits and contact all stakeholders; it is a good way to get ideas and develop a project taking into account the concerns of the actors involved (Becker et al., 2003).

An early assessment of the area of influence will extract social data relevant to the project, serving as a prediction of the future by determining how the research will influence the affected society. This will provide answers to what kind of change is expected with the implementation of the project, where this change will occur, what effects it will have and whether this effect is important for the society (Helming et al., 2011). It is also used to gather expert opinions and compare experiences from other projects and ex post evaluations (Vanclay et al., 2015).

The development of this phase is perhaps the most complex part, as there are problems that appear in the execution or completion of the project that the evaluators have not been able to predict at this stage. To prevent this from happening, good planning is necessary in which three to five scenarios of possible future contexts are designed, a theoretical model that simulates what could happen in each of the cases. These simulations can be carried out in several rounds to correct weaknesses and classify strategies according to the type of scenario. The complexity can be increased by adding possible incidents. This planning also includes the adverse impact mitigation strategy (Becker, 2001).

Once the project is underway, the social impact assessment should be followed up with an in itinere assessment. In this phase, the planning agreed in the previous phase is followed. The social aspects are monitored to see whether the change is being implemented as planned. In case of deviations, previously developed mitigation measures are applied to eradicate the adverse impact and redirect the investigation. During this phase, continuous reporting on the status of the project is carried out, involving stakeholder consultation and feedback (Macombe and Loeillet, 2017; Vanclay et al., 2015).

At the end of the project, an ex post social impact assessment should be carried out, either in the short term or in the long term (Flecha, 2018). This timeframe will vary depending on the subject of the project. As an example Li et al. (2014) propose for housing projects to carry out the evaluation one year after the end of the project. In this way, all social impacts arising from the project are captured in a final report. This type of evaluation is becoming increasingly common among funding agencies, as it allows the most impactful research and researchers to be identified in order to receive more funding in future calls for proposals.

A study carried out by the European Research Council (ERC), a body dedicated to funding quality research in Europe, found that 59 per cent of 225 completed projects under the EU's Seventh Framework Programme had a significant scientific breakthrough and that more than half had an impact on the economy, society and policy-making. This study was carried out in 2018 by 25 expert panels (ERC, 2019), suggesting a concern about the impact of funded research.

4   Assessing the social impact of tourism research

The complexity of tourism sometimes makes impact impossible to measure (McCombes et al., 2015). Research assessing the social impact of tourism research is virtually non-existent, with the exception of the study by Viana-Lora and Nel·lo-Andreu (2020), which uses the social impact of social media as an indication of the benefit of research on society, and the analysis by Brauer et al. (2019), on the impact of UK tourism research according to data provided by the Research Excellence Framework (REF). Although the latter article does not focus on the social impact of research or the impact of researchers on society, it does highlight the improvement of quality of life, environmental sustainability and social sustainability as the type of impact of the studies analysed.

In the field of tourism, the focus has historically been on highlighting the positive and negative impact of the activity as such, but there is no trace of evaluation of the research carried out. There is no action, for example, to create a body that describes what social benefits tourism is intended to achieve in order to guide research in pursuit of these benefits.

Due to the lack of such assessments in the field of tourism, this chapter provides a brief analysis of the social impact of tourism research in three assessment tools, the Research Excellence Framework (REF), the Engagement and Impact Assessment (EI) and Social Impact Open Repository (SIOR). For the field of tourism these are the only tools that assess completed research and have online and open access to the data.

4.1   Method

The method carried out consists of extracting from each tool, the Research Excellence Framework (REF), the Engagement and Impact Assessment (EI) and Social Impact Open Repository (SIOR), the research related to tourism, using the following keywords: tour, tourism, tourist, touristy, vacation, adventure, resort, retreat, travel, traveller, journey, destination, holiday, visit and pilgrimage, in order to carry out a content analysis and detect the social impact present in this research.

4.2   Results

This section contains the results obtained in the analysis of each tool by subsection.

4.2.1   Research Excellence Framework

The REF was created in the United Kingdom in 2014 by the four bodies financing higher education. It is a revision process in pairs consisting of panels of experts who assess the quality of the results, the non-academic impact and the research environment. It aims to compare research so as to establish reputation criteria, provide responsibility for public investment and inform on fund assignment (REF, 2019).

REF classifies the research in the United Kingdom using different filters, and one of them is the field of research, and it shows 36; the field of tourism is unit 26 (Sport and Exercise Sciences, Leisure and Tourism). The percentage in field 26 is fairly low, 1.84 per cent, with 122 case studies against the 6637 total number of studies. Another classification is made by research area and within this, by subarea, and out of the 22 areas of research there is one called Commerce, Management, Tourism and Services which has 347 researches, 5.23 per cent of the total, and within this, the subarea for tourism has 7 case studies, i.e. 0.11 per cent of the total.

This tool includes any non-academic impact, but incorporates a filter according to the type of impact; Political, Health, Technological, Economic, Legal, Cultural and Societal. A social impact filter is run to select projects. Social impact includes 1723 case studies, and it is the type of impact with the most research. When filtering by field 26, we find 82 case studies, 3 of which have the tourism filter as area of research. However, if the tourism filter as research subarea is applied to the 1723 cases with social impact, 4 cases appear, and this is because one case is classified within the field of Business and Management Studies.

In order to prevent other tourism researches with social impact being classified in other fields or other areas of research, various searches are conducted with the above-mentioned key words. After eliminating the duplications, we collect 478 case studies, out of which 21 are related to tourism.

This result reflects the little presence of case studies regarding tourism with an impact on society; only 21 cases out of the 1723 reveal some social impact, which would mean 1.22 per cent of the total.

4.2.2   Engagement and impact assessment

In Australia, the Australian Research Council (ARC), the government's research advisory body, developed the Engagement and Impact Assessment (EI) tool and carried out the first pilot test in 2017. It aims to represent the impact of Australian research beyond the academic contribution, in terms of economic, environmental, social, cultural and other types of benefits. This way, it identifies how institutions translate research into impact through mainly qualitative, tangible results (ARC, 2015). The research is classified into 22 fields of research, and tourism occupies the 15th (Commerce, Management, Tourism and Services).

Its first results were submitted in 2019, where one can find a total of 245 researches. By applying the above-mentioned key words, we find a total of 56 researches. Content analysis and filtering are carried out to select the studies affecting tourism and to avoid the keywords inserting studies from other fields. After completing this process, we are left with 12 studies related directly or indirectly to the tourism sector, where some social impact is noticed. One example is the improvement of the transport infrastructure, which leads to; a saving on travel time, better efficiency, safety and comfort, and prioritizing public investment in road safety.

Once again, there is scarce representation in total research, this time in Australia, and a very limited presence of tourism, 4.90 per cent if we consider the 12 cases selected out of the 245 total case.

4.2.3   Social Impact Open Repository

In Spain, the SIOR was created in 2017 as the world's first open access, free-of-charge repository to show, share and store the social impact of the results of research. It essentially works by rating in pairs the social impact of projects, from 1 to 10, based on their connection to the Sustainable Development Goals (SDGs), the percentage of improvement obtained with respect to the initial situation, the replicability of the impact, the social impact published in scientific journals and the sustainability obtained through the project findings (SIOR, 2017).

Using the keywords associated with tourism, we find one single project, "Ecosocial behaviour of the hominids in the Atapuerca Mountain range during the Quaternary period". This is not a project directly related to tourism, but it reflects a social impact on the local population because of the increase in employment thanks to tourism.

This tool does not reflect the reality of the social impact of research in Spain, as only 33 projects are represented.

5   Limitations and problems of social impact assessment

The three tools described above use case study methodology, which is a complex process that requires a lot of effort, but seems to be the most effective way to measure social impact (Bornmann, 2012). However, these tools have some limitations, because the systems are not standardized (Lauronen, 2020), which makes it impossible to compare different systems and countries, and they do not represent the total research. There is no successful measurement model (Bornmann, 2012). Moreover, in all cases an ex post evaluation is carried out. Social impact assessment does not capture scientific impact, and therefore approaches that combine scientific and social impact assessment in one applicable framework are needed.

In seeking to make the social impact of research tangible, a number of problems arise. The attribution problem is the most discussed, based on how to know whether the impact was actually produced by the research (Permanyer-Miralda et al., 2016; Bornmann et al., 2019; Sivertsen and Meijer, 2020; Tahamtan and Bornmann, 2020), also called "attributable change", i.e. that the change was caused by a particular research (Reale et al., 2017). Another problem is the time lag; it can take between 3 and 9 years for the societal benefit to occur, in medical sciences up to 17 years have passed between medical trials and the demonstration of benefit to society (Ozanne et al., 2017). It is also the case that SIA is conducted out of obligation and compliance, without concern for society and without taking into account the real societal issues (Aucamp and Lombard, 2018). Determining the size of the study to establish the number of people needed to carry it out is another of the problems found in the literature (Becker, 2001).

6   Conclusion

There is no doubt about the complexity of measuring the social impact of research; there are a number of problems in the evaluation process that are currently unsolvable. There is no accepted framework for measuring the social impact of science (Bornmann, 2014). Some of the problems discussed in the previous section could be solved, as in the case of the attribution problem, with the use of process indicators; in this case the constant monitoring of the research makes it possible to clarify how the knowledge contributed to the achievement of the concrete benefit (De Jong et al., 2014).

Tourism has limitations in its research related to its multidisciplinary nature and the lack of interaction between stakeholders, so much so that sometimes its complexity causes research to take certain values or knowledge for granted, leading to unintended consequences in the research results (Tribe, 2004).

The lack of studies on the social impact of tourism research leads to this analysis, which detects that the social benefits generated by tourism research are poorly represented in the tools examined. This may be due to the lack of social orientation in the research carried out. It is essential to incorporate social objectives and to consider society in research planning (Pejić Bach et al., 2020), in order to respond to social demands and thus ensure that knowledge is appropriately focused (Lauronen, 2020). It has been shown that researchers most concerned with the social impact of their research are those who engage most with stakeholders (Olmos-Peñuela et al., 2014). Interaction with stakeholders already demonstrates an effort to generate benefits for society (Hill, 2016). It is considered a necessary condition for successful research (Molas-Gallart and Tang, 2011).

The tools analysed perform an ex post evaluation of the science and, therefore, it is unknown whether this research has been aimed at achieving societal benefits or whether the benefits achieved have been the result of chance.

On the other hand, researchers are often unaware that their research has a social impact (Bornmann, 2012). For this reason, it is necessary to engage them through awareness-raising to help improve engagement with society and visualize the potential social impact (Olmos-Peñuela et al., 2014).

7   Future research

Future research can be directed towards the design of a clear, measurable and universal system of indicators to measure the social impact of research at all stages of research, thus enabling its monitoring. In this way, its application will make it possible to visualize whether the research developed in tourism so far has had a social impact and will serve as a basis for applying it to future research projects. A universal measurement system could be used by funding agencies, both to grant funding and to monitor research.

Since the search for social benefit in research is increasingly desired, it would be interesting to explore how these funding agencies treat social impact in public calls for proposals, in order to detect the importance or weight of social aspects as opposed to other aspects such as scientific impact. It has been shown that research with a high scientific impact does not necessarily generate benefits for society (Bornmann, 2012).

Especially in tourism, few studies focus on achieving a beneficial social impact on the population. Another opportunity for future research would be to conduct an in-depth analysis involving all stakeholders in the tourism industry to gather their views and develop a framework for action. This framework will serve to design research projects taking into account the social problems identified and the potential social impact; perhaps this action will help to avoid problems such as "tourism phobia", as the views of the local residents would be taken into account before planning any tourism typology or space.

A future line of research can be directed towards discovering how tourism research affects the daily lives of citizens, i.e. how the research is applied to generate social benefit.

Acknowledgement

This publication has been possible with the support of the Ministerio de Ciencia, Innovación y Universidades (MICINN)/the European Social Fund (ESF) (PRE2018-085470), the POLITUR project (CSO2017-82156-R) and the Department of Research and Universities of the Catalan Government (2017SGR22).

References

Ahmadvand, M., and Karami, E. (2017). Social impacts evaluation and insider-outsider paradigm: Floodwater spreading project on the Gareh-Bygone plain as an illustrative case. *Evaluation and Program Planning, 65,* 69–76.

Antonson, H., and Levin, L. (2018). A crack in the Swedish welfare façade? A review of assessing social impacts in transport infrastructure planning. *Progress in Planning, 138.*

ARC (2015). *About the Australian Research Council.* https://www.arc.gov.au/.

Arce-Gomez, A., Donovan, J. D., and Bedggood, R. E. (2015). Social impact assessments: Developing a consolidated conceptual framework. *Environmental Impact Assessment Review, 50,* 85–94.

Aucamp, I., and Lombard, A. (2018). Can social impact assessment contribute to social development outcomes in an emerging economy? *Impact Assessment and Project Appraisal, 36*(2), 173–185.

Bakar, A. A., Osman, M. M., Bachok, S., and Zen, I. (2015). Social impact assessment: How do the public help and why do they matter? *Procedia–Social and Behavioral Sciences, 170,* 70–77.

Becker, D. R., Harris, C. C., McLaughlin, W. J., and Nielsen, E. A. (2003). A participatory approach to social impact assessment: The interactive community forum. *Environmental Impact Assessment Review, 23*(3), 367–382.

Becker, H. A. (2001). Social impact assessment. *European Journal of Operational Research, 128*(2), 311–321.

Bornmann, L. (2012). Measuring the societal impact of research: Research is less and less assessed on scientific impact alone – we should aim to quantify the increasingly important contributions of science to society. *EMBO Reports, 13*(8), 673–676.

Bornmann, L. (2013). What is societal impact of research and how can it be assessed? A literature survey. *Journal of the American Society for Information Science and Technology, 64*(2), 217–233.

Bornmann, L. (2014). Do altmetrics point to the broader impact of research? An overview of benefits and disadvantages of altmetrics. *Journal of Informetrics, 8*(4), 895–903.

Bornmann, L., Haunschild, R., and Adams, J. (2019). Do altmetrics assess societal impact in a comparable way to case studies? An empirical test of the convergent validity of altmetrics based on data from the UK research excellence framework (REF). *Journal of Informetrics, 13*(1), 325–340.

Brauer, R., Dymitrow, M., and Tribe, J. (2019). The impact of tourism research. *Annals of Tourism Research, 77,* 64–78.

Burdge, R. J. (2002). Why is social impact assessment the orphan of the assessment process? *Impact Assessment and Project Appraisal, 20*(1), 3–9.

Burdge, R. J., and Robertson, R. A. (1990). Social impact assessment and the public involvement process. *Environmental Impact Assessment Review, 10*(1–2), 81–90.

De Jong, S., Barker, K., Cox, D., Sveinsdottir, T., and Van den Besselaar, P. (2014). Understanding societal impact through productive interactions: ICT research as a case. *Research Evaluation, 23*(2), 89–102.

Dendena, B., and Corsi, S. (2015). The environmental and social impact assessment: A further step towards an integrated assessment process. *Journal of Cleaner Production, 108,* 965–977.

ERC (2019). *Qualitative Evaluation of Completed Projects Funded by the European Research Council 2018*. https://erc.europa.eu/sites/default/files/document/file/2019-qualitative-evaluation-projects.pdf.

Esteves, A. M., Factor, G., Vanclay, F., Götzmann, N., and Moreira, S. (2017). Adapting social impact assessment to address a project's human rights impacts and risks. *Environmental Impact Assessment Review, 67*, 73–87.

Esteves, A. M., Franks, D., and Vanclay, F. (2012). Social impact assessment: The state of the art. *Impact Assessment and Project Appraisal, 30*(1), 34–42.

Finsterbusch, K. (1977). The potential role of social impact assessment in instituting public policies. In K. Finsterbusch and C. Wolf (eds.), *Methodology of Social Impact Assessment*. Stroudsburg, PA: Dowden, Hutchinson and Ross, pp. 2–12.

Flecha, G. R. (2018). Evaluación del impacto social de la investigación. *Revista de Fomento Social, 291–292*, 485–502.

Freudenburg, W. R. (1986). Social impact assessment. *Annual Review of Sociology, 12*(1), 451–478.

Glasson, J., Therivel, R., and Chadwick, A. (2013). *Introduction to Environmental Impact Assessment*, 3rd edition. Abingdon: Routledge.

Harvey, B. (2011). Foreword: SIA from a resource developer's perspective. In F. Vanclay and A. M. Esteves (eds.), *New Directions in Social Impact Assessment: Conceptual and Methodological Advances*. Cheltenham, UK and Northampton, MA, USA: Edward Elgar Publishing.

Helming, K., Diehl, K., Bach, H., Dilly, O., König, B., Kuhlman, T., … Wascher, D. (2011). Ex ante impact assessment of policies affecting land use. Part A: Analytical framework. *Ecology and Society, 16*(1).

Hill, S. (2016). Assessing (for) impact: Future assessment of the societal impact of research. *Palgrave Communications, 2*(1), 1–7.

Interorganizational Committee on Guidelines and Principles (1995). Guidelines and principles for social impact assessment. *Environmental Impact Assessment Review, 15*(1), 11–43.

Kolotzek, C., Helbig, C., Thorenz, A., Reller, A., and Tuma, A. (2018). A company-oriented model for the assessment of raw material supply risks, environmental impact and social implications. *Journal of Cleaner Production, 176*, 566–580.

Lauronen, J. P. (2020). The dilemmas and uncertainties in assessing the societal impact of research. *Science and Public Policy, 47*(2), 207–218.

Li, D., Chen, H., Hui, E. C. M., Yang, H., and Li, Q. (2014). A methodology for ex-post assessment of social impacts of an affordable housing project. *Habitat International, 43*, 32–40.

Lima, G. D. M. R., and Wood, T. (2014). The social impact of research in business and public administration. *Revista de Administração de Empresas, 54*(4), 458–463.

Lingane, A., and Olsen, S. (2004). Guidelines for social return on investment. *California Management Review, 46*(3), 116–135.

Macombe, C., and Loeillet, D. (2017). Instruments to assess the social impacts of value chains. In E. Biénabe, A. Rival, and D. Loeillet (eds.), *Sustainable Development and Tropical Agri-Chains*. Dordrecht: Springer, pp. 257–265.

McCombes, L., Vanclay, F., and Evers, Y. (2015). Putting social impact assessment to the test as a method for implementing responsible tourism practice. *Environmental Impact Assessment Review, 55*, 156–168.

Millar, R., and Hall, K. (2013). Social return on investment (SROI) and performance measurement: The opportunities and barriers for social enterprises in health and social care. *Public Management Review, 15*(6), 923–941.

Molas-Gallart, J., and Tang, P. (2011). Tracing "productive interactions" to identify social impacts: An example from the social sciences. *Research Evaluation*, *20*(3), 219–226.

Momtaz, S., and Kabir, Z. (2013). *Evaluating Environmental and Social Impact Assessment in Developing Countries*. Amsterdam: Elsevier.

Olmos-Peñuela, J., Castro-Martínez, E., and d'Este, P. (2014). Knowledge transfer activities in social sciences and humanities: Explaining the interactions of research groups with non-academic agents. *Research Policy*, *43*(4), 696–706.

Ozanne, J. L., Davis, B., Murray, J. B., Grier, S., Benmecheddal, A., Downey, H., … Seregina, A. (2017). Assessing the societal impact of research: The relational engagement approach. *Journal of Public Policy and Marketing*, *36*(1), 1–14.

Pejić Bach, M., Pulido, C. M., Suša Vugec, D., Ionescu, V., Redondo-Sama, G., and Ruiz-Eugenio, L. (2020). Fostering social project impact with Twitter: Current usage and perspectives. *Sustainability*, *12*(15), 6290.

Penfield, T., Baker, M. J., Scoble, R., and Wykes, M. C. (2014). Assessment, evaluations, and definitions of research impact: A review. *Research Evaluation*, *23*(1), 21–32.

Permanyer-Miralda, G., Hinrichs-Krapels, S., and Adam, P. (2016). The social impact of cardiology research: Beyond management. *Revista Española de Cardiología* (English Edition), *69*(7), 639–643.

Reale, E., Avramov, D., Canhial, K., Donovan, C., Flecha, R., Holm, P., … Primeri, E. (2017). A review of literature on evaluating the scientific, social and political impact of social sciences and humanities research. *Research Evaluation*, *27*(4), 298–308.

REF (2019). *Research Excellence Framework*. https://www.ref.ac.uk/.

SIOR (2017). *Social Impact Open Repository*. https://sior.ub.edu/.

Sivertsen, G., and Meijer, I. (2020). Normal versus extraordinary societal impact: How to understand, evaluate, and improve research activities in their relations to society? *Research Evaluation*, *29*(1), 66–70.

Spaapen, J., and Van Drooge, L. (2011). Introducing "productive interactions" in social impact assessment. *Research Evaluation*, *20*(3), 211–218.

Tahamtan, I., and Bornmann, L. (2020). Altmetrics and societal impact measurements: Match or mismatch? A literature review. *El profesional de la información (EPI)*, *29*(1).

Tang, B. S., Wong, S. W., and Lau, M. C. H. (2008). Social impact assessment and public participation in China: A case study of land requisition in Guangzhou. *Environmental Impact Assessment Review*, *28*(1), 57–72.

Tribe, J. (2004). Knowing about tourism. In J. Phillimore and L. Goodson (eds.), *Qualitative Research in Tourism: Ontologies, Epistemologies and Methodologies*. London: Routledge, pp. 46–62.

Vanclay, F. (1999). Social impact assessment. In J. Petts (ed.), *Handbook of Environmental Impact Assessment*. Oxford: Blackwell Science, pp. 301–326.

Vanclay, F. (2003). International principles for social impact assessment. *Impact Assessment and Project Appraisal*, *21*(1), 5–12.

Vanclay, F., Esteves, A. M., Aucamp, I., and Franks, D. (2015). *Evaluación de impacto social: Lineamientos para la evaluación y gestión de impactos sociales de proyectos*. IAIA Asociación Internacional para la Evaluación de Impactos.

Viana-Lora, A. and Nel·lo-Andreu, M. (2020). Alternative metrics for assessing the social impact of tourism research. *Sustainability*, 12(10), 4299.

5 Social impacts of tourism activities: a social life-cycle assessment perspective

Irene Huertas-Valdivia

Introduction

Since the early 1970s, sustainability has attracted the attention of society and research. Several United Nations conferences have stressed the importance of promoting economic growth in the context of positive social development (e.g., the 1972 United Nations Conference on the Human Environment in Stockholm and the 1992 United Nations Conference on Environment and Development in Rio de Janeiro), urging companies worldwide to address social issues in management practices (Iofrida et al., 2018). More recently, the United Nations (UN) Sustainable Development Goals, launched in 2015, address current global challenges by setting seventeen goals (divided into 129 targets) to achieve worldwide by 2030. Eleven of these goals involve social impacts. Furthermore, the EU Non-financial Reporting Directive (Directive 2014/95/EU) encourages value chains worldwide to respect human rights. Since 2018, companies with more than 500 employees are required to include non-financial and diversity information in their annual reports (for more information, see https://ec.europa.eu/info/business-economy-euro/company -reporting-and-auditing/company-reporting/non-financial-reporting_en).

Social issues have indeed become a central concern for academics and practitioners in all economic sectors, including tourism. Sustainability issues are becoming integral components of tourism policy and strategy and have received a dizzying amount of research attention in recent years (Garrigos-Simon et al., 2018).

Tourism has powerful transformational effects on the territories and societies in which it is developed. It is a dynamic industry driver for socio-economic progress, with direct and indirect consequences for the social, cultural, educational, environmental, and economic aspects of communities (Michailidou et al., 2016). Tourism businesses' products are the provision of transportation, accommodation, food and beverage, entertainment, recreation, and other activities. In tourism, production and consumption occur simultaneously; the product cannot be stored for later use. Tourism services are mainly based on *experiences*. The tourist experience is thus a complementary, holistic product resulting from close cooperation of agents in multiple subsectors: public authorities, residents, private companies, and visitors. The different stakeholders that intervene in the tourism ecosystem are highly interdependent, such that damage to one part directly or indirectly affects the others (Jiang et al., 2019).

Tourism business decisions affect not only the environment (in terms of waste generation, gas emissions, energy consumption, noise, etc.) but also people (customers, employees, administration, society in general, etc.), either directly through their operations or indirectly through their value chain collaborators. Now more than ever, tourism companies are expected to deliver their services within a sustainable paradigm, seeking a balance between economic, environmental, and social concerns at different levels. Public opinion and potential customers often demand transparency in these companies' method of operations and are increasingly requiring companies to answer questions about their environmental and social performance to enable potential customers to make more informed purchase decisions.

Not all tourism business models are equally socio-ethically sustainable. In fact, two companies located in the same area and producing the same service may have completely different social impacts due to various factors, such as managerial approaches, the way they treat their employees, or their relationship with other stakeholders. To be sustainable, tourism activities should meet "the needs of the present without compromising the ability of future generations to meet their own needs" (World Commission on Environment and Development, 1987, p. 15).

Assessing sustainability in tourism

In recent decades, various methodologies have been developed to assess sustainability of the three pillars *People, Planet, and Profit*, also known as the *triple bottom line*. Life-cycle methodologies have introduced a long-term perspective on sustainability approaches, enlarging the scope of assessment and of stakeholders' responsibility to all phases of the product life-cycle (*cradle to grave* or *cradle to cradle*). *Life-cycle sustainability assessment* (*LCSA*) integrates three methodologies: environmental life-cycle assessment (E-LCA), Life-Cycle Costing (LCC), and social life-cycle assessment (S-LCA).

Among these methods, environmental life-cycle assessment (E-LCA) is the most established in international contexts, as it has been monitored by ISO standards such as ISO 14040-14044. E-LCA is organized into four standardized steps: *definition of goal and scope, inventory analysis, impact assessment, and interpretation*. E-LCA has focused predominantly on product assessment, and Gauthier (2005) identified adaptation of E-LCA methodology to the service sector as a valuable research avenue. E-LCA methodology has previously been applied to tourism, but in a limited way. For example, Castellani and Sala (2012) analysed the environmental sustainability of "one week of a spa holiday" and "one bednight" in different types of accommodation structures in northern Italy. Integrating two methodologies, E-LCA and ecological footprint, these authors assessed the impacts of different consumption activities (food, housing, mobility, goods and services, and waste). Michailidou et al. (2016) performed a similar analysis in the Greek Chalkidiki region, also including multi-criteria analysis and surveying hoteliers about the hotels' energy and water consumption, waste generation, carbon footprint, etc. Recently, Soratana et al. (2021) have applied E-LCA to different tourism subsectors as well.

As to social impacts, the significance of assessing the social consequences of private business and public policy decisions has been increasing since the 1990s. Social phenomena can be studied using many different approaches. Within the LCSA framework, S-LCA aims at "facilitating companies to conduct business in a socially responsible manner by providing information about the potential social impacts on people caused by the activities in the life cycle of their products" (Dreyer et al., 2006, p. 88). The main aim of S-LCA is thus to improve social performance of the product or service through a methodology that assesses positive and negative social impacts on the different groups of stakeholders involved throughout the entire product/service life-cycle.

In 2009, the United Nations Environmental Programme/Society of Environmental Toxicology and Chemistry (UNEP/SETAC) developed the *Guidelines for Social Life Cycle Assessment of Products* as a reference framework for social impact analysis. The guidelines identified five categories of stakeholders: workers, local community, consumers, society, and value chain actors. The most recent version of the guidelines (UNEP, 2020) included a sixth stakeholder category, children. Social impacts are classified by stakeholder categories and operationalized through inventory indicators grouped into subcategories that vary depending on the stakeholder analysed (see

Table 5.1). In 2013, the *Methodological Sheets for Social Life Cycle Assessment* (UNEP/SETAC, 2013) defined generic and specific indicators for each sub-category (e.g., human rights, working conditions, health and safety, cultural heritage, governance, and socio-economic repercussions).

In 2020, a new version of the *Guidelines* was published that provided a more practical reference for those wanting to learn about and apply S-LCA methods. These new *Guidelines* summarize the pros and cons of each method and describe in detail the tasks to be performed in each step of S-LCA analysis (UNEP, 2020).

Arcese et al. (2013) are the first and among the few authors to date to propose applying the S-LCA methodology to the tourism sector, assessing the social criticalities of a Bed and Breakfast company. They studied the business's social impact, using multiple tools available to analyse information obtained through social accounting and business management tools. Their approach gave prominence to relationships between tourist accommodation services and the local community, while also referencing company networks.

Application of S-LCA to tourism activities

S-LCA is a methodology that combines quantitative and qualitative indicators to assess potential (and actual) positive and negative impacts of products and services (throughout their life cycle) on different stakeholders. Like the modelling capabilities and systematic assessment process of E-LCA, the S-LCA framework follows a four-step process: (1) goal and scope of the analysis, (2) social life-cycle inventory, (3) social life-cycle impact assessment, and (4) interpretation of results (see Figure 5.1).

Goal and scope of the analysis
Specification of question(s) to be answered by S-LCA
The goals of S-LCA case studies can be oriented to designing sustainable products, identifying social hotspots along the value chain and throughout the life-cycle of the products and services, quantifying and qualifying the potential social performance of products, and examining potential social improvement options throughout the life-cycle. The goal of such study is to understand whether the product value chain contributes to social development of its stakeholders (UNEP, 2020).

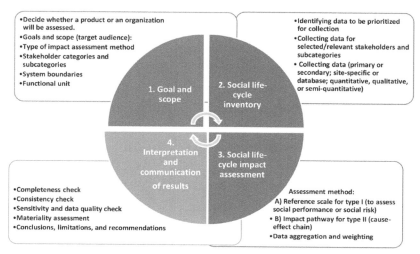

Source: Adapted from Benoît Norris et al. (2012) and UNEP (2020)

Figure 5.1   The four iterative steps of S-LCA

Application of S-LCA to tourism could answer some of the following questions: What are the *social hotspots* of one guest night/a seven-day holiday in a specific destination's life-cycle? What overall social impact does the value chain of a certain restaurant or transport company produce? How would social impacts be affected if we switched to an alternative travel operator/holiday destination?

Stakeholders

In addition to specifying research questions or goals, we must also identify the stakeholders affected (e.g., workers, consumers, local community).

Many stakeholders affect and are affected by the actions, decisions, policies, practices, or goals of the tourism organizations. Table 5.1 displays a complete list of stakeholders' categories and subcategories, as per the 2020 UNEP *Guidelines*. Nevertheless, authors such as Sousa-Zomer and Cauchick Miguel (2018) assert that only a few indicators of the S-LCA guidelines are appropriate for comparative analyses in service systems.

To conduct a global sustainability assessment, Castellani and Sala (2012, p. 136) divide the tourism sector into three main areas of activity, each related to specific stakeholders (local administrators, entrepreneurs, and tourists,

Table 5.1   Stakeholder classification

Stakeholder categories	Subcategories	Example of indicator
Workers	1. Freedom of association and collective bargaining. 2. Child labour. 3. Fair salary. 4. Working hours. 5. Forced labour. 6. Equal opportunities / discrimination. 7. Health and safety. 8. Social benefits / Social security. 9. Employment relationship. 10. Sexual harassment. 11. Smallholders including farmers.	1. Workers are free to join unions of their choosing. 4. Number of hours that employees will effectively work / Respect for contractual agreements concerning overtime. 5. Workers are free to terminate their employment within the established limits. 6. Total number of incidents of discrimination and actions taken. 8. Percentage of permanent workers receiving paid time off.
Local community	1. Access to material resources. 2. Access to immaterial resources. 3. Delocalization and migration. 4. Cultural heritage. 5. Safe and healthy living conditions. 6. Respect for indigenous rights. 7. Community engagement. 8. Local employment. 9. Secure living conditions.	1. Development of project-related infrastructure with mutual community access and benefits. 2. Strength of community education initiatives. 3. Number of individuals who resettle (voluntarily and involuntarily) that can be attributed to the organization. 7. Diversity of community stakeholder groups that engage with the organization. 8. Percentage of workforce that could be hired / Percentage of spending on locally based suppliers. 9. Efforts to strengthen community health / Efforts to minimize use of hazardous substances.

Stakeholder categories	Subcategories	Example of indicator
Society	1. Public commitment to sustainability issues. 2. Contribution to economic development. 3. Prevention and mitigation of armed conflicts. 4. Technology development. 5. Corruption. 6. Ethical treatment of animals. 7. Poverty alleviation.	1. Presence of mechanisms to follow up on fulfilment of promises. 2. Contribution to economic progress. 4. Investments in technology development / Technology transfer to society. 5. The organization installs or cooperates with internal and external controls to prevent corruption.
Consumers	1. Health and safety. 2. Feedback mechanism. 3. Consumer privacy. 4. Transparency. 5. End-of-life responsibility.	1. Presence of management measures to assess consumer health and safety. 2. Presence of feedback mechanisms (e.g., related to process of service provision). 3. Number of consumer complaints related to breach of privacy or loss of data within the last year.
Value chain actors (not including consumers)	1. Fair competition. 2. Promotion of social responsibility. 3. Supplier relationships. 4. Respect for intellectual property rights. 5. Wealth distribution.	1. Contribution to strategic positioning and competitiveness of companies in the value chain. 2. Percentage of suppliers the enterprise has audited with regard to social responsibility in the last year. 4. Use of local intellectual property.
Children	1. Education provided in the local community. 2. Health issues for children as consumers. 3. Child-related marketing practices concerns.	

Source: UNEP/SETAC (2013); UNEP (2020); Sousa-Zomer and Cauchick Miguel (2018)

respectively): (1) "the construction of tourism facilities consisting mainly of hospitality structures"; (2) "the holiday itself that includes the activities that tourists do at the determined destination"; and (3) "the travel involved in getting to and from the tourist destination". The stakeholders identified in Mohaddes Khorassani et al.'s (2019) case study of fortress restoration are workers at the museum, workers at the construction company, consumers (museum visitors, tourists, and scholars), local community (measuring its well-being), and society (involvement and cultural value).

Social impacts on workers due to working conditions have been studied in greater depth than impacts on other stakeholders in the literature, although in sectors other than tourism (Huertas-Valdivia et al., 2020). Some workplace practices experience negative externalities such as "reduced" outcomes for psychological, social, and work-related health and well-being (e.g., work-related exhaustion and burnout, stress-related sleep disorders, depression that disrupts family's/couple's lives, crossover of work-family conflict, etc.). Mariappanadar (2014) developed a specific index to capture harm to psychological, social, and work-related health and the associated costs of harm due to work intensification and high stress (derived from high-performance work practices).

Iofrida et al. (2018) use the S-LCA impact pathway to assess psychosocial risk factors in citrus-growing industry workers, using odds ratios to explain the relationship between working conditions and health problems (in terms of risks of specific disorders or diseases). Their study can be extended to the tourism sector, as workers from its subsectors (restaurants, hospitality, cruise industry) are commonly exposed to stressing situations such as emotional labour, changing shifts, long working hours, and heavy workload during peak season (Tongchaiprasit and Ariyabuddhiphongs, 2016).

System boundaries and functional unit

At this preliminary stage, it is also fundamental to determine which processes to analyse by setting the system boundaries and activity variables for a specific quantity (e.g., housekeeping tasks, F&B services, maintenance duties, administrative activities, etc. related to *one guest night*). System boundaries can be outlined by determining length of stay in the establishment (arrival, duration of stay, end of stay, and departure of the visitor), and whether social impacts will be assessed starting at the visitor's departure from origin or upon arrival at the tourism destination. Following Arcese et al. (2013), the functional unit of a hospitality company can be, for example, *a guest night* in *a two-day service*. Soratana et al. (2021) suggest other functional units, such as *tourist per one trip* or *per one meal* in other related subsectors.

Type of impact assessment method

The impact assessment method must also be determined from the following types:

- Type I. Reference Scale Approach: assesses the product system in terms of social performance or social risk, based on performance reference points.
- Type II. Impact Pathway Approach: entails predicting cause-effect relationships established through characterization of models or qualitative descriptions of existing relationships along an impact pathway.

Social life-cycle inventory

Collection of inventory data

Next, inventory data must be collected to identify social impacts within the tourism product system. The inventory data are related to the stakeholder categories and subcategories defined in Step 1 (e.g., restaurant *workers'* conditions: working hours, wages, number of accidents in workplace, etc.; conditions in the *local community* surrounding a hotel: e.g., local employment, safe and healthy living conditions, access to drinking water, etc.).

Actors can be involved through participatory methods. In Arcese et al. (2013), approaching hotel managers was crucial to collecting data from hotels. Mohaddes Khorassani et al. (2019) interviewed 54 visitors at the fortress museum.

Inventory results from primary data (e.g., retrieved from questionnaires administered to employees and clientele) can be combined with secondary data from tourism sector databases and specific country or/and sector databases (e.g., Product Social Impact Life Cycle Assessment Database (PSILCA) or Social Hotspots Database (SHDB)) (Benoît-Norris et al., 2012). Robust S-LCA results depend on both data consistency and representativeness (UNEP, 2020).

Social life-cycle impact assessment

Translation of data collected

At this third stage, the data and information collected must be translated into a resulting social impact or risk of a social impact, applying one of the two aforementioned approaches:

1. If the aim is to describe a product system with focus on its social performance or social risk, Type I, Reference Scale Approach, should be used.

A reference scale enables benchmarking of impact indicators to rank social hotspots or social performance on a scale from +2 to −2 (where +2 indicates ideal performance, and −2 a non-compliance situation); or from *very high risk* to *very low risk* (see Mohaddes Khorassani et al., 2019 for an example).

2. If the goal is to predict the consequences of the product system, with emphasis on characterizing potential social impacts, the Impact Pathway Approach should be used. This approach focuses on tracing the real chain of causes and effects, for example, "lower future well-being related to poor nutrition because of wages unpaid" (UNEP, 2020).

Both approaches assess impacts throughout the value chain. Impacts have the potential to be aggregated (to obtain a measure of the social impact of the product in relation to a particular social issue and a stakeholder, or a single total score), with some weighting (percentage weight assigned to the social topic score per stakeholder group).

Because S-LCA is an iterative process (assessment can be improved over time through several assessment loops), repeating the analysis can track the effect of changes with increasing accuracy over time, moving from more generic/potential results to more site- and case-specific ones (UNEP, 2020).

Interpretation (and communication) of results

Interpretation of the results detects hotspots and areas for improvement. A social hotspot is a location and/or activity in the life-cycle's stages or processes where a social impact and/or social risk is likely to occur. Results must be communicated in a relevant, reliable, clear, accessible, and transparent way.

Need for further development of S-LCA in tourism

Rooted in and inspired by international conventions and globally agreed-upon documents (Universal Declaration of Human Rights, International Labour Organization conventions and recommendations, Brundtland Report, Global Reporting Initiative (GRI), Social Accountability standards, country norms, etc.), S-LCA has rapidly attracted research interest, despite its newness as a method, due to its utility in supporting decision making. Decisions based on S-LCA analysis will produce more socially beneficial situations (Jørgensen, 2013; Sousa-Zomer and Cauchick Miguel, 2018).

Given its overall, synthetic approach, S-LCA could complement existing corporate social responsibility (CSR) tools to assess social sustainability of products and services in the tourism sector. Additional methods must be devised, however, to measure social impacts of services – which are labour- and relationship-intensive. Most studies in the literature have focused on *product* analysis (Sousa-Zomer and Cauchick Miguel, 2018), and it would be of great utility to apply S-LCA indicators to unravel how development of a tourism *service* could affect the social fabric of the location where it is delivered.

Social sustainability can be measured at individual, relational, and institutional level (Hale et al., 2019) using many models of indicators with different nature and composition. Since S-LCA is a relatively new approach based on multi-layered social phenomena, it still lacks a homogeneous and standardized model for impact assessment. In addition to the difficulties determining a functional unit, choosing system boundaries and cut-off criteria, and including qualitative data, impacts are not always easy to quantify and may depend greatly on the observer's perception, interpretation, and epistemological position (Iofrida et al., 2018). Further research efforts are thus necessary to develop valid indicators to measure the social value and social impacts of service systems, especially of tourism activities. Only so will studies be able to predict the consequences of organizational or structural changes in the life-cycles of tourism products. Of paramount importance in alerting companies and tourism destinations to possible negative impacts, such instruments are crucial to sustainable tourism management and planning. Tourism impact measures should be not only methodologically consistent and easy to apply, but also generally agreed upon in the scientific and expert community (del Río-Vázquez et al., 2019).

As a decision tool, S-LCA enables organizations to choose among different products, production methods, materials, and even partners by identifying the path (realized vs. non-realized situation) to the most favourable social impacts and thus fostering a change of behaviour in the company by modelling impacts. S-LCA methodology identifies not only negative but also positive social impacts. For example, tourism can produce positive social impacts in terms of cultural heritage preservation and related employment generated, facilities and accessibility, and other society-wide improvements. In their case study based on restoration of a medieval fortress, Mohaddes Khorassani et al. (2019) demonstrate that guidelines for the S-LCA of products are appropriate for evaluating social issues related to enhancement of cultural heritage in cultural heritage interventions. Furthermore, the authors note benefits beyond merely environmental benefits (energy saving). Social benefits from preserving heritage buildings extend to issues such as place identity, social cohesion, and sense of belonging to the community.

It is crucial that organizations maintain good relationships and communication with their stakeholders in any S-LCA process. At individual level, *worker* is the stakeholder category that has received the most research attention. This attention may be due to the development of prior social accountability standards, such as SA8000, the first auditable social standard based on the international workplace standards of the International Labour Organization, as well as the United Nations' Universal Declaration of Human Rights (Arcese et al., 2013). Further studies should enlarge the scope of analysis to consumers, residents, and other actors in the supply chain.

The new *Guidelines for Social Life Cycle Assessment of Products and Organizations*, published by UNEP in 2020, include innovations in method and practice, such as social organizational LCA (SO-LCA). Adopting a life-cycle perspective within a single organization, SO-LCA combines and assesses social and socio-economic issues (and their related impacts) associated with the organization *as a whole* (going beyond focus on the product). It complements the S-LCA approach by helping to assess the organization's social performance (UNEP, 2020). A company displays its social consciousness not only through its intentions, but also through the specific actions – or lack of action – that the company performs in many aspects of its business.

Having the ability to identify and report the positive social impacts of their activities can motivate companies to advance in social sustainability strategy. Positive impacts normally imply proactive behaviour that includes encouraging performance beyond compliance. Moreover, a good S-LCA score can become a powerful market parameter, "creating some kind of market advantage for producers living up to certain social standards" to push companies to comply with social standards (Jørgensen et al., 2012, p. 831). Tourism businesses need to rethink their responsibility in order to reformulate their current business models to pursue a more socially responsible orientation. Similarly, the European Ecolabel for accommodation facilities (http://ec.europa.eu/ecat/hotels-campsites/en), a distinction granted to reward tourism businesses' real commitment to social issues, could be extended to foster social sustainability efforts in service organizations. For example, recognition could be granted to tourism companies that apply more sustainable human resources management (SHRM) practices. SHRM practices are bundles of HR practices that "enhance both profit maximization for the organization and also 'reduce the harm' on employees, their families and communities" (Mariappanadar, 2014, p. 313). The main goal of these practices is achievement of the triple bottom line principles, thereby enhancing economic prosperity, environmental integrity, and social equality (Santana and Lopez-Cabrales, 2019). Tourism companies should train their leadership to be conscious of the ethical dimension of their relationship to stakeholders. Managers must be willing to revise practices to increase care and reduce negative impacts of their company's tourism activity.

In 2016, the European Union proposed a measurement system of 43 basic indicators to assess essential aspects of a destination's sustainability, including a social and cultural dimension evaluating aspects such as inclusion, accessibility, and gender equality (https://ec.europa.eu/growth/sectors/tourism/offer/sustainable/indicators_en). This Tourism Indicators System (ETIS) seems to be designed, however, for destination managers and public authorities. Further, use is voluntary. It could thus be valuable to reinforce its results with other qualitative or more subjective indicators (such as residents' perceptions) and extend its use to tourism businesses.

Since public procurement promotes responsible behaviour, it can facilitate changes in unsustainable production and consumption models. For example, del Río-Vázquez et al. (2019) argue that environmentally, socially, and economically sustainable criteria should be of utmost importance in tourism-related public tenders, beyond mere pricing references. These authors note the need for new criteria to detect and measure the social value generated. To this end, they recommend specific training of personnel involved in a public procurement process.

Universities can also play a crucial role in increasing awareness of the importance of social sustainability by teaching ethical leadership principles (Brown and Treviño, 2006). Training undergraduate students in *workplace sustainability leadership* is critical to developing future leaders who can recognize relationships between environmental, social, and economic impacts. Sustainability leadership can help students to evaluate a range of alternative solutions and to identify the solution that achieves the best balance of environmental, social, and economic outcomes, minimizing negative impacts to the physical environment and to the community (Thomas et al., 2020).

References

Arcese, G., Lucchetti, M. C., and Merli, R. (2013). Social life cycle assessment as a management tool: Methodology for application in tourism. *Sustainability*, 5(8), 3275–3287.

Benoît-Norris, C., Cavan, D. A., and Norris, G. (2012). Identifying social impacts in product supply chains: Overview and application of the social hotspot database. *Sustainability*, *4*(9), 1946–1965.

Brown, M. E. and Treviño, L. K. (2006). Ethical leadership: A review and future directions. *Leadership Quarterly*, *17*(6), 595–616.

Castellani, V. and Sala, S. (2012). Ecological footprint and life cycle assessment in the sustainability assessment of tourism activities. *Ecological Indicators*, *16*, 135–147.

del Río-Vázquez, M. E. S., Rodríguez-Rad, C. J., and Revilla-Camacho, M. Á. (2019). Relevance of social, economic, and environmental impacts on residents' satisfaction with the public administration of tourism. *Sustainability (Switzerland)*, *11*(22), 6380.

Dreyer, L., Hauschild, M., and Schierbeck, J. (2006). A framework for social life cycle impact assessment. *International Journal of Life Cycle Assessment*, *11*(2), 88–97.

Garrigos-Simon, F. J., Narangajavana-Kaosiri, Y., and Lengua-Lengua, I. (2018). Tourism and sustainability: A bibliometric and visualization analysis. *Sustainability (Switzerland)*, *10*(6), 1976.

Gauthier, C. (2005). Measuring corporate social and environmental performance: The extended life-cycle assessment. *Journal of Business Ethics*, *59*(1–2), 199–206.

Hale, J., Legun, K., Campbell, H., et al. (2019). Social sustainability indicators as performance. *Geoforum*, *103*, 47–55.

Huertas-Valdivia, I., Ferrari, A. M., Settembre-Blundo, D., et al. (2020). Social life-cycle assessment: A review by bibliometric analysis. *Sustainability*, *12*(15), 6211.

Iofrida, N., De Luca, A. I., Silveri, F., et al. (2018). Psychosocial risk factors' impact pathway for social life cycle assessment: An application to citrus life cycles in South Italy. *International Journal of Life Cycle Assessment*, *24*(12).

Jiang, Y., Ritchie, B. W., and Verreynne, M. L. (2019). Building tourism organizational resilience to crises and disasters: A dynamic capabilities view. *International Journal of Tourism Research*, *21*(6), 882–900.

Jørgensen, A. (2013). Social LCA: A way ahead? *The International Journal of Life Cycle Assessment*, *18*(2), 296–299.

Jørgensen, A., Dreyer, L. C., and Wangel, A. (2012). Addressing the effect of social life cycle assessments. *International Journal of Life Cycle Assessment*, *17*(6), 828–839.

Mariappanadar, S. (2014). Stakeholder harm index: A framework to review work intensification from the critical HRM perspective. *Human Resource Management Review*, *24*(4), 313–329.

Michailidou, A. V., Vlachokostas, C., Moussiopoulos, N., et al. (2016). Life cycle thinking used for assessing the environmental impacts of tourism activity for a Greek tourism destination. *Journal of Cleaner Production*, *111*, 499–510.

Mohaddes Khorassani, S., Ferrari, A. M., Pini, M., et al. (2019). Environmental and social impact assessment of cultural heritage restoration and its application to the Uncastillo Fortress. *International Journal of Life Cycle Assessment*, *24*, 1297–1318.

Santana, M. and Lopez-Cabrales, A. (2019). Sustainable development and human resource management: A science mapping approach. *Corporate Social Responsibility and Environmental Management*, *26*(6), 1171–1183.

Soratana, K., Landis, A. E., Jing, F., and Suto, H. (2021). *Supply Chain Management of Tourism Towards Sustainability*. Cham: Springer.

Sousa-Zomer, T. T. and Cauchick Miguel, P. A. (2018). The main challenges for social life cycle assessment (SLCA) to support the social impacts analysis of product-service systems. *International Journal of Life Cycle Assessment*, *23*(3), 607–616.

Thomas, I., Holdsworth, S., and Sandri, O. (2020). Graduate ability to show work-place sustainability leadership: Demonstration of an assessment tool. *Sustainability Science, 15*(4), 1211–1221.

Tongchaiprasit, P. and Ariyabuddhiphongs, V. (2016). Creativity and turnover intention among hotel chefs: The mediating effects of job satisfaction and job stress. *International Journal of Hospitality Management, 55,* 33–40.

UNEP (2020). *Guidelines for Social Life Cycle Assessment of Products and Organizations 2020.* https:// www .lifecycleinitiative .org/ library/ guidelines -for -social -life -cycle -assessment-of-products-and-organisations-2020/.

UNEP/SETAC (2013). *The Methodological Sheets for Sub-Categories in Social Life Cycle Assessment (S-LCA).* United Nations Environment Programme and Society for Environmental Toxicology and Chemistry.

World Commission on Environment and Development (1987). *Our Common Future.* United Nations. https://www.are.admin.ch/are/en/home/sustainable-development/ international -cooperation/ 2030agenda/ un - _ -milestones -in -sustainable -development/1987--brundtland-report.html.

6   Tourism and citizenship: time to readjust the focus?

Tim Coles

Introduction

According to the famous saying, nothing in the world is certain except death and taxes. Usually attributed to Benjamin Franklin in a letter of 1789 (NCC, 2020), this aphorism points to the fact that, as human beings, we cannot control in which state we are born nor to which state(s) we are initially ascribed citizenship with all this subsequently entails. It also reminds us that our perspectives on the world, both as researchers and as human beings, are positioned and framed by the contexts we assume, experience and are immersed in.

Sitting at home in the United Kingdom (UK) since the start of the pandemic and watching its effects unfold around the world, it has been startling just how many orthodoxies and traditions that were taken for granted before, have been challenged. In summer 2020, UK citizens – as elsewhere – were left wondering where they could go for their summer holidays and what would be the implications of their travel upon their return, especially if the government changed the safety status of their destination (Clatworthy et al., 2020). Almost unfettered freedom of movement had become implicit and time-honoured since the Cold War. Abruptly ending in the spring, it compounded uncertainties brought about by Brexit (Hall, 2020; Andrews, 2020) and the UK's departure from the EU in January 2020. Equally remarkable were some of the earliest pronouncements, especially from politicians and destination management organizations, urging visitors to exercise their discretion, act responsibly and *not* to travel for early season getaways or to second homes (BBC, 2020a). For five decades prior, the UK tourism policy paradigm had been one of continuous growth (Coles, 2021). When the original lockdown in England was lifted in July 2020 the Prime Minister exhorted people to continue to behave responsibly, not least by observing 'social distance' (BBC, 2020b). Media reports in the days afterwards showed beaches replete with visitors, suggesting this plea had been largely ignored (BBC, 2020c). In parallel, the Spanish government encouraged British holidaymakers and second home owners to exert their rights to international travel, by removing the obligation to quarantine on arrival (BBC, 2020d).

Occurrences of this nature were not unique to the UK. Similar things were happening elsewhere around the world. These particular experiences though demonstrate a much wider point. Much of the framing of tourism mobilities in the context of the Coronavirus pandemic has, if not explicitly in these terms, focused on citizenship-related issues; that is to say, the intersection of rights and responsibilities of travellers, residents, communities, business owners and operators, and even politicians and law-makers in the mediation (or not) of travel experiences. Although enduring, there is more to the concept of citizenship than state-based models and those that focus minutely on the interaction of 'rights' and 'responsibilities', not least the relational nature of its definition and its lasting nature (cf. Jones and Gaventa, 2002; Menéndez and Olsen, 2020). Accepting this to be the case, and although well established in the conceptual canon of the social sciences, citizenship widely writ has not been as widely or overtly used in tourism studies as perhaps may have been anticipated. As argued below, this continues to be a missed opportunity for the current and future tourism research agenda on the social impacts of tourism, particularly but not exclusively as it relates to COVID-19. Before developing this argument further, the next section selectively examines some of the central ideas underpinning the concept of citizenship, as it more immediately relates to travel and tourism.

Citizenship: a brief conceptual recap

For keen observers, the invocation of 'rights' and 'responsibilities' as defining characteristics points to a particular, state-based mode of understanding citizenship. Perhaps most notably associated with T. H. Marshall, they attempt to capture the interface between the individual and the state, as well as their respective roles in the organization of modern society (Marshall and Bottomore, 1992). In the case of the latter, the state has significant roles to play –responsibilities of its own, as it were – in the provision of health, security, defence, welfare, education and culture and so on, for or on behalf of its 'citizens'; that is, those individuals it counts among its 'members'. In a somewhat instrumental arrangement, in return for these benefits bestowed on them by the state, individuals are expected to demonstrate their loyalty to the state by subscribing to the principles established for the collective and observed by other fellow group members.

This is clearly a highly abridged summary, and Marshall identified three types of citizenship that had developed over time. There is not space here to discuss the emergence of the civil, political and social citizenships he identified, the latter he argued to be a twentieth-century phenomenon (see Coles, 2007, 2008). Rather, it is germane to note the obvious linkages between this approach to citizenship and mobility, with the latter effectively being the expression of a right to move, the freedom to travel ascribed by the home state. Thus, perhaps one of the most tangible manifestations of state-based citizenship is the passport (Coles, 2008). Through this artefact the state effectively empowers the citizen with the capacity to move beyond its borders and entitles access to the state's representation, facilities and presentation in third countries. Interestingly though, a passport has not always been accompanied by the automatic right to exit a country nor conversely with the automatic right to re-enter a (home) country. While it may be tempting to associate this with totalitarian regimes (Semmens, 2005), several non-political reasons exist for restricting entry, as Australian citizens located in India discovered during April 2021 when their return home was prohibited during the pandemic (BBC, 2021b). Temporary or permanent exclusion orders may form appropriate interventions when travel acts as a major vector for the spread of pathogens (Iaquinto, 2020) and international terrorism (9/11 Commission, 2004).

The Marshallian view of citizenship is not without sustained criticism (cf. Murray, 2007; Revi, 2014), not least because it presents a much simpler, almost early-to-mid twentieth-century view of the relationship between citizen and state that does not capture the social diversity, plurality and complexity associated with the conditions of contemporary (post-modern) society (Isin, 1997; Isin and Wood, 1999). Nor does it adequately deal with the apparent power asymmetries in favour of the state. In presenting the relationship between the state and citizen in an abstract manner, the original view is somewhat agnostic, and in a great many cases the individual citizen needs the state more than the state needs the individual citizen. Yet its core ideas have continued to be evident in, and used by, many societies as conceptual 'building blocks' for how state and citizen relate in civil society. Precisely this type of language was used by the British Prime Minister Tony Blair, and the Labour government after 1997 (Blair, 2002; MoJ, 2009). Even a cursory inspection of public pronouncements on the Coronavirus by politicians and public health officials around the world reveals that similar language and thinking is being used as the state attempts to balance the rights of (sovereign) citizens with their responsibilities to society at various spatial scales (BBC, 2020b; WHO, 2020).

As a concept, citizenship is concerned with how social groups with common interests and shared identities emerge and function. Considering the basic duality of rights and responsibilities, albeit in a state-based view of citizen-ship, is critically and analytically helpful to tourism studies because it further implies a more complex form of social politics than might first meet the eye in host–guest encounters. For instance, there are important questions of 'rights to what?' and 'responsibilities to whom?' As a form of 'othering' it is easy to assume, somewhat lazily, that those travelling from home and the everyday, away to the exotic will encounter people from different groups, more so where this involves state citizenship and cross-border travel. Within domestic tourism, this is not necessarily the case nor in the European Union where pre-scriptions for supra-national forms of citizenship form part of a greater project for social cohesion.

Unpacking the concept further, there is an implicit assumption that all citizens have equal rights and hence access to resources, services and facilities provided by the state. In practice, this is not the case, and instead it leads to situations of relative advantage, disadvantage and inequality among individuals and social groups including how, when and where they travel (Coles, 2008; Bianchi and Stephenson, 2014). To this point, the concepts of 'rights' and 'responsibilities' have been presented in this account in an unfussy, matter-of-fact manner as if there is an implicit, singular and common understanding of what they are, shared by all citizens, equally and invariably. Clearly, this is not the case and there are variations in how they are perceived, understood and interpreted within and among social groups depending on how they are positioned – perhaps with respect to existing social structures and frameworks (Bianchi and Stephenson, 2014) – and position themselves in society. Moreover, notions of 'rights' and 'responsibilities' are presented as a mutually-dependent duality, almost in a form of conceptual equilibrium: awareness of, or action resulting from, one should not exist without reference to the other or its effects on the other. For many citizens and in a wide range of human behaviours though, the two ideas are separate. A perceptual disjuncture exists between the rights afforded to the individual to act and observance of the responsibilities that enacting these rights entails, such that rights to act are not commensurately (or sometimes at all) accompanied by consideration of the responsibilities following on from action. In other words, there is almost a 'responsibility gap' akin to the 'intention-behaviour gap' widely discussed in behavioural research, not least on personal health (Faries, 2016) and sustainable development (Barr et al., 2011; Hall, 2014). For instance, in many advanced economies, including the UK, reducing air pollution is regarded a priority, a responsibility for all in society. Notwithstanding, this does not prevent many city-dwellers from exercising their rights as consumers to buy the most polluting vehicles (Stacey, 2021).

Despite the limitations of state-based approaches to conceptualizing citizenship, one of their enduring legacies has been to point to notions of shared identity, group membership and belonging as foundational elements in social group formation as well as pointing to the possibility of alternative citizenships. Greater political, economic and social liberalization in the 1970s and 1980s suggested that other ways of understanding citizenship were necessary to reflect changing contexts and conditions. In a highly influential contribution, Isin and Wood (1999) argued that contemporary citizenship was no longer exclusively associated with the nation-state, polity and the dominance of the political and legal. Instead, alternative forms of citizenship had emerged which depended on common interests and reciprocal social relations. Some argued that citizenship rights existed at the sub-state level (Murphy and Harty, 2003), for instance relating to ethnic groups (Pearson, 2002). Other commentators noted the relevance of 'post-sovereign' citizenships (Murphy and Harty, 2003), especially relating to indigenous peoples (Mörkenstam, 2015), and 'global citizenship' (Schattle, 2005).

In the case of the latter, social groups existing across geographical borders have coalesced around shared awareness of, willingness to act on, and mutual interdependency relating to, issues playing out at the global level. In the case of the former, institutions with sovereignty over a territory no longer exclusively ascribe citizenship rights. In an increasingly plural and cosmopolitan world, individuals are subject to multiplied citizenships and belong to a wider range of social groups based on, and further shaping, their identities. For Isin and Wood (1999) these included participating in diasporic and aboriginal citizenship, sexual citizenship, cosmopolitan citizenship and cultural citizenship. As noted elsewhere (Coles, 2008, p. 58), among the latter are those 'who are defined by their rights to consume goods and services' as forms of consumer citizenship while the past decade has witnessed the rise of 'green' (Gabrielson, 2008) and 'environmental' citizenships. As such, it may be awkward for individuals to reconcile their memberships to multiple groups simultaneously.

Citizenship in current tourism research

Essays of this nature almost inevitably have to be selective in their coverage and keen scholars of citizenship will immediately recognize that the previous account is deliberately curated. It is not intended as a full or up-to-date review of recent advances in citizenship studies. For instance, it could have discussed further the role of the World Wide Web, digital technology and other infrastructures in the material politics that mediate or constrain forms of citizenship (Amelung et al., 2020). Issues of surrounding lived citizenship (Kallio et al., 2020), revoking citizenship rights (Carey, 2018) or deliberative citizenship (Smith, 2019) have clearly added to the body of knowledge in citizenship studies, and on subjects that should also resonate with scholars of travel and tourism. Rather, in going 'back to basics' as it were, the previous section was intended as a starting point in a provocation for a renewed research agenda on the social impacts of tourism informed and motivated by a greater awareness and understanding of citizenship, which is elaborated in the remainder of the chapter.

Before this, it is useful to survey, again briefly, work that has connected tourism and citizenship. As I have argued elsewhere, there are some obvious and literal examples of social policy and legislation around the rights to paid holidays that reflect the Marshallian view, and which served to catalyse domestic tourism in industrial societies, both in the inter-war and post-war periods (Coles, 2008). Conversely, 'although in many countries people may believe that they have an intrinsic right to travel, no such legal rights exist under international law, with the decisions and declarations of the World Tourism Organization only constituting a form of "soft" international law in contrast to "hard" international and domestic law' (Coles and Hall, 2011, p. 209). Bianchi et al. (2020, p. 290) add to the complexity by arguing that 'rather than a mere reflection of accumulated political rights (citizenship)', the differential nature and levels of mobilities are embedded in, and 'conditioned by a complex assemblage of discursive frameworks and structural forces that are played out in specific historical-geographic contexts'.

Views of this nature demonstrate that it is not as a simple explanatory variable but rather as an additional conceptual (and contextualized) lens that citizenship contributes further clarity to our understanding of the social impacts of travel and tourism. In one immediate manner, consideration of citizenship shifts the unit of analysis from the individual, the traveller, the visitor, towards social groups; that is, collectives of individuals drawn together, their members defined by common denominators – be they travelling or non-travelling members – and their impacts, whether in the destinations and communities they travel to or within the groups themselves as social relationships are renewed, revisited, and reinterpreted (Coles and Timothy, 2004).

Before returning to this point later, it is germane to note though that even at the level of individuals, citizenship casts further, alternative light by which to re-read their interactions. Almost all travel episodes at one time or another require the traveller to come into contact with other people whether as service providers, members of host communities and so on. Both hosts *and* guests have rights *and* responsibilities in the Marshallian view. While to some this may seem like a trope and too focused on the content of citizenship (Isin, 1997), it precipitates reflection on, and alternative modes for understanding issues related to, equity, equality and social justice. This is especially timely when such issues are at the forefront of discussion about the relevance and application of the Sustainable Development Goals (SDGs) in travel and tourism (Saarinen, 2020).

Although consideration of citizenship contributes nuance and insight, this conceptual toolbox has yet to be fully embraced in tourism studies despite several calls for its adoption (Rojek, 1998; Coles, 2007, 2008; Bianchi and Stephenson, 2014). This is not intended to seem unduly contrary when data-bases of academic publications may, superficially at least, suggest the opposite. A search for the keywords of 'tourism' and 'citizenship' reveals over 360 entries from Scopus over the period 2006 to 2021.

There is not space to review this apparently substantive body of knowledge in any great depth nor is this especially necessary or appropriate here. Closer inspection does though reveal three key features. The first is that, although well established in the conceptual canon of the social sciences, few studies have presented extended theoretical or conceptual discussions of the implications and potentials of employing citizenship thinking in understanding the social impacts of tourism. As a notable exception Bianchi and Stephenson (2013, 2014) take a similar line to earlier contributions (Coles, 2007, 2008; Rojek, 1998), to argue for a move beyond the casual invocation of the term in the context of tourism, to engaging with citizenship more actively and in more conceptually and theoretically informed ways. For them, the appeal of engaging with citizenship thinking is that:

> tourism both bears the imprint of existing models of citizenship that have been forged within the containers of the nation-state, as well as acting as a vector through which notions of citizenship, moulded by the forces of globalization, transnationalism and extensive, albeit uneven, cross-border mobilities, are being extended, redefined and contested. (Bianchi and Stephenson, 2013, p. 18)

The second feature is that, when observed in the wider context of scholarship on tourism, citizenship has not been widely, nor always overtly, used as a core foundational element in, or central design feature of, tourism studies. Indeed, the reverse may also be true: in a keyword search for 'tourism' of the leading subject journal, *Citizenship Studies*, only one of the leading 30 articles by relevance of 138 in total, included tourism in its title (Prokkola and Ridanpää, 2017). Be that as it may, apparently numerous studies on travel and tourism invoke the term to one degree or another; they are indexed by it; and they may even selectively deploy features in citizenship thinking, sometimes indirectly or obliquely, especially in framing their research questions. Within this body of knowledge there is a diverse array of thematic touchpoints. Since the start of 2020, the term has been invoked, *inter alia*, in studies on: sense-making among small tourism business owners and operators (Tomassini et al., 2023); the practices and consequences of birth(right) tourism (Choi and Lai, 2022; Lozanski, 2020); differential citizenship rights and inequalities of access to health and welfare facilities by travellers (Stan et al., 2021); and the role of organizational citizenship in the delivery of environmental management measures (Luu, 2020). In one of the few contributions to employ explicitly the rights and responsibilities duality, Weaver et al. (2022, p. 897) argue that citizenship is 'a compelling basis for attaining sustainable and resilient tourism which [furthermore] complements ongoing dominant narratives of "resident" or "community"'.

Of course, this brief selection represents just a subjective choice from the more than 50 articles tagged with these keywords and in the public domain since 2020. Taking a longer view and again selective by virtue of the medium, the most prominent and enduring topic appears to have been 'global citizenship' or the notion that an individual's identity transcends international frontiers, and that one's role and place in the world is better conceptualized with reference to humanity per se rather than the nation-state or other citizenship groups. In one of the earliest contributions, Wilson and Harris (2006) explored women's stories of travel noting that connections with others as a form of shared global citizenship were a way in which travel became meaningful. The role of tourism in how individuals conceptualize global citizenship has been a recurrent theme (Baker and Dredge, 2019; Hermann et al., 2019; Molz, 2017; Cheung, 2017) and subject to critique (Butcher, 2017; Lyons et al., 2012). Ormond and Vietti (2022, p. 533) note that tourism acts as a vector for the mediation of global citizenship, arguing that '"visiting" is a key mode of civic learning', while others have noted the role of more formalized educational programmes (Tarrant et al., 2014). In much of this work, volunteering is presented as an embodiment of the individual's perception of, or their learning about, their global citizenship (Crossley, 2017). Several studies have examined the practices of voluntourism (Bone and Bone, 2018; Gray et al., 2017) and the effects this has on local communities, in particular the appropriateness and direction of knowledge exchange in educational contexts and other settings (Prince, 2019; McLennan, 2019; Cheung, 2017).

A third and final feature is the apparent 'absences'; that is, those aspects of, or pertaining to, tourism and citizenship which we may have reasonably expected to have been included. For instance, it is notable that within this corpus of work relatively few studies deal with other forms of 'alternative citizenships'. Diaspora is a distinct form of citizenship (Isin and Wood, 1999) and tourism (Coles and Timothy, 2004). Yet, only 26 studies variously connected these topics while consumer citizenship apparently featured in 89 studies. The latter result is inflated mainly due to common usage of 'consumer' while the former's suggestion of a paucity of interest is misleading. Separate keyword searches for 'tourism consumer citizen' and 'diaspora tourism' yielded 16 and 339 results respectively. The latter deserves more reflection. It appears that tourism scholars working on diaspora may not necessarily identify their work as contributing to understanding contemporary citizenship (or vice versa). Moreover, the limits to indexing terms in bibliographical databases may lead to misrepresentation of the actual coverage of higher level concepts.

Citizenship and future tourism research

So, where next for tourism research on citizenship? Obviously it is tempting to suggest that there is considerable scope for further examination of the social impacts of tourism, teasing out the well-woven strands of current scholarship further to their logical conclusions. As critical reviews of global citizenship (Butcher, 2017; Lyons et al., 2012) suggest, there is still much to discuss about the role and value of travel and tourism in mediating this more recent, non-state-based mode of citizenship. Arguably, as the relative paucity of coverage on consumer citizens hints, there is further research to be conducted on other alternative citizenships of the types identified by, or perhaps emerging since the provocations of, Isin and Wood (1999). Stubborn questions persist about the perception, nature and practice of 'environmental' or 'green' citizenship (Weaver et al., 2022) among visitors and the juxtaposition in their citizenship behaviours at home and away (Barr et al., 2011). Even in what may appear to be a more mature corpus of work, there are still significant unanswered questions relating to diaspora and tourism. Diaspora is far from a static concept (Story and Walker, 2016). Ways of experiencing and being in diaspora are evolving, with implications for how we understand current and future travel and tourism. As noted above, work on digital citizenship has pointed to technology and infrastructure in mediating connectedness and membership (Amelung et al., 2020). While even a decade ago, travelling was considered one if not the main way of keeping in touch with family and relatives at 'home' and 'in diaspora', the widespread access to relatively low-cost communications using the World Wide Web has the potential to reduce the need for in-person diasporic travel. As plausible as a working hypothesis of this nature may seem, it remains to be investigated.

However, if the Coronavirus pandemic has taught us anything then probably it is time to readjust the dial. Beyond the continuation of ideas from the 'old normal', a more ambitious research agenda on the social impacts of tourism would return to the established conceptual building blocks of rights and responsibilities, belonging, community, membership and group affiliation, to investigate a series of research questions about the 'new normal'. Indeed, prima facie, it should contribute to critical examination of the rhetoric as to whether there is a 'new normal', what it looks like, and how it differs from the 'old normal'.

That is a longer term intellectual project of much wider scope. More immediately, it is pertinent to note that several tourism-specific topics issues relating to citizenship have been central to the lived experiences of the Coronavirus pandemic and are worthy of dedicated attention moving forward. Perhaps most obviously, one aspect of this should examine the effects of imposing and releasing travel restrictions on destinations while another should focus on travellers and tourists as citizens (in other words, the impacts or not, on particular social groups). Of course, mobility is relative, it is defined by reference to others and, as a topic, immobility has been the poor relation of tourism *mobilities* (Coles, 2015). In a very literal sense, the pandemic raises questions about who is (or has been) able to travel, when, where and in what manner (or not as the case may be).

On the former – the regulation of travel – some work has already peripherally examined the relationship between state citizenship and travel. Farzanegan et al. (2021) examine the relationship between international tourism and associated deaths in 90 states. They observed that a 1 per cent higher level of inbound and outbound tourism is associated with 1.2 per cent and 1.4 per cent higher levels of confirmed cases and deaths respectively. Another way of reading this is that states granting higher levels of freedom to enter and exit have been worse hit. Moving forward, there is even greater scope and relevance to examining the effects of the differential imposition and/or removal of travel restrictions among country dyads. In a similar manner to Neumayer's (2010) work on visa restrictions and bilateral travel, this would allow for greater precision in identifying the impacts that citizens from country X have on destination country Y when country X imposes (or releases) restrictions on travel to Y. Such work also offers insights into the effectiveness and success of policy instruments and arrangements, such as the creation and utilization of 'air bridges' between the United States of America (Ledsom, 2021) and the UK or 'travel bubbles' between Australia and New Zealand (McDonald, 2021).

Arguably, research of this nature has a primarily economic orientation, for instance looking at the effects on the visitor economy (i.e. spend, jobs, tax take) associated with changes (increases or decreases) in visitor numbers from state X to Y because of Y's specific policy interventions affecting X's citizens. However, as yet only fragmentary evidence points to the social impacts on citizens and communities induced by the economic outcomes, including job losses, the damage to livelihoods, business failures, falling quality of life and standard of living, limited access to services and amenities, and threats to the social fabric of communities, including the most vulnerable and marginalized in society (cf. OECD, 2020a).

In this context, it is worth noting that many narratives have focused on the effects on citizens (e.g. entrepreneurs, their businesses, the communities they live in). In contrast, the role of the state as a provider (or perhaps better put, as a guarantor) of rights has yet to be critically examined. Recast under a Marshallian hue, the state proffers citizens with rights to expect a certain quality of life, to welfare services, and to opportunities to make a living. In order to deliver their responsibilities to their citizens, a range of policy interventions were introduced (OECD, 2020b, 2020c; WTTC, 2021). Several states operated furlough, employment protection and business support schemes in multiple guises. Yet, the efficacy and effects of these schemes on their intended recipients in the tourism sector remain to be systematically documented and appraised.

The challenge then is to move from ad hoc consideration of the issues to a more systematic and robust evidence base on the effects and how long they may last and indeed have lasted. In the case of the latter – the effects on citizens – the potential importance of the topic area is again largely intimated by reportage. For example, the limited availability of, and exorbitant costs for, flights home to Australia resulted in many of its citizens being stranded overseas for extended periods (O'Connor, 2020). Unable to travel home or to connect with friends and relatives, several encountered physical and mental health problems which may act as longer-term legacies of their trips. Very little systematic attention though, if any, has been afforded the psychological and sociological effects of quarantine episodes on travellers and tourists having to experience them. In professional sport, the concept of 'bubble fatigue' has been reported, perhaps most notably among cricketers. As a form of sport tourism (Higham and Hinch, 2009), many elite professional cricketers were temporarily away from home for short periods in 2020 and 2021. Several of them had to return home due to the demands on them relating, *inter alia*, to isolation, boredom, distress and de facto incarceration (Schout, 2020). Relative confinement and limited in-person social interactivity has also affected many young people, in particular students (Elmer et al., 2020; Odriozola-González et al., 2020). Many travelling overseas for study have been subject to similar conditions, both at initial entry and then in their regular (term-time) accommodation as a result of national lockdowns.

Little is known about these experiences and how the associated perception of risk may factor into, and endure as features in, future decision-making about personal travel, tourism and mobility in the short to medium term. With vaccines offering greater protection against the most dangerous medical effects of the disease but not necessarily preventing those inoculated from acting as vectors in the spread of the virus, the dangers of new strains will loom large for several years to come. In 2020 when international travel bans, restrictions and regulations (i.e. quarantine) were variously introduced, revised or lifted at short notice (cf. Mullens-Burgess and Nickson, 2021), there was clear jeopardy associated with departing under one regime, returning under another, and potentially being subject to increased costs (i.e. paying for quarantine hotels and board, loss of earnings from work) and extra time for travel (i.e. being quarantined in-destination and/or on return). This was in addition to the not-so-small matters of possibly being exposed to the Coronavirus and/or contracting COVID-19 while travelling!

Personal travel was then effectively a trade-off between the risks of being exposed to the virus and/or of a change in quarantine regulations, against the perceived need to have a break from an everyday that had come to include lockdowns, in order to aid physical and mental well-being. Vaccination presented a means to overcome these forms of 'travel gamble' in the short term. Discussion turned to whether mass vaccination more generally and 'vaccination passports' in particular offer the key to restarting tourism, especially international travel, on a large-scale (EC, 2021). Travel was presented as being safer for those who received their vaccination (and for those in the host communities and businesses that received them); moreover, those who were able to demonstrate they had been vaccinated (or had received recent negative tests) should not be subject to the same restrictions as those who had not (EC, 2021; BBC, 2021a).

The nature of this discourse is especially relevant here. Once more it invokes both the conceptual framework of citizenship (i.e. rights to travel, the responsibility to travel safely, to comply with requests for vaccination) and one major manifestation of state-based models of citizenship (i.e. the passport). Arguably, these sorts of arrangements would also create new (post-modern) citizenship groups – the vaccinated and the not-vaccinated – with common identities, shared values (i.e. a belief in the importance of being vaccinated and their civic duty to receive a vaccine) and membership criteria (Isin and Wood, 1999; Bailey, 2020). As some critics have noted, the emergence of these groups would be accompanied by new forms of inequality and disadvantage in terms of access to resources, services and facilities (Bailey, 2020; Baral et al., 2021; Papazoglu, 2021). In most advanced economies, the elderly as the most vulnerable and – it should be noted – some of the most immobile in society, were vaccinated first. Conversely, young people as the least vulnerable and the more mobile, were being vaccinated later (Murkett, 2021). Further layers of complexity relate to differential rates among sections of society. In the UK, vaccine hesitancy and slower uptake from citizens from Black and Minority Ethnic (BAME) communities were reported (Razai et al., 2021). Beyond travellers, discussion turned to whether vaccination (and certification) may be compulsory for employees in travel and tourism enterprises as 'people businesses' (Schraer, 2021).

Vaccination passports generated so many research questions that they were, and continue to be, worthy of a research agenda of their own. For instance, did those able to demonstrate they have been vaccinated actually travel more than those who did not? Did travellers really feel safer because of the vaccine and did they travel more as a result? In other words, was advocacy of vaccine passports as an enabling mechanism borne out by travel behaviours? Did destinations and events allowing freer access to those with vaccination passports enjoy greater visitor numbers in the short term as well as faster, more sustained recoveries? Alternatively, did destinations or even travel and tourism businesses insisting on or privileging vaccination passports, suffer reputational damage as a result? What will visitor profiles in destinations look like if vaccination passports are made compulsory, to what extent will they be different from pre-pandemic profiles, and what will be the social impacts on destinations? How will a system that privileges vaccination passports be enacted, regulated or 'policed'? The private sector, not the state and public sector, appears to have been the primary delivery mechanism for the New York trial of vaccination passports to facilitate entry to events (Holland et al., 2021). In some societies, especially those with public health care systems and those with enhanced personal privacy and data protection laws, the concept of the state ceding responsibility for the administration and management of vaccination passports to private enterprises may be extremely uncomfortable, not to say even unpalatable. In which case, how might this impact outbound travel for citizens of such countries where the international destinations they visit and the businesses (i.e. airlines, tour operators, hotel chains) they use, have alternative value sets and operate under different regulatory conventions? Within these countries, what will be the consequences for domestic tourism?

For humans to be mobile with a dangerous pathogen at large, careful consideration is required of the public health risks and possible consequences of travel, the associated mitigation factors and measures, and the extent to which guidance and requirements can and will be observed. 'Social distancing' is a noun-verb that has entered the English language since early 2020, while the wearing of face masks and hand sanitization have become routine in many countries. New or revised public health guidance has been published for airlines, attractions, events, hospitality and accommodation providers to make operations safe for visitors. App-based digital tracing systems were developed and rolled out to track where infected citizens were and to alert those who had been in proximity with them, with a view to their self-isolating.

Key knowledge gaps exist in terms of the extent to which guidance is observed and/or understood, how far such measures have been, and are, adopted in the production and consumption of travel and tourism, and how either willingness or actual compliance changes (i.e. possibly drops off?) over time. In other words, is there a responsibility gap, does it close or widen over time, and what are the implications or social impacts of non- or partial compliance? While there are several examples of successful tracking schemes, particularly in Korea, Singapore and China, research has pointed to lower levels of uptake and effectiveness of the technology in other countries notwithstanding its importance to monitoring and managing the spread of further waves of the pandemic (Lancet, 2020). Personal tourism has routinely been conceptualized as a time when many citizens typically suspend their everyday routines, relax and try to forget about their other, more mundane or routine citizenship obligations such as to the environment (Barr et al., 2011). Yet, there is currently no data on the extent to which visitors are willing to use – or actually do use – tracing systems in their travel away from home and the everyday, nor the potential barriers to their use, possibly including language difficulties and different cultural norms for international visitors.

Widening the scope, other questions relate to whether there are particular types or groups of visitors who disregard public health advice to one degree or another, perhaps who are unable and/or unwilling to use tracing systems. This prompts further consideration of how can they be encouraged to act more responsibly to protect other citizens, both fellow travellers and members of the local communities they visit? Each country had a system of sanctions for those contravening the regulations, yet little is known – perhaps from an experimental approach – about the relationship (trade-off) between sanctions and willingness to contravene (aspects of) the regulations. Similar questions apply to businesses but are probably unresearchable: it is unclear who would openly admit to this in a survey environment and hence how accurate and meaningful the findings would be.

Finally, among citizen-visitors, it is worth noting that much of the guidance to behave responsibly constitutes a form of social marketing (Hall, 2014). A frequent approach in social marketing has been to segment populations into groups with shared attributes and common characteristics on particular behavioural issues, and then to develop targeted approaches, messaging and interventions to effect behaviour change among them (Barr et al., 2011; Borden et al., 2017). Critical appraisals of social marketing have also been interested in the nature, construction and reception of messages among segments, often through testing alternatives. A greater research effort in both these spaces has potential value in the delivery of clearer, understandable messaging directed at different groups of visitors to ensure a more inclusive, cohesive and effective response among society. In 2020, even the British Prime Minister was unable to articulate correctly the rules that his government had established for post-lockdown behaviour (Woodcock, 2020). Subtlety, complexity and variation of regulation have become issues that may frustrate citizens in their attempts to close the responsibility gap. For instance, while there has been much overlap, each of the devolved administrations in the UK enacted different regulations such that there were differences for Welsh citizens travelling to England compared to English citizens travelling to Wales. Within Germany, in addition to the federal level, each of the *Bundesländer* enacted separate regulation with subtle variations in how many people may meet, where and how. A visitor arriving at Frankfurt airport as a major international hub and travelling onwards to visit the vineyards in Rhineland-Pfalz was potentially subject to four sets of regulations and guidelines as they crossed internal (and invisible) borders (i.e. Bund, Hessen, Baden-Württemberg, and Rhineland-Pfalz).

Conclusion

This chapter started by observing that citizenship is a positioned concept; perspectives on citizenship are framed by social, political and cultural contexts, among many others, at any given moment. Not surprisingly then, this chapter has presented a perspective that leans heavily on UK experiences and contexts. Moreover, the Coronavirus pandemic has featured prominently in this chapter because of its importance at the time of writing, its capacity to illuminate the issues discussed here, and the major research imperatives it has precipitated.

While others have debated the apparent transformative capacity of the pandemic or whether there would be a 'new normal' and what this would look like (cf. Lew et al., 2020; Sigala, 2020), from a perspective of tourism studies one of the most important aspects of recent developments has been to highlight the significant, yet taken-for-granted nature of citizenship in travel and tourism. It also challenges orthodoxies in our thinking. The global pandemic reminds us that hosts and guests have an obligation to keep the other safe even if, somewhat perversely, this means non-visitation with all the implications this entails for local communities, their prosperity, standard of living and quality of life.

As a major concept in the social sciences, citizenship has not featured as obviously or frequently in the research agenda of tourism studies, as may have been anticipated. Rather, citizenship has been more a selective concern, although the ideas it presents and the ways of understanding it foster, proffer valuable critical and analytical insights on contemporary travel, tourism mobilities and immobilities. The time is right to turn the academic gaze directly onto citizenship and apply a much sharper focus. Refocusing the research agenda relating to the social impacts of tourism in this way is not just about adding to our understanding of the nature and array of social impacts and the groups who generate and experience them. The Coronavirus pandemic has raised a series of altogether new questions about the social impacts of tourism that relate to it specifically and which have greater salience in building knowledge to a post-pandemic world, possibly towards tackling future episodes of similar scale and magnitude.

More extensive engagement with citizenship, then, has implications for knowledge production and exchange, the usefulness of what we do as an academy, and the impact of the academy beyond its hallowed halls and ivory towers to address what Brauer et al. (2019) have termed a 'significance gap'. Some (but not all) have optimistic views for the future with tourism scholars as part of the solution, even a transformation (cf. Lew et al., 2020). Citizenship, travel and tourism featured in the management of the pandemic and moreover proposals on how to recover from it (Ateljevic, 2020). If there really is a desire to produce impactful, relevant knowledge to the betterment of society as a whole, one of the challenges for tourism scholars is going to be to align their interests with others both beyond the academy and – as citations within this text demonstrate – beyond the traditional boundaries of tourism studies. In this respect, citizenship is not a legacy concept from the 'old normal', just to be picked up for short-term convenience. With a pandemic challenging our freedoms, rights and responsibilities, it is only going to become a more significant consideration in the future of tourism and its management.

References

9/11 Commission (2004). *The 9/11 Commission Report*. https://govinfo.library.unt.edu/911/report/911Report.pdf.

Amelung, N., Gianolla, C., Solovova, O., and Sousa Ribeiro, J. (2020). Technologies, infrastructures and migrations: Material citizenship politics. *Citizenship Studies*, 24(5), 587–606.

Andrews, H. (ed.) (2020). *Tourism and Brexit: Travel, Borders and Identity*. Clevedon: Channel View.

Ateljevic, I. (2020). Transforming the (tourism) world for good and (re)generating the potential 'new normal'. *Tourism Geographies*, 22(3), 467–475.

Bailey, A. (2020). The argument in favour of COVID-19 immunity passports. *The Conversation*, 23/12/2020. https://theconversation.com/the-argument-in-favour-of-covid-19-immunity-passports-151627.

Baker, H. and Dredge, D. (2019). Narratives of global citizenship, ethics and tourism: A Danish perspective. *Hospitality and Society*, 9(1), 9–30.

Baral, S., Rwema, J., and Phaswana-Mafuya, N. (2021). Covid-19 vaccine passports will harm sustainable development (thebmjopinion). https://blogs.bmj.com/bmj/2021/03/30/covid-19-vaccine-passports-will-harm-sustainable-development/.

Barr, S. W., Shaw, G., and Coles, T. E. (2011). Times for (un)sustainability? Challenges and opportunities for developing behaviour change policy. A case-study of consumers at home and away. *Global Environmental Change*, 21, 1234–1244.

Bianchi, R. and Stephenson, M. (2013). Deciphering tourism and citizenship in a globalized world. *Tourism Management*, 39, 10–20.

Bianchi, R. and Stephenson, M. (2014). *Tourism and Citizenship: Rights, Freedoms and Responsibilities in the Global Order*. Abingdon: Routledge.

Bianchi, R., Stephenson, M., and Hannam, K. (2020). The contradictory politics of the right to travel: Mobilities, borders and tourism. *Mobilities*, 15(2), 290–306.

Blair, T. (2002). Full text of Tony Blair's speech on welfare reform. *The Guardian*, 10/06/2002. https:// www .theguardian .com/ society/ 2002/ jun/ 10/ socialexclusion .politics1.

Bone, J. and Bone, K. (2018). Voluntourism as cartography of self: A Deleuzian analysis of a postgraduate visit to India. *Tourist Studies*, 18(2), 177–193.

Borden, D. S., Coles, T. E., and Shaw, G. (2017). Social marketing, sustainable tourism and small/medium-size tourism enterprises: Challenges and opportunities for changing guest behaviour. *Journal of Sustainable Tourism*, 25, 903–920.

Brauer, R., Dymitrow, M., and Tribe, J. (2019). The impact of tourism research. *Annals of Tourism Research*, 77, 64–78.

British Broadcasting Corporation (BBC) (2020a). Coronavirus: 'Tourists will put services under pressure'. https://www.bbc.co.uk/news/uk-england-cornwall-51975411.

British Broadcasting Corporation (BBC) (2020b). Coronavirus: Lockdown to be relaxed in England as 2m rule eased. https://www.bbc.co.uk/news/uk-53152416.

British Broadcasting Corporation (BBC) (2020c). Coronavirus: PM warns over virus rules after beach crowds. https://www.bbc.co.uk/news/uk-53190209.

British Broadcasting Corporation (BBC) (2020d). Coronavirus: Spain to allow UK tourists without quarantine. https://www.bbc.co.uk/news/uk-53122825.

British Broadcasting Corporation (BBC) (2021a). Coronavirus: Spain hopes for tourists as EU votes on digital passports. https:// www .bbc .co .uk/ news/ world -europe -56912667.

British Broadcasting Corporation (BBC) (2021b). Australia's India ban criticised as 'racist' rights breach. https://www.bbc.co.uk/news/world-australia-56967520.

Butcher, J. (2017). Citizenship, global citizenship and volunteer tourism: A critical analysis. *Tourism Recreation Research*, *42*(2), 129–138.

Carey, B. (2018). Against the right to revoke citizenship. *Citizenship Studies*, *22*(8), 897–911.

Cheung, J. (2017). Class and global citizenship: Perspectives from non-elite young people's participation in volunteer tourism. *Tourism Recreation Research*, *42*(2), 164–175.

Choi, S. and Lai, R. (2022). Birth tourism and migrant children's agency: The 'double not' in post-handover Hong Kong. *Journal of Ethnic and Migration Studies*, *48*(5), 1193–1209.

Clatworthy, A., Gregory, A., and Conradi, P. (2020). Coronavirus holiday misery for British tourists in Spain as quarantine returns. *The Sunday Times*, 26/07/2020. https://www.thetimes.co.uk/article/coronavirus-holiday-misery-for-british-tourists-in-spain-as-quarantine-returns-vbzdtkrwc.

Coles, T. E. (2007). Telling tales of tourism: Mobility, media and citizenship in the 2004 EU Enlargement. In P. Burns and M. Novelli (eds.), *Tourism and Mobilities*. Wallingford: CABI.

Coles, T. E. (2008). Citizenship and the state: Hidden features in the internationalisation of tourism. In T. E. Coles and C. M. Hall (eds.), *International Business and Tourism: Global Issues, Contemporary Interactions*. London: Routledge.

Coles, T. E. (2015). Tourism mobilities: Still a current issue in tourism? *Current Issues in Tourism*, *18*(1), 62–67.

Coles, T. E. (2021). Tourism, Brexit and net-zero emissions in the United Kingdom: On connecting different forms of crisis. *Journal of Sustainable Tourism*, *29*(1), 1–18.

Coles, T. E. and Hall, C. M. (2011). Rights and regulation of travel and tourism mobility. *Journal of Policy Research in Tourism, Leisure and Events*, *3*(3), 209–233.

Coles, T. E. and Timothy, D. J. (eds.) (2004). *Tourism, Diasporas and Space*. London: Routledge.

Crossley, E. (2017). Cosmopolitan empathy in volunteer tourism: A psychosocial perspective. *Tourism Recreation Research*, *42*(2), 150–163.

Elmer, T., Mepham, K., and Stadtfeld, C. (2020). Students under lockdown: Comparisons of students' social networks and mental health before and during the COVID-19 crisis in Switzerland. *PLoS ONE*, *15*(7). https://doi.org/10.1371/journal.pone.0236337.

European Commission (EC) (2021). Coronavirus: Commission proposes a Digital Green Certificate. Press release, 17 March 2021. https://ec.europa.eu/commission/presscorner/detail/en/IP_21_1181.

Faries, M. (2016). Why we don't 'just do it': Understanding the intention-behaviour gap in lifestyle medicine. *American Journal of Lifestyle Medicine*, *10*(5), 322–339.

Farzanegan, M. R., Gholipour, H. F., Feizi, M., Nunkoo, R., and Andargoli, A. E. (2021). International tourism and outbreak of Coronavirus (COVID-19): A cross-country analysis. *Journal of Travel Research*, *60*(3), 687–692.

Gabrielson, T. (2008). Green citizenship: A review and critique. *Citizenship Studies*, *12*(4), 429–446.

Gray, N., Meeker, A., Ravensbergen, S., Kipp, A., and Faulkner, J. (2017). Producing science and global citizenship? Volunteer tourism and conservation in Belize. *Tourism Recreation Research*, *42*(2), 199–211.

Hall, C. M. (2014). *Tourism and Social Marketing*. Abingdon: Routledge.

Hall, D. (2020). *Brexit and Tourism: Process, Impacts, and Non-Policy*. Clevedon: Channel View.

Hermann, I., Weeden, C., and Peters, K. (2019). Connecting the dots: Ethics, global citizenship and tourism. *Hospitality and Society*, 9(1), 3–8.

Higham, J. and Hinch, T. (2009). *Sport and Tourism: Globalization, Mobility and Identity*. Abingdon: Routledge.

Holland, J., Lee, J., and Iafolla, R. (2021). Big tech unleashes vaccine passports as privacy questions loom. *Bloomberg Law*, 19/04/2021. https:// news .bloomberglaw .com/ us -law-week/big-tech-unleashes-vaccine-passports-as-privacy-questions-loom.

Iaquinto, B. L. (2020). Tourist as a vector: Viral mobilities of COVID-19. *Dialogues in Human Geography*, 10(2), 174–177.

Isin, E. (1997). Who is the new citizen? Towards a genealogy. *Citizenship Studies*, 1(1), 115–132.

Isin, E. and Wood, P. (1999). *Citizenship and Identity*. London: Sage.

Jones, E. and Gaventa, J. (2002). Concepts of citizenship: A review. *IDS Development Bibliography*, 19. https:// assets .publishing .service .gov .uk/ media/ 57a08 d3ce5274a2 7b2001709/db19.pdf.

Kallio, K., Wood, B., and Häkli, J. (2020). Lived citizenship: Conceptualising an emerging field. *Citizenship Studies*, 24(6), 713–729.

Lancet, The (2020). Contact tracing: Digital health on the frontline. https:// www .thelancet .com/ journals/ landig/ article/ PIIS2589 -7500(20)30251 -X/ fulltext #coronavirus-linkback-header.

Ledsom, A. (2021). UK/US travel: Carriers push for air bridge to resume in May due to vaccination success. https:// www .forbes .com/ sites/ alexledsom/ 2021/ 04/ 12/ ukus-travel-carriers-push-for-air-bridge-to-resume-on-17-may-due-to-vaccination -success/?sh=144acfd939bf.

Lew, A., Cheer, J., Haywood, M., Brouder, P., and Salazar, B. (2020). Visions of travel and tourism after the global COVID-19 transformation of 2020. *Tourism Geographies*, 22(3), 455–466.

Lozanski, K. (2020). Mobilizing mobilities: Birthright tourists as willful strangers in Canada. *Mobilities*, 15(2), 146–160.

Luu, T. T. (2020). Integrating green strategy and green human resource practices to trigger individual and organizational green performance: The role of environmentally-specific servant leadership. *Journal of Sustainable Tourism*, 28(8), 1193–1222.

Lyons, K., Hanley, J., Wearing, S., and Neil, J. (2012). Gap year volunteer tourism: Myths of global citizenship? *Annals of Tourism Research*, 39(1), 361–378.

Marshall, T. H. and Bottomore, T. (1992). *Citizenship and Social Class*, updated edition. London: Pluto Press. Originally, T. H. Marshall, published under the same title in 1950. Cambridge: Cambridge University Press.

McDonald, T. (2021). Is the Australia–New Zealand travel bubble the way ahead? https://www.bbc.co.uk/news/business-56796943.

McLennan, S. J. (2019). Global encounters: Voluntourism, development and global citizenship in Fiji. *Geographical Journal*, 185, 338–351.

Menéndez, A. J. and Olsen, E. D. H. (2020). The concept and the conception of citizenship. In *Challenging European Citizenship: Ideas and Realities in Contrast*. Palgrave Studies in European Union Politics. Cham: Palgrave Macmillan.

Ministry of Justice (MoJ) (2009). *Rights and Responsibilities: Developing our Constitutional Framework*. https:// assets .publishing .service .gov .uk/ government/ uploads/system/uploads/attachment_data/file/228938/7577.pdf.

Molz, J. (2017). Giving back, doing good, feeling global: The affective flows of family voluntourism. *Journal of Contemporary Ethnography, 46*(3), 334–360.

Mörkenstam, U. (2015). Recognition as if sovereigns? A procedural understanding of indigenous self-determination. *Citizenship Studies, 19*(6–7), 634–648.

Mullens-Burgess, E. and Nickson, S. (2021). *Hotel Quarantine*. Institute for Government. https://www.instituteforgovernment.org.uk/explainers/hotel-quarantine.

Murkett, K. (2021). Vaccine passports are a kick in the teeth for young people. *The Spectator*, 7/12/2021. https://www.spectator.co.uk/article/vaccine-passports-are-a-kick-in-the-teeth-for-young-people.

Murphy, M. and Harty, S. (2003). Post-sovereign citizenship. *Citizenship Studies, 7*(2), 181–197.

Murray, G. (2007). Who is afraid of T. H. Marshall? Or, what are the limits of the liberal vision of rights? *Societies Without Borders, 2*(2), 222–242.

National Constitution Center (NCC) (2020). Benjamin Franklin's last great quote and the Constitution. https://constitutioncenter.org/blog/benjamin-franklins-last-great-quote-and-the-constitution.

Neumayer, E. (2010). Visa restrictions and bilateral travel. *The Professional Geographer, 62*(2), 171–181.

O'Connor, M. (2020). Coronavirus: 'We're Australian but we're trapped in the UK'. https://www.bbc.co.uk/news/uk-54279802.

Odriozola-González, P., Planchuelo-Gómez, Á., Irurtia, M. J., and de Luis-García, R. (2020). Psychological effects of the COVID-19 outbreak and lockdown among students and workers of a Spanish university. *Psychiatry Research, 290*, 113108. https://doi.org/10.1016/j.psychres.2020.113108.

Organisation for Economic Co-operation and Development (OECD) (2020a). Rebuilding tourism for the future: COVID-19 policy responses and recovery. 14 December 2020. https://www.oecd.org/coronavirus/policy-responses/rebuilding-tourism-for-the-future-covid-19-policy-responses-and-recovery-bced9859/.

Organisation for Economic Co-operation and Development (OECD) (2020b). Tourism policy responses to the Coronavirus (COVID-19). https://www.oecd.org/coronavirus/policy-responses/tourism-policy-responses-to-the-coronavirus-covid-19-6466aa20/#tablegrp-d1e645.

Organisation for Economic Co-operation and Development (OECD) (2020c). Mitigating the impact of COVID-19 on tourism and supporting recovery. OECD Tourism Papers, 2020/03. http://dx.doi.org/10.1787/47045bae-en.

Ormond, M. and Vietti, F. (2022). Beyond multicultural 'tolerance': Guided tours and guidebooks as transformative tools for civic learning. *Journal of Sustainable Tourism, 30*(2–3), 533–549.

Papazoglu, A. (2021). Is there a way to make vaccine passports ethically acceptable? *The Guardian*, 27/02/2021. https://www.theguardian.com/commentisfree/2021/feb/27/vaccine-passports-alternatives-mills-harm-principle-discrimination.

Pearson, D. (2002). Theorizing citizenship in British settler societies. *Ethnic and Racial Studies, 25*(6), 989–1012.

Prince, S. (2019). Volunteer tourism and the eco-village: Finding the host in the pedagogic experience. *Hospitality and Society, 9*(1), 71–89.

Prokkola, E. and Ridanpää, J. (2017). Youth organizations, citizenship, and guidelines for tourism in the wake of mass tourism in Finland. *Citizenship Studies, 21*(3), 359–377.

Razai, M., Osama, T., and McKechnie, D. (2021). Covid-19 vaccine hesitancy among ethnic minority groups. *British Medical Journal, 372*, n513.

Revi, B. (2014). T. H. Marshall and his critics: Reappraising 'social citizenship' in the twenty-first century. *Citizenship Studies*, *18*(3–4), 452–464.

Rojek, C. (1998). Tourism and citizenship. *Cultural Policy*, *4*(4), 291–310.

Saarinen, J. (ed.) (2020). *Tourism and Sustainable Development Goals: Research on Sustainable Tourism Geographies*. Abingdon: Routledge.

Schattle, H. (2005). Communicating global citizenship: Multiple discourses beyond the academy. *Citizenship Studies*, *9*(2), 119–133.

Schout, D. (2020). Cricket prepares for mental health challenges thrown up by bubble life. *The Guardian*, 7/11/2020. https://www.theguardian.com/sport/2020/nov/08/cricket-prepares-for-mental-health-challenges-thrown-up-by-bubble-life.

Schraer, R. (2021). Covid vaccine passports could discriminate, experts warn. https://www.bbc.co.uk/news/health-56125142.

Semmens, K. (2005). *Seeing Hitler's Germany: Tourism in the Third Reich*. Basingstoke: Palgrave Macmillan.

Sigala, M. (2020). Tourism and COVID-19: Impacts and implications for advancing and resetting industry and research. *Journal of Business Research*, *117*, 312–321.

Smith, W. (2019). Deliberative citizenship: A critical reappraisal. *Citizenship Studies*, *23*(8), 815–830.

Stacey, T. (2021). Polluting SUVs will be on roads for the next two decades – what should we do with them? https://theconversation.com/polluting-suvs-will-be-on-roads-for-the-next-two-decades-what-should-we-do-with-them-158594.

Stan, S., Erne, R., and Gannon, S. (2021). Bringing EU citizens together or pulling them apart? The European Health Insurance Card, east–west mobility and the failed promise of European social integration. *Journal of European Social Policy*, *31*(4), 409–423.

Story, J. and Walker, I. (2016). The impact of diasporas: Markers of identity. *Ethnic and Racial Studies*, *39*(2), 135–141.

Tarrant, M., Lyons, K., Stoner, L., Kyle, G., Wearing, S., and Poudyal, N. (2014). Global citizenry, educational travel and sustainable tourism: Evidence from Australia and New Zealand. *Journal of Sustainable Tourism*, *22*(3), 403–420.

Tomassini, L., Lamond, I., and Burrai, E. (2023). Global citizenship & parrhesia in small values-based tourism firms. *Leisure Sciences*, *45*(7), 628–646.

Weaver, D., Moyle, B., and McLennan, C. (2022). The citizen within: Positioning local residents for sustainable tourism. *Journal of Sustainable Tourism*, *30*(4), 897–914.

Wilson, E. and Harris, C. (2006). Meaningful travel: Women, independent travel and the search for self and meaning. *Tourism*, *54*(2), 161–172.

Woodcock, A. (2020). Coronavirus: 'Grossly incompetent' Boris Johnson forced to apologise for getting rules wrong. *The Independent*, 05/10/2020. https://www.independent.co.uk/news/uk/politics/boris-johnson-speech-today-north-east-coronavirus-restrictions-b692358.html.

World Health Organization (WHO) (2020). Public health considerations while resuming international travel. https://www.who.int/news-room/articles-detail/public-health-considerations-while-resuming-international-travel.

World Travel and Tourism Council (WTTC) (2021). COVID-19 related policy shifts supportive of [the] travel and tourism sector. https://wttc.org/Portals/0/Documents/WTTC %20COVID-19 %20Strong %20Policies %2007 .04 .pdf ?ver = 2021 -04 -08 -112055-103.

7 Two pathways towards synergies between the right to live and the right to travel

Jeroen Nawijn, Ondrej Mitas and Jeroen Klijs

Introduction

In times of uncertainty (Gössling et al., 2021), preceded by an undesirable growth in tourist arrivals at certain destinations (Cheer et al., 2019), there is a definite need to examine the processes underlying desirable visitor and resident experiences, and how these may interact (Perkumienė & Pranskūnienė, 2020). Although not a new issue per se (e.g., Allen et al., 1993), the extent to which discrepancies between the two main stakeholder groups are expressed in the media (Phi, 2020) and the academic attention to a need for new strategies and measures is remarkable (cf. Cheung & Li, 2019). Meanwhile, some tourism destinations do not recognize the problem in the first place and their destination marketing/management organizations (DMOs) continue with growth strategies (or are at least aiming for post-coronavirus growth). Yet other destinations, that do recognize to reconsider the growth paradigm, struggle to develop and implement strategies to address tourism impacts (cf. Koens et al., 2019). Perkumienė and Pranskūnienė (2020) framed the quest for a renewed balance as a struggle between tourists' right to travel versus the local residents' right to live. Despite this need and the influx in academic and industry attention for strategic solutions, the status quo is that often we discuss destination management and marketing in terms of as-is and not in terms of what should-be.

In this chapter, we discuss well-established theories related to attitudes towards tourism and tourism development and connect these to more recent empirical work on the management of impacts of tourism. Next, we identify potential synergies between the right to travel and the right to live via two interrelated pathways. We discuss these two pathways from a local resident and visitor/tourist perspective, while addressing the interaction between these two groups. Finally, we formulate several strategic implications to implement these pathways in destination management and marketing practice.

Literature review

One of the most cited works in the field of tourism is the first publication on the Tourist Area Life Cycle (TALC) by Butler (1980). This early model of tourism development at destinations was rooted in evolutionary thinking and built heavily on the Product Life Cycle model (Vernon, 1966). In essence, the TALC describes the life cycle of tourism destinations in relation to tourist arrivals and residence support for tourism development over time. Like any social scientific model, the TALC has not been generally applicable to all contexts (cf. Ma & Hassink, 2013). Regardless, the general idea that tourism destinations develop over time and the notion that resident attitudes towards these developments change is apparent. Theoretically, it is assumed that residents will become antagonists of tourism development (Doxey, 1975) and may temporarily or permanently move to other locations (Ap & Crompton, 1993) if they perceive that their area of residence has overshot its carrying capacity for tourism. According to Watson and Kopachevsky (1996), carrying capacity may refer to capacity in terms of ecology-environment, physical-facility, social-perception, economics, and psychology. Initial views of local residents about carrying capacity shift over time and may differ between stakeholders (cf. McKercher & Prideaux, 2014). Carrying capacities are thus best used in relative ways, not via absolute numbers (Watson & Kopachevsky, 1996).

While evolutionary models are useful in describing and partly explaining changes over time, to understand resident attitudes towards tourism at a certain point in time, other theoretical approaches are more useful. A core theory that attempts to explain resident attitudes towards tourism is social exchange theory. Originally a sociological theory (Homans, 1958), social exchange theory applied to tourism destinations suggests a trade-off between costs and benefits resulting in an attitude towards tourism development (Ward & Berno, 2011). This rational approach to human behavior is still in use but is nowadays often supplemented or exchanged for more affective understandings of human behavior.

Emotional solidarity theory, for example, has repeatedly been used to understand resident support for tourism development. Originating from early sociological work (cf. Durkheim, 1915), emotional solidarity theory has taken many forms (Woosnam, 2012). Woosnam (2012) defined local residents' emotional solidarity as having a welcoming nature, feeling emotional closeness, and having a sympathetic understanding towards tourists. Jointly, these dimensions of emotional solidarity partly explain residents' support for tourism development (Woosnam, 2012). Social exchange theory is considered an antecedent to emotional solidarity (e.g., Erul et al., 2023).

Regarding the support of tourists for tourism at a destination, individuals generally do not view themselves as typical tourists, but prefer to believe they are more authentic travelers and that they travel for different reasons compared to a mass tourist (Doran et al., 2015). According to Holloway et al. (2011, p. 235), "[t]he presence of other tourists is an inevitable part of the tourist experience," suggesting that visiting a crowded destination as part of a tourist "throng" is not desirable for many tourists. Yet, there is relatively little empirical assessment of how tourists view other tourists and how other tourists' presence affects their experience at destinations. Recent qualitative work suggests that indirect interaction with other tourists has a stronger effect on the tourist experience than direct interaction with other tourists, regardless of whether this interaction is viewed negatively or positively (Han et al., 2021). In any case, observing other tourists is inherently connected to stereotypical projections of who is seen as a tourist and who is not. Tourists that blend in may be observed as local residents, whereas local residents may be mistakenly interpreted as being tourists.

Recent empirical work on tourists' and local residents' support for tourism – or lack thereof – deals with the concept of overtourism (e.g., Cheer et al., 2019; Cheung & Li, 2019; Koens et al., 2019). The United Nations World Tourism Organization (UNWTO) defines overtourism as a state in which tourism "excessively influences the perceived quality of life of citizens and/or quality of visitors' experiences in a negative way" (UNWTO, 2018, p. 6). Cheung and Li (2019) consider degrowth and resilience as strategies for future tourism development. However, these authors pose concerns and question whether a reduction in tourist arrivals (i.e., degrowth) will provide a change in local residents' perceptions of how tourism affects their quality of life. They propose a hysteresis hypothesis, which suggests that a tipping point may have been reached, causing irreversible impacts. Thus, they reason, removing the original causes of overtourism may not affect the perceived exceeding of a destination's carrying capacities by local residents.

In advocating resilience, Cheung and Li (2019) seem to imply that the guiding principles in destination development should not automatically include a pro-tourism stance. Next to that, they acknowledge a need for long-term planning and thinking, using predictive models to detect potential exceeding of carrying capacities in the future and anticipate on this predicted development via preventive measures.

In sum, numerous destinations have drawn numbers of tourists which led to conflict with local residents, some of whom perceive that carrying capacities have been exceeded. While some of this conflict is rationally driven, relationships between local residents and tourists clearly have a large affective component as well. Resilience and prediction are posited as promising approaches. Potential strategic implications for these approaches should be understood from the theoretical perspective of the right to travel and the right to live.

The right to travel and the right to live

We now discuss theoretical assumptions and empirical evidence related to the right to travel and the right to live. We organize this discussion in terms of two possible pathways towards synergies between the two rights that are based on (1) stimulating the openness of residents and tourists to mutually desirable interaction, (2) attracting the "right" type of tourists, namely tourists that (are perceived to) practice their right to travel in a way that does not reduce the possibilities for local residents to exercise their right to live. Subsequently, we posit strategic implications for both pathways that can effectuate these synergies.

Openness of residents and tourists to mutually desirable interaction

Interaction between local residents and tourists typically occurs when purchasing products or services, when using the same facilities (e.g., attractions, accommodation), and in public spaces. Intentional or unintentional, desired or undesired, consciously or unconsciously, these interactions shape views of the other (cf. Hsu & Chen, 2019). Contact theory suggests that interaction under appropriate circumstances lessens negative social phenomena, such as prejudices, bias, stereotyping, and social distance (Allport, 1954). Çelik (2019) reviewed existing theoretical and empirical evidence on the interaction between local residents and tourists and concludes that most studies on local residents' attitudes towards tourists show a positive change in attitude when there is or has been interaction with tourists. Earlier work by Tomljenović (2010) suggested a number of antecedents for the quality of contact between tourists and local residents. This included type of travel arrangement, destination characteristics, travel motivations, personality, initial attitude, and socio-cultural attitudes. During trips, contact opportunities are of utmost importance for determining the quality of contact (Tomljenović, 2010). However, the hysteresis hypothesis posed by Cheung and Li (2019) suggests these antecedents and the contact hypothesis itself fail when a tipping point has been reached at a destination. Overtourism is said to be a gamechanger in this respect. Thus, it is necessary to reconsider approaches to overtourism and clearly distinguish between a pre-overtourism approach and a post-overtourism approach. We adopt such an approach in our strategic implications at the end of this chapter.

Targeting the "right" type of tourist

Two types of tourists that might be right for the destination – because the way they (are perceived to) behave is not reducing the possibility for inhabitants to exercise their right to live – are domestic (or close-by) tourists and loyal tourists (i.e., repeat visitors). Differences in (perceived) impacts on the right to live, compared to other types of tourists, might, for example, stem from the fact that they know the destination better and understand the local culture, are less likely to go to crowded hotspots, have preferences and attitudes that are like those of local residents and/or are not recognized as being tourists.

Domestic tourists

Over thirty-five years ago, Jafari (1986, p. 491) noted that "[a]lthough almost all travel is domestic, international tourism occupies the main position in tourism research." Perhaps due to publication bias (Franco et al., 2014), and despite continued extensive evidence suggesting that domestic tourism is "far more important than international tourism" (Bigan et al., 2007, p. 157), times have not changed much since Jafari's initial observation. Yet we do know a bit more about domestic travel in general. In terms of decision-making, it appears that choices related to domestic travel are very similar to those for international travel (Huybers, 2003). Joo et al. (2018) studied local residents' attitudes towards domestic tourism. Basing their hypotheses on existing theories and empirical work on international tourism (e.g., Yilmaz & Tasci, 2013), they managed to partially support all their hypotheses, consequently validating contact theory in a domestic tourism context. Taking the tourist perspective, in terms of tourists' life satisfaction, hedonic experience, and broader indicators of their wellbeing, there seem to be only a few and minor differences in outcomes between domestic and exotic or long-haul vacations (cf. De Bloom et al., 2017; Nawijn & Peeters, 2010). These characteristics of domestic tourism inform our suggested strategic considerations for tourism destinations.

Loyal tourists

Loyalty is considered a driving force behind the success of companies and destinations (Oppermann, 2000). The concept of loyalty is complex as trip purposes may differ from visit to visit, repeat visit frequency fluctuates, and complex longitudinal datasets are needed to do destination loyalty justice (Oppermann, 2000). Consequently, the drivers of destination loyalty are not yet fully understood. Using large datasets, Tasci (2017) managed to establish that loyal tourists differ from non-loyal tourists to a large degree and on different levels (e.g., behavior, socio-demographics). Additionally, she found that attitudinal loyalty is a better indicator of destination loyalty than past visits or visit intention. To some extent this is a positive observation as attitudes are easily measured via cross-sectional data, whereas past visits are best measured using longitudinal data and intentions are generally poor indicators of actual visits (McKercher & Tse, 2012). However, behavior is still important to address for two reasons. First, behavior shapes preferences and attitudes, and in turn, these shape behavior (cf. Allen et al.; Allport, 1954). Second, behavior has observable effects, including pollution, income, and cultural valuation or erosion (Sharpley, 2014). In this way, behavior impacts carrying capacities and overtourism.

Concerning interactions between tourists and local residents, Ribeiro et al. (2018) found that emotional solidarity affects loyalty, both directly and indirectly via satisfaction. Stylidis et al. (2020) distinguished three tourist consumer segments, varying in their levels of emotional solidarity and, to some extent, loyalty. Both studies contained samples of international visitors only and do not specifically address destinations suffering from overtourism. Addressing domestic tourists, Patwardhan et al. (2020) found links between emotional solidarity and destination loyalty, comparable to those found by Ribeiro et al. (2018) for international tourists. This suggests that the paths between emotional solidarity and destination loyalty do not differ between international and domestic tourists, although the evidence is scarce. Unfortunately, as far as the authors are aware, no extant studies take the local resident perspective on these variables into account, and no extant studies deal with destination loyalty in an overtourism context either.

We have examined potential synergies between the right to travel and the right to live via two interrelated pathways: openness of residents and tourists to mutually desirable interaction and attracting the "right" type of tourists, namely those that exercise their right to travel in such a way that it does not reduce local residents' right to live. We found that these pathways feature distinct local resident and visitor/tourist perspectives and differ between pre-overtourism and post-overtourism phases. Based on these assertions, we offer several evidence-based strategic implications in the form of strategies and directions for future research.

Discussion

We now discuss strategic implications for destination management and marketing. Our discussion on future research addresses data use for DMOs and three gaps we identified in academic work.

Attitudinal loyalty

In terms of destination marketing, the existing evidence implies that DMOs focus on establishing positive attitudinal loyalty among desired tourist consumer segments. It is likely that these consumer segments contain more domestic than international tourists, but this is not a given, as contextual differences between destinations and nations may vary. DMOs should focus on attitudinal loyalty in both stages of overtourism. In the pre-overtourism stage, such an approach will serve as a preventive measure to large numbers of tourists, as the literature suggests that tourists with a positive attitudinal disposition do travel to the destination, but not necessarily frequently. In doing so, the focus should be generating revenue rather than aiming to increase tourist arrivals at the destination. This suggested focus on revenue rather than arrivals is opposite to well-established theories on tourism development.

Selectivity

Fed by the overtourism discussion, destinations are gradually shifting from the perspective that more tourists is always better and are becoming more selective about type and number of tourists they would like to attract. This should result in a different approach to destination marketing. Although there are practical and ethical considerations to a shift from mass tourism towards attracting (only) high-spending tourists who are conscious of their own potential social and environmental impacts, destinations are becoming more selective, for example by aiming for different target markets across different destinations within a single region (e.g., domestic tourists).

Persistent contact

Regarding destination management, our review of the literature suggests that contact between local residents and tourists is generally good in the pre-overtourism stage. Yet, it seems that local residents' involvement in tourism development is limited to the pre-overtourism stage only. In the post-overtourism stage, local residents seemingly want to push back against tourism development and thus often protest rather than cooperate with multi-stakeholder efforts aimed at tourism policy. In terms of destination management, this situation suggests that DMOs should enable and promote contact between local residents and tourists, but instead of doing this only pre-overtourism, the emphasis should be on establishing active involvement of local residents in the post-overtourism stage.

Spreading

Spreading of tourists is an issue of marketing and management. Pre-visit spreading should aim at spreading visitors over time (pre-visit) and thus involves marketing the low season and demarketing the high season. During visits, spreading involves dispersing tourists spatially across the destination as a way to mitigate carrying capacities. This is a management and marketing task. Marketing may target less visited areas at the destination and management should enhance the tourist offer at such locations and enable the connections between these locations and the most visited parts of the destination.

Future research

In terms of market research, the emphasis on attitudinal loyalty indicates that cross-sectional consumer data can be used as attitudinal measurements. Next to such cross-sectional data on desired tourist consumer segments, DMOs do need to have access to longitudinal data, but these data should focus mostly on behavior at the destination. The purpose is partly to quantify carrying capacities over time, mainly onsite spreading to monitor physical carrying capacities. Rather though, its purpose is mainly to assess the subjective interpretations of other carrying capacities over time and thus be aware of possible shifts in carrying capacity views by stakeholders (e.g., local residents).

In terms of academic work, the review presented in this chapter points towards three main gaps in the tourism literature. The first concerns destination loyalty, specifically for destinations that deal with overtourism where empirical evidence is non-existent. Second, regarding domestic tourists, little is known (Patwardhan et al., 2020), although, based on our review, we may not assume major differences exist. Last, there is little research on how tourist consumer segments view each other.

Conclusion

We identified (1) openness of residents and tourists to mutually desirable interaction and (2) attracting domestic tourists and loyal tourists, as *the* two pathways towards a balance between the right to travel and the right to live. Strategic solutions need to distinguish between pre-overtourism and post-overtourism phases. The purpose of destination marketing should be to create attitudinal loyalty, to spread tourists over the year, and to target domestic tourists. The purpose of destination marketing ought to be to facilitate contact between local residents and tourists, especially in the post-overtourism phase. Continuous data collection is required for marketing and management purposes, with cross-sectional data to monitor attitudinal loyalty and longitudinal data to monitor behavior in terms of annual spreading of tourist arrivals and tracking of onsite tourist behavior to monitor crowding.

References

Allen, C. T., Machleit, K. A., & Kleine, S. S. (1992). A comparison of attitudes and emotions as predictors of behavior at diverse levels of behavioral experience. *Journal of Consumer Research, 18*(4), 493–504.

Allen, L. R., Hafer, H. R., Long, P. T., & Perdue, R. R. (1993). Rural residents' attitudes toward recreation and tourism development. *Journal of Travel Research, 31*(4), 27–33.

Allport, G. W. (1954). *The Nature of Prejudice.* Cambridge, MA: Addison-Wesley.

Ap, J., & Crompton, J. L. (1993). Residents' strategies for responding to tourism impacts. *Journal of Travel Research, 32*(1), 47–50.

Bigan, A., Hamilton, J. M., Lau, M., Tol, R. S. J., & Zhou, Y. (2007). A global database of domestic and international tourist numbers at national and subnational level. *International Journal of Tourism Research, 9*(3), 147–174.

Butler, R. W. (1980). The concept of the tourist area cycle of evolution: Implications for management of resources. *Canadian Geographer, 24*(1), 5–12.

Çelik, S. (2019). Social psychological effects of tourism: Evaluation of the tourist–local people interaction within the context of Allport's intergroup contact theory. In D. Gursoy & R. Nunkoo (Eds.), *The Routledge Handbook of Tourism Impacts: Theoretical and Applied Perspectives* (pp. 242–251). Abingdon: Routledge.

Cheer, J. M., Milano, C., & Novelli, M. (2019). Tourism and community resilience in the Anthropocene: Accentuating temporal overtourism. *Journal of Sustainable Tourism, 27*(4), 554–572.

Cheung, K. S., & Li, L.-H. (2019). Understanding visitor–resident relations in overtourism: Developing resilience for sustainable tourism. *Journal of Sustainable Tourism, 27*(8), 1197–1216.

De Bloom, J., Nawijn, J., Geurts, S., Kinnunen, U., & Korpela, K. (2017). Holiday travel, staycations, and subjective wellbeing. *Journal of Sustainable Tourism, 25*(4), 573–588.

Doran, R., Larsen, S., & Wolff, K. (2015). Different but similar: Social comparison of travel motives among tourists. *International Journal of Tourism Research, 17*(6), 555–563.

Doxey, G. V. (1975). A causation theory of visitor-resident irritants: Methodology and research inferences. Paper presented at the Impact of Tourism, Sixth Annual Conference of the Travel Research Association, San Diego, California.

Durkheim, E. (1915). *The Elementary Forms of Religious Life.* New York: Free Press.

Erul, E., Woosnam, K. M., Ribeiro, M. A., & Salazar, J. (2023). Complementing theories to explain emotional solidarity. *Journal of Sustainable Tourism, 31*(2), 229–244.

Franco, A., Malhotra, N., & Simonovit, G. (2014). Publication bias in the social sciences: Unlocking the file drawer. *Science, 345*(6203), 1502–1505.

Gössling, S., Scott, D., & Hall, C. M. (2021). Pandemics, tourism and global change: A rapid assessment of Covid-19. *Journal of Sustainable Tourism, 29*(1), 1–20.

Han, X., Praet, C. L. C., & Wang, L. (2021). Tourist–tourist social interaction in the co-creation and co-destruction of tourism experiences among Chinese outbound tourists. *Tourism Planning & Development, 18*(2), 189–209.

Holloway, D., Green, L., & Holloway, D. (2011). The intratourist gaze: Grey nomads and "other tourists". *Tourist Studies, 11*(3), 235–252.

Homans, G. C. (1958). Social behavior as exchange. *American Journal of Sociology, 63*(6), 597–606.

Hsu, C. H. C., & Chen, N. (2019). Resident attribution and tourist stereotypes. *Journal of Hospitality & Tourism Research, 43*(4), 489–516.

Huybers, T. (2003). Domestic tourism destination choices: A choice modelling analysis. *International Journal of Tourism Research, 5*(6), 445–459.

Jafari, J. (1986). On domestic tourism. *Annals of Tourism Research, 13*(3), 491–496.

Joo, D., Tasci, A. D. A., Woosnam, K. M., Maruyama, N. U., Hollas, C. R., & Aleshinloye, K. D. (2018). Residents' attitude towards domestic tourists explained by contact, emotional solidarity and social distance. *Tourism Management, 64*, 245–257.

Koens, K., Melissen, F., Mayer, I., & Aall, C. (2019). The smart city hospitality framework: Creating a foundation for collaborative reflections on overtourism that support destination design. *Journal of Destination Marketing & Management, 19.* https://doi.org/10.1016/j.jdmm.2019.100376.

Ma, M., & Hassink, R. (2013). An evolutionary perspective on tourism area development. *Annals of Tourism Research, 41*, 89–109.

McKercher, B., & Prideaux, B. (2014). Academic myths of tourism. *Annals of Tourism Research, 46*, 16–28.

McKercher, B., & Tse, T. S. M. (2012). Is intention to return a valid proxy for actual repeat visitation? *Journal of Travel Research, 51*(6), 671–686.

Nawijn, J., & Peeters, P. M. (2010). Travelling "green": Is tourists' happiness at stake? *Current Issues in Tourism, 13*(4), 381–392.

Oppermann, M. (2000). Tourism destination loyalty. *Journal of Travel Research*, *39*(1), 78–84.

Patwardhan, V., Ribeiro, M. A., Payini, V., Woosnam, K. M., Mallya, J., & Gopalakrishnan, P. (2020). Visitors' place attachment and destination loyalty: Examining the roles of emotional solidarity and perceived safety. *Journal of Travel Research*, *59*(1), 3–21.

Perkumienė, D., & Pranskūnienė, R. (2020). Overtourism: Between the right to travel and residents' rights. *Sustainability*, *11*, 1–17.

Phi, G. T. (2020). Framing overtourism: A critical news media analysis. *Current Issues in Tourism*, *23*(17), 2093–2097.

Ribeiro, M. A., Woosnam, K. M., Pinto, P., & Silva, J. A. (2018). Tourists' destination loyalty through emotional solidarity with residents: An integrative moderated mediation model. *Journal of Travel Research*, *57*(3), 279–295.

Sharpley, R. (2014). Host perceptions of tourism: A review of the research. *Tourism Management*, *42*, 37–49.

Stylidis, D., Woosnam, K. M., & Ivkov, M. (2020). Tourists' emotional solidarity with residents: A segmentation analysis and its links to destination image and loyalty. *Journal of Destination Marketing & Management*, *17*, 1–9.

Tasci, A. D. A. (2017). A quest for destination loyalty by profiling loyal travelers. *Journal of Destination Marketing & Management*, *6*(3), 207–220.

Tomljenović, R. (2010). Tourism and intercultural understanding or contact hypothesis revisited. In O. Moufakkir & I. Kelly (Eds.), *Tourism, Progress and Peace* (pp. 17–34). Wallingford: CABI.

UNWTO (2018). *"Overtourism"? Understanding and Managing Urban Tourism Growth Beyond Perceptions*. Madrid: World Tourism Organization.

Vernon, R. (1966). International investment and international trade in the product cycle. *The Quarterly Journal of Economics*, *80*(2), 190–207.

Ward, C., & Berno, T. (2011). Beyond social exchange theory: Attitudes toward tourists. *Annals of Tourism Research*, *38*(4), 1556–1569.

Watson, G. L., & Kopachevsky, J. P. (1996). Tourist carrying capacity: A critical look at the discursive dimension. *Progress in Tourism and Hospitality Research*, *2*(2), 169–179.

Woosnam, K. M. (2012). Using emotional solidarity to explain residents' attitudes about tourism and tourism development. *Journal of Travel Research*, *51*(3), 315–327.

Yilmaz, S. S., & Tasci, A. D. A. (2013). Internet as an information source and social distance: Any relationship? *Journal of Hospitality and Tourism Technology*, *4*(2), 188–196.

8 New perspectives of community-based tourism: a universal approach to tourism development

Thanakarn Bella Vongvisitsin and Antony King Fung Wong

Introduction

In the past decades, an increased realization of tourism impacts that affect local communities has led to an emergence of a community-based approach to sustainable development that addresses local issues, such as resident demands, physical and social carrying capacities, and local participation in decision-making process (Murphy, 1983; Richards & Hall, 2000; Singh et al., 2003). As guided by global organizations, such as the United Nations, the International Labour Organization and the World Bank, a community-based approach is the key to sustainable development and the foundation of a democratic system (Moser, 1989; Simmons, 1994). Although it is sometimes criticized as a Westernized ideology, many developing countries comply with these guidelines towards inclusive and sustainable tourism introduced by the United Nations World Tourism Organization (2015). Applied in tourism, this approach is considered as a fundamental and integral component of tourism development that safeguards community rights to access basic needs, increases self-reliance and improves the effectiveness of the development projects (Boyd & Singh, 2003; Bulatovic & Rajovic, 2016; Moser, 1989). However, this approach is contextually dependent and requires a deeper understanding of the application in different types of communities (Mayaka et al., 2018).

Community-based tourism (CBT) has been used as a concept in tourism academia and become highly relevant in tourism planning and development practices. Generally, CBT addresses local needs and benefits and guides the direction of tourism development towards more sustainable outcomes (Telfer, 2003). Instead of accommodating tourist demands, the core of CBT is to engage stakeholders in destination communities and ensure their inclusive representation and participation in the process (Boyd & Singh, 2003; Bramwell & Sharman, 2000; Hwang & Stewart, 2017). In particular, the focus of CBT is often on empowering the poor, marginalized or grassroots people to participate in the decision-making process and receive more benefits from tourism development (Telfer, 2003; Tosun, 2000, 2006). By highlighting community participation, tourism can tackle community issues, generate local benefits and enhance their economic and social prosperity (Edgell et al., 2008; Giampiccoli & Mtapuri, 2012; Richins, 2011). As a result, CBT is suggested as a solution to mitigate the perceived undesirable local impacts generated by tourism and tourists (Ashworth & Page, 2011).

The concept of CBT has been heavily applied to rural communities that offer alternative tourism products, such as homestay tourism, village tourism, agritourism and indigenous tourism (Boonratana, 2010; Kontogeorgopoulos et al., 2015). To extend CBT to other types of communities may draw scepticism due to a deeply rooted bias that CBT is applicable to only the rural development context (Bellini & Pasquinelli, 2017). Specifically, the implementation of the CBT concept in the urban context demonstrates a paradox between localization and globalization and a potential for integrating sustainable tourism with urban planning and development (Ashworth & Page, 2011). Besides the urban context, CBT is useful for understanding how different groups of people who share common characteristics or values may adopt tourism as a tool for achieving their collective goals (Singh et al., 2003). Given these perspectives, CBT is proposed by this chapter as a universal approach to tourism development in which the communities regardless of identity are embraced and empowered by the process and ensured a fair distribution of benefits. This chapter discusses how CBT has been adopted by urban communities in Bangkok and LGBTQ+ communities in Hong Kong.

CBT as a universal approach to tourism development

CBT has been positioned as an approach to tourism planning and development that tackles generated pressures or impacts in the local communities (Murphy, 1983). In particular, the local communities usually comprise poor or marginalized groups of people, such as women, young people, informal workers, immigrants, ethnic groups and squatters (Ahmed, 2019; Lahiri-Dutt, 2004; Moser, 1989; Nunkoo, 2017; Stone & Stone, 2011). In many cases, the term CBT has been interchangeably used to describe tourism products that are connected to local and indigenous communities despite the extent to which the communities are actively engaged or inclusively benefited from tourism (Boonratana, 2010). However, CBT is not limited to only indigenous communities but also applicable to different groups of people who share common characteristics or values (Singh et al., 2003). Particularly, CBT is defined as tourism that is owned and/or managed by the community and intended to generate benefits for its members (Goodwin & Santilli, 2009). Besides, CBT ultimately aims at increasing awareness of the communities and their ways of living and tackling local issues that undermine environmental and socio-cultural sustainability (Kontogeorgopoulos et al., 2015).

The core element of the CBT approach is community participation where the community members play a significant role in tourism planning and development (Tolkach & King, 2015). Effective community participation requires mobilization of the community members, facilitation of diverse social groups, representation of different voices and interests, and distribution of benefits (Boyd & Singh, 2003; Burgos & Mertens, 2017; Richards & Hall, 2000). Specifically, community participation refers to a process that empowers individuals or communities of interest to involve themselves in problem identification, decision-making, implementation and benefit sharing (France, 1998; Marzuki et al., 2012). Regardless of participatory platform, the individuals, groups or the community as a whole take part in either institutions, programmes or environments (Jordan et al., 2013). Grounded on the Western ideology of democracy, community participation usually implicates election of representatives to ascertain its performance (Bramwell & Sharman, 2000; Jordan et al., 2013). Nevertheless, community participation may be ineffective when some voices are excluded in certain stages of the process especially in the context where centralism of administration, shortcomings of coordination or barriers to access resources exist (Keogh, 1990; Nault & Stapleton, 2011; Simmons, 1994; Wang et al., 2010).

To achieve sustainable tourism, CBT with an inclusive participation is considered as a cornerstone of the overall development process (Loukissas, 1983; Moser, 1989; Murphy, 1983; Richards & Hall, 2000; Simmons, 1994). With the inclusion of communities, tourism development can focus on specific target groups of beneficiaries, including grassroots communities, and empower them to participate in the process (Telfer, 2003). Additionally, inclusive participation leads to larger and more balanced benefits generated by tourism development for the communities (Tosun, 2006). Although inclusive participation is proposed as an idealized model (Idziak et al., 2015; Moscardo, 2008; Murphy & Murphy 2004), many studies confirmed that local circumstances present unique challenges, such as limited resources and capabilities, power structures, socio-cultural norms, apathy and other life priorities (Jamieson, 2006; Li, 2006;

Mayaka et al., 2018; Nault & Stapleton, 2011; Sood et al., 2017; Taylor, 2017; Tosun, 2000). Moreover, another challenge for inclusive participation in CBT is to align different needs of the community members, especially isolated or disadvantaged individuals, with community-wide goals (Ishihara & Pascual, 2009).

Rethinking the meaning of community and CBT

A deeply rooted anti-urban bias in the meaning of 'community' has led to a traditional understanding of communities as traditionally tight-knit villages or small towns situated in the rural areas (Tonnies, 2001). In other words, urban areas are perceived as places where 'serious' activities, such as administration and trading, take place while small communities are marginalized (Ashworth & Page, 2011; Bellini & Pasquinelli, 2017). Specifically, the urban communities are large-scale social units that demonstrate more complex characteristics than their rural counterparts, such as the presence of secondary groups and greater heterogeneity or diversity of people (Beeton, 2006; Edwards et al., 2008; Hillery, 1955). Due to urbanization and industrialization, social relations are greatly dispersed and the urban communities are weakened (Hofferth & Iceland, 1998). In tourism studies, the notion of urban communities focuses on dynamics of mobility that lead to spatial restructuring of destinations and pluralization of stakeholders (Dredge & Jamal, 2013). Since CBT is usually adopted as a policy solution to over-tourism in the cities and a strategy to disperse tourists out of the urban areas (Kontogeorgopoulos et al., 2015), the poor or marginalized urban communities may be included as target beneficiaries. Besides the geographically bounded rural-urban continuum of communities, the community can be grounded on a socio-anthropological paradigm and seen as a group of people who share either tangible (e.g., language, dress, cuisine, festivities, settlement types and lifestyle) or intangible (e.g., beliefs, ethics and attitudes) commonalities (Singh et al., 2003). While traditionally seen as an important element of the community, geographical area and its social ties are not necessary for defining boundary of the community (Hillery, 1955). Particularly, the community involves a group of people with social or professional commonalities or even a philosophical or psychological commitment to certain lifestyles or special interests, such as scientist community, artistic community, academic community, Jewish community, LGBTQ+ community and online community (Bradshaw, 2008; Lyon & Driskell, 2012). Given that the meaning of community can transcend geographical or spatial boundaries to 'non-place' communities (Beeton, 2006), therefore, both geographical and socio-anthropological perspectives are discussed in this chapter by exemplifying the cases of urban and LGBTQ+ communities and rethinking the usage of CBT.

Urban communities in Bangkok metropolis

Bangkok, locally known as 'Krung Thep Maha Nakhon', was founded in 1782 and has become one of the fastest growing and most urbanized Asian mega-cities where a rapid process of urbanization has been juxtaposed with the abundance of historical communities (Storey, 2012). In particular, Rattanakosin Island is the oldest area in Bangkok that is home to historical sites, such as palaces, temples, traditional administrative buildings and residences. This area comprises much of the inner part that has been mostly gentrified for heritage conservation and the outer part that has been settled by many living urban communities (Department of City Planning and Urban Development, 2016). Since 1961, Bangkok has been considered as the national primate city with extensive modernization and industrialization. Given the rapid expansion of the metropolitan area, Bangkok has been upgraded as a special administrative area, namely Bangkok Metropolitan Region, and extended to other eight surrounding provinces (Tangchonlatip, 2007). From having merely a million residents in 1950, the city is currently accommodating up to 12 million people (Fraser, 2002).

Despite the governmental attempts in decentralizing economic prosperity to other regions, Bangkok has been prioritized as the focus of national economic development (Kaothien, 1991; Phuttharak & Dhiravisit, 2015). Traditional livelihoods of the urban communities in Bangkok have been greatly influenced by the Westernized paradigm of urban development, modernized housing style, increased land price and territorial demarcation (Evers, 1966; Noparatnaraporn & King, 2007). Since the urbanization has increased the disparity of socio-economic classes and transformed local identities, the conditions of the urban communities in Bangkok, especially the urban poor, have become controversial and raised several issues about the rapid and extensive development activities (McGrath et al., 2017). Bangkok's socio-economic fabric has gradually evolved through the ongoing city expansion sprawling its business and entertainment districts to other areas (Jiraratanapon, 2007). As a result, the evolution has led to continuously changing faces and challenges for the urban communities, especially those which are located in the old-town districts.

Specifically, the urban communities in Bangkok have been encountering several challenges, including land expropriation and gentrification. For example, an expansion of Mass Rapid Transport (MRT) to the old-town districts of Bangkok has led to an increased land price and produced threats to the stability of the urban communities (Kangwanpoom, 2014). As a consequence, the surrounding areas of newly built MRT stations are prone to expropriation for commercialization especially when a land ownership right does not belong to the residents like in Nang Loeng communities (Butkotorn, 2013). In addition, many urban communities in the old-town area have been affected by gentrification projects, such as waterway cleaning and beautification, pedestrian area reclamation and riverfront development (Boonjubun, 2017; Storey, 2012). For example, gentrification of the riverfront area, including some parts of Talad Noi communities, has been proposed as one of the mega-projects (Bangkok Metropolitan Administration, 2015). One of the most significant failures of gentrification in Bangkok took place at the Pom Mahakan community that has been completely demolished by the BMA ordered by the Administrative Court (Sittichok, 2018).

Urban CBT in Bangkok

In Bangkok, CBT has been adopted by a number of urban communities as an approach to community development and emerged as a social movement advocating for community issues. The urban CBT communities have been mobilized in many ways, such as a network, individual community, specific project or event. For example, the Civil Society Tourism Network (CSTN) has been convened by the BMA's Culture, Sports and Tourism Department and established as the largest not-for-profit network involving seven urban CBT communities in Bangkok. Moreover, CBT projects in Nang Loeng communities, such as community walking tours, arts and musical events, have been initiated by small groups of community residents (e.g., E-Loeng) with various external supports. Furthermore, Chomrom Khon Rak Talad Noi (KRTN) has gathered volunteers in Talad Noi communities and been created as an informal group by urban development projects executed by Arsom Silp Institute of the Arts whose project leader later turned the projects into a social enterprise called Pan Muang. Besides, in Banglamphu communities, Chomrom Kesorn Lamphu has emerged from Prachakhom Banglamphu as an informal group of youth guides organizing community walking tours for visitors and partnering with Pipit Banglamphu Museum.

The advantages of urban CBT are also seen by many urban communities in Bangkok as a tool for tackling the issues that affect their livelihoods, such as loss of traditional jobs, deterioration of cultural identity and heritage, lack of public space, and imminent threats of expropriation. Particularly, one of the historic movements in Banglamphu communities was initiated by conflicts between the Treasury Department, BMA and the community residents. The conflicts were aggravated by the Treasury Department's plan to demolish the Kurusapha Press building and gentrify its area as an extended part of the BMA's Santi Chaiprakarn Park. To preserve the building and reserve community rights to public space, Prachakhom Banglamphu has successfully registered the Press building as an ancient monument legally protected by the Fine Arts Department since 2001. As a result, the Treasury Department was obligated to halt its gentrification plan and comply with conservation guidelines. In collaboration with Prachakhom Banglamphu and Kesorn Lamphu, the Press building has been renovated as Pipit Banglamphu Museum where the community residents exhibit their stories and artefacts and use the area as a public space for organizing community events and activities, including community walking tours led by Kesorn Lamphu's youth guides.

In Talad Noi communities, KRTN serves as a community working group that coordinates with the community residents on organizing CBT events and activities. One of the major CBT events is the annual Chinese vegetarian or Nine Emperor Gods Festival that attracts a lot of visitors to Talad Noi communities to participate in religious rituals at Zu Shi Gong Shrine and buy traditional vegetarian food. With support from Pan Muang social enterprise, KRTN arranges small alleys around the shrine as a communal space where the community residents are allocated to different food vending stalls. Apart from the vegetarian festival, KRTN attempts to revive other important Chinese festivals, such as Lunar New Year, Yuan Xiao Festival and Mid-Autumn Festival. In every Mid-Autumn Festival, for instance, KRTN collaborates with CSTN on organizing community walking tours in which the visitors can indulge their Chinese nostalgia or learn about Chinese traditions, such as moon worshipping ritual, Basket Ghost summoning, lantern decoration and mooncake tasting. Another group, Sapa Kafae, emerged from a group of residents in Trok Tan alley and also organized a community event to share nostalgic memories with the visitors. Moreover, similarly to Banglamphu communities, the Treasury Department has gentrified an old machinery shop and its area adjacent to Phanu Rangsi pier to include a community exhibition hall and park utilized as a public space for community events and activities.

Due to a lack of land ownership rights, several historic urban communities, such as Pom Mahakan and Woeng Nakhon Kasem, have been expropriated for commercialization and beautification purposes. Additionally, local livelihoods, such as flower market vendors at Pak Klong Talad and street merchants and hawkers at Saphan Lek, have been eliminated by authorities due to their illegal street market establishments. Given these issues, other urban communities, including Nang Loeng, increasingly perceive pressures and fears over instability of their lands and properties that are not privately owned. In addition, the construction of Lan Luang MRT station is planned to expropriate some parts of Nang Loeng communities, including traditional Thai performance (i.e., Lakorn Chatri) troupes. The community issues in Nang Loeng led to numerous attempts in search of channels to negotiate with authorities, such as landowners (i.e., Crown Property Bureau) and government agencies (e.g., Ministry of Culture). Collaborating with social enterprises, academic institutions and development agencies, the E-Loeng group is one of the community groups that adopt a CBT approach to voicing the issues by organizing community walking tours, community events and activities, and participating in the urban planning process. Meanwhile, Nang Loeng Research Committee has been set up to mainly conduct research and establish a cultural learning centre within the community.

Despite being one of the most visited global destinations, the urban communities may not be the main focus of the overall tourism development in Bangkok. Urban CBT is seen as a tool for solving different community issues in the urbanized cities, such as loss of traditional jobs, deterioration of cultural identity and heritage, lack of public space, and imminent threats of expropriation. Due to a lack of negotiation power, CBT has also been sought to provide the urban communities with social capital and assist them in accessing resources, skills and knowledge and inclusive participation in the decision-making process (Edgell et al., 2008; Rinsin, 2019; Tolkach & King, 2015). The inclusion of urban community voices in tourism planning and development is important for coping with community rights violations by elites in power and addressing local needs and pressures (Boonjubun, 2017; Erickson, 2017; Imai, 2012). Since urban destinations often encounter challenges in implementing the profit-driven policies that maximize local benefits, a bottom-up approach (i.e., CBT) is recommended to achieve tourism growth while sustaining a balance of competing interests and needs (Ashworth & Page, 2011; Edwards et al., 2008; Ugur, 2017; UNWTO, 2012).

LGBTQ+ communities in Hong Kong

In Hong Kong, LGBTQ+ communities have been struggling for equal rights and social acceptance since the 1970s. Due to the British colonial rule applied to Hong Kong, social awareness of LGBTQ+ issues initially emerged from extensive public debates on criminalization and life imprisonment of homosexual people (The Law Reform Commission of Hong Kong, 1983). In 1991, the Legislative Council of Hong Kong (1991) or LegCo passed the Crimes (Amendment) Bill to give effect to the Law Reform Commission (LRC) recommendation to 'decriminalize homosexuality'. Moreover, the age of consent for gay sex was challenged in 2005 when Hong Kong's Government decided to lower it from 21 to 16 (LRC, 2010). Nevertheless, the legal process towards equal rights of LGBTQ+ people in Hong Kong is stagnant due to hesitation of the authorities to advance the laws on 'controversial' issues. For example, the LegCo overruled the motion on equal rights for people of different sexual orientations in 2012 (Hong Kong Sex Culture Society, 2012), vetoed the motion on the 'Marriage (Amendment) Bill 2014' for equality rights of LGBTQ+ couples to marriage (Hong Kong Special Administrative Region, 2014), and revoted the motion on investigating formulation of policies for homosexual couples to enter into unions (Legislative Council, 2018).

Despite the unproductive legislative process, there have been different forms of social movements advocating for LGBTQ+ rights, such as non-governmental organizations (NGOs) and networks of corporates and professionals. For instance, Rainbow of Hong Kong (2017) campaigns on different aspects of LGBTQ+ wellbeing, such as safe sex education and HIV prevention, and mobilizes LGBTQ+ communities through discussion groups, workshops and recreational activities. Moreover, Big Love Alliance (2017) promotes equal rights of LGBTQ+ communities through its connections with celebrities and politicians and continuous engagement on social media, publications, cultural events (e.g., Pink Dot). Pink Alliance (2021) also advocates for LGBTQ+ rights, social acceptance and dignity of LGBTQ+ individuals by organizing LGBTQ+ events (e.g., International Day Against Homophobia, Biphobia, Intersexphobia and Transphobia, Pink Season) and cooperates with other LGBTQ+ NGOs. Furthermore, the Hong Kong Lesbian and Gay Film Festival (2021) is an annual LGBTQ+ film event that promotes equal opportunities and anti-discrimination against LGBTQ+ people through cinematography. Apart from NGO perspectives, the advocacy of LGBTQ+ communities has expanded to corporate and professional networks in private sectors. Since Hong Kong is home to large-scale international corporates, social movement on LGBTQ+ inclusion in the workplace is seen as unique and prominent compared with other Asian territories (Vongvisitsin & Wong, 2021). For example, Community Business (2021) has established Diversity and Inclusion in Asia Network (DIAN) since 2008 with a handful group of pioneering corporates that implement diversity and inclusion (D&I) in the workplace. Specifically, the Hong Kong LGBT Inclusion Index and Awards initiative has been created to annually recognize the companies that demonstrate exceptional dedication and achievements in promoting LGBTQ+ inclusion in Hong Kong (Community Business, 2019). Besides, some networks of LGBTQ+ professionals have been established to advocate for LGBTQ+ rights in specific sectors. For example, Hong Kong LGBT+ Attorneys Network (2019) represents a network of supportive law firms and individuals, including lawyers, trainees, paralegals, employees, students, recruiters and academics in the legal field. In addition, Hong Kong LGBT+ Interbank Forum (2021) has been founded as an inter-organizational forum for LGBTQ+ professionals in the financial sector.

Unlike traditionally segregated spaces known as gay districts or villages in the Western cosmopolitan cities (Gorman-Murray & Nash, 2017), the social network of LGBTQ+ communities in Hong Kong is more dispersed to different organizations that target specific issues or beneficiary groups. Gay and lesbian bars and saunas are not prevalent or openly promoted in Hong Kong. Meanwhile, gay saunas are hidden as a space mainly for sexual activities due to social stigma against same-sex relations. The online community serves as a social platform where LGBTQ+ communities, especially young generation, are connected through conventional social media or LGBTQ+ specific mobile applications. Given this unique context, the connections amongst LGBTQ+ people are not geographically bounded. Instead, LGBTQ+ advocates tend to be socially connected through other formats, such as events and activities organized by LGBTQ+ NGOs, corporate and professional networks. To exemplify, the Hong Kong Pride Parade (2020) was considered as the largest LGBTQ+ event in Hong Kong that provided networking opportunities for LGBTQ+ communities with increased figures of participants from 100 in 2004 to 12,000 in 2018. More importantly, the event has gathered people who share common values towards social justice and inclusion.

CBT towards LGBTQ+ inclusive tourism in Hong Kong

Given that private sectors play a significant role in advocating for equal rights of LGBTQ+ communities in Hong Kong, the hospitality and tourism sectors are considered as a part of the social movements. Although CBT has not been clearly mentioned as the approach adopted by LGBTQ+ communities in hospitality and tourism sectors, community participation is regarded as the means to tourism planning and development that includes LGBTQ+ voices ranging from employees to customers. By involving LGBTQ+ NGOs in delivering trainings and workshops, several hospitality and tourism companies attempted to create awareness on LGBTQ+ issues amongst their employees that leads to a better understanding and treatment of their LGBTQ+ customers (Vongvisitsin & Wong, 2021). For example, Encompass HK (2021) is a social enterprise that promotes a diverse and inclusive workplace culture and assists practitioners to achieve standards guided by sustainable development goals. Also, Pride Lab (2020) delivered LGBTQ+ trainings for many organizations in Hong Kong. Besides, LGBTIQ+ Tourism Asia (2021) has been founded to engage with hospitality and tourism practitioners and provide them with consultancy services, such as sexuality and gender sensitization, organizational development, product and service design, marketing and communications and community engagement.

Emerged from D&I interventions in Hong Kong, LGBTQ+ inclusion is seen as the agenda in which LGBTQ+ communities are engaged by different hospitality and tourism stakeholders in the planning and development process. For example, Cathay Pacific (2019a), the largest Hong Kong-based airline, imposed well-rounded policies, including anti-harassment, D&I and non-discrimination policies that are applied not exclusively to its employees but also responsibly to its customers and local LGBTQ+ suppliers and communities. Additionally, 'Fly with Pride' has been launched as a network for advancing social awareness of LGBTQ+ people and voicing on-the-ground issues of LGBTQ+ employees (Cathay Pacific, 2019b). Also, as part of social marketing campaigns, its 'Move beyond Labels' advertisement featuring a same-sex couple attracted public discussions across Hong Kong's society on the controversial ban of its exposure in major public transport facilities (Lee, 2019; Luo & Wan, 2019; Tam, 2019). Eventually, Cathay Pacific has built its 'LGBTQ+ inclusive' brand as a part of tourism development that addresses the needs and concerns of LGBTQ+ communities.

Moreover, the hotel sector is seen as one important stakeholder that adopted a CBT approach in encouraging participation of and contributing benefits to local LGBTQ+ communities. For example, Eaton Hotel provided its space for supporting LGBTQ+ activists to organize community events and activities. Besides the policies, Eaton Hotel demonstrated LGBTQ+ friendliness through its decorations (e.g., billboard, paintings) and provision of facilities (e.g., gender-neutral toilets) (Hong Kong Free Press, 2018; World Rainbow Hotel, 2018). Moreover, Hotel ICON (2021) claimed to be the first hotel to organize D&I conferences in Hong Kong that are seen as a significant milestone to enhancing awareness of LGBTQ+ inclusion, exchanging ideas with LGBTQ+ communities and encouraging representation and inclusion of LGBTQ+ communities especially in its human resources process. Furthermore, The Peninsula Hong Kong (2020) initiated its 'Stay for Love' package that attracted same-sex couples to spend holidays in its premises and financially contributed to support the marriage equality movement in Hong Kong.

Furthermore, the CBT approach has been used by a tour operator that introduced LGBTQ+ themed tour products and engaged with LGBTQ+ communities and other hospitality and tourism stakeholders. Specifically, Walk in Hong Kong (2021) is committed to CBT by developing community walking tours and engaging with local small enterprises and guides, including its 'LGBT in the City' that connects customers with local guides and LGBTQ+ entrepreneurs through the tour programme. In addition, collaboration within hospitality and tourism sectors leads to greater impacts generated by CBT to the target beneficiaries. Particularly, Walk in Hong Kong also collaborated with several hotels in delivering its CBT programme as a part of alternative packages made available to the hotel guests. For example, Hotel ICON (2020) launched its 'ICON Pride' package which offers an additional tour option for its guests that are interested in LGBTQ+ culture in Hong Kong. Also, Hyatt Centric Victoria Harbour Hong Kong curated 'Centric Pride' festivals by displaying rainbow installations and photobooths, serving rainbow-inspired dishes and drinks, and offering Pride-themed goody bags (Cam, 2023). Although LGBTQ+ communities in Hong Kong are dispersed, CBT can convey the voices of LGBTQ+ people and connect with the mainstream through the tourism supply chain in which LGBTQ+ communities can participate.

Apart from hospitality and tourism practitioners that individually adopted CBT to create their own LGBTQ+ focused tourism initiatives, Hong Kong has been designated to host the international multi-sports, arts and cultural events (i.e., Gay Games) that connect both local and international LGBTQ+ communities. With shared sexual and gender characteristics and values towards equal rights and inclusive environments for LGBTQ+ communities, Gay Games 11 Hong Kong 2023 or GGHK (2023) is adopting a CBT approach by communicating its three principles, including participation, inclusion and personal best, through its sports, arts and cultural events. By integrating a CBT concept in the ground principles, GGHK has initiated a network of volunteers, sponsors and advisory council members to build participation of the LGBTQ+ communities in Hong Kong and hospitality and tourism practitioners who share common values in favour of LGBTQ+ communities. Despite blurred social boundaries of LGBTQ+ communities, CBT is, therefore, proved to be a means to creating inclusive community participation from socio-anthropological perspectives.

Conclusions

Whist CBT has been frequently used as an effective tool for developing rural destinations (Boonratana, 2010; Giampiccoli & Mtapuri, 2012; Kontogeorgopoulos et al., 2015), this chapter shows extensive potentials of CBT concept that are applicable to other types of communities. Tracing back to the original definition of community, its meanings are varied by heterogeneity in types, scales and functions based on geographical and socio-anthropological perspectives (Singh et al., 2003). However, the terms *community* and *CBT* have been deeply biased with the rigid conception of community as a small and secluded village (Ashworth & Page, 2011; Bellini & Pasquinelli, 2017). Therefore, CBT is often limited to homestay tourism, village tourism or indigenous tourism as the alternative tourism products in the rural areas (Boonratana, 2010; Kontogeorgopoulos et al., 2015; Sood et al., 2017). By taking broader perspectives towards communities into account, CBT can be positioned as the universal approach to tourism planning and development in which either rural, urban or other socially constructed communities play an active role and enjoy larger and more balanced benefits in response to their needs (Tosun, 2006).

Besides the potentials for alleviating poverty and conserving cultural and environmental resources, CBT can tackle unique contextual issues experienced by different types of communities. For instance, the urban communities are distinctively featured with a highly complex nature in terms of natural environments, social groups and relationships, power structures, physical mobility, individualism, segmentations of life, access to services and education (Ashworth & Page, 2011; Beeton, 2006; Edwards et al., 2008; Hillery, 1955; Hofferth & Iceland, 1998; Mahjabeen et al., 2009). As a consequence, the urban communities employ a CBT approach to address more specific problems, such as fading traditional jobs, deteriorating cultural identity and heritage, limited public space, expropriation and gentrification, and profit-driven policies. As the approach to enhancing more inclusive participation, CBT serves as the platform for the urban communities to take part in the planning and development process, communicate their needs and concerns, and gain more power in negotiation with authorities and elites. In the long run, the urban communities can also monitor the urban development interventions and provide recommendations to policymakers to ensure fair distribution of benefits.

On the other hand, the CBT concept may not have been used directly to describe how 'non-place' communities adopt tourism to address their needs and solve their issues. By taking socio-anthropological perspectives on the communities, CBT can be geographically unbounded and extended to other socially constructed communities that may share either tangible or intangible commonalities (Singh et al., 2003). This chapter explored how LGBTQ+ communities have been engaged in NGOs, private organizations, including hospitality and tourism corporates, and professional networks, to create Hong Kong as a more inclusive and friendly destination. Given the issues experienced by both LGBTQ+ residents and visitors, such as discrimination, exclusion and mistreatment, hospitality and tourism practitioners (e.g., airlines, hotels, tour operators, events) utilized community participation as the core element for developing LGBTQ+ inclusive tourism. Particularly, LGBTQ+ communities have been involved in tourism planning and development to various extents, ranging from leading the initiatives by themselves to participating in certain activities of the overall process, either actively or passively. Although LGBTQ+ communities are dispersed, CBT serves as a platform where they are gathered to collectively participate in and gain benefits from tourism development.

Limitations and future research directions

This chapter proposes a research agenda that expands the knowledge horizons of CBT that lead to wider social impacts in different types of communities. Whilst CBT has been positioned as the universal approach to tourism development, the case studies exemplified by this chapter are groundbreaking but relatively new for CBT research. The extension of the CBT concept to different types of communities other than the rural still attracts scepticism from tourism scholars about its objectives and practicalities. However, this chapter shows how the understanding of CBT can be reframed in different contexts. Since the CBT concept highlights the importance of inclusive community participation in tourism planning and development, this chapter suggested several directions for future research, such as patterns of participation, social capital and relationships in the CBT landscape, power structures, and barriers to participation. Additionally, to investigate different types, scales and functions of the communities leads to a fruitful knowledge base of CBT and its potentials to generate social impacts to wider populations especially the poor and marginalized. With extensive research on CBT in various perspectives, as a result, the CBT claim as the universal approach to tourism development can be strengthened and generalized.

References

Ahmed, K. G. (2019). Instinctive participation: Community-initiated mechanisms for managing and maintaining urban poor settlements in Cairo, Egypt. *Urban Research and Practice, 12*(4), 341–371.

Ashworth, G., & Page, S. J. (2011). Urban tourism research: Recent progress and current paradoxes. *Tourism Management, 32*, 1–15.

Beeton, S. (2006). *Community Development through Tourism.* Collingwood: Landlinks Press.

Bellini, N., & Pasquinelli, C. (2017). *Tourism in the City: Towards an Integrative Agenda on Urban Tourism.* Cham: Springer.

Big Love Alliance (2017). *About Biglove.* http:// biglovealliance .org/ about -biglove/ (accessed 10 April 2021).

Boonjubun, C. (2017). Conflicts over streets: The eviction of Bangkok street vendors. *Cities, 70*, 22–31.

Boonratana, R. (2010). Community-based tourism in Thailand: The need and justification for an operational definition. *Kasetsart Journal (Social Sciences), 31*, 280–289.

Boyd, S. W., & Singh, S. (2003). Destination communities: Structures, resources and types. In S. Singh, D. J. Timothy, & R. K. Dowling (Eds.), *Tourism in Destination Communities* (pp. 19–33). Wallingford: CABI Publishing.

Bradshaw, T. K. (2008). The post-place community: Contributions to the debate about the definition of community. *Community Development, 39*(1), 5–16.

Bramwell, B., & Sharman, A. (2000). Approach to sustainable tourism planning and community participation: The case of the Hope Valley. In G. Richards & D. Hall (Eds.), *Tourism and Sustainable Community Development* (pp. 17–35). London: Routledge.

Bulatovic, J., & Rajovic, G. (2016). Applying sustainable tourism indicators to community-based ecotourism tourist village Eco-katun Štavna. *European Journal of Economic Studies, 16*(2), 309–330.

Burgos, A., & Mertens, F. (2017). Participatory management of community-based tourism: A network perspective. *Community Development, 48*(4), 546–565.

Cam, L. (2023, 8 June). 6 Pride events in Hong Kong in June 2023, from drag queen shows to cocktail parties and an exhibition about a pioneering Chinese-American lesbian. *South China Morning Post.* https://www.scmp.com/lifestyle/entertainment/ article/3223354/6-pride-events-hong-kong-june-2023-drag-queen-shows-cocktail -parties-and-exhibition-about-pioneering (accessed 24 August 2023).

Cathay Pacific (2019a). *Human Rights Policy.* https://www.cathaypacific.com/content/ dam/ focal -point/ cx/ about -us/ responsible -business/ Cathay -Pacific -Airways -Limited_Human-Rights-Policy.pdf (accessed 14 April 2021).

Cathay Pacific (2019b). *Sustainable Development Report 2018.* https://www.swire.com/ en/sustainability/sd_reports/cx_2019.pdf (accessed 14 April 2021).

Community Business (2019). *2019 Hong Kong LGBT+ Inclusion Index (index).* https:// www .communitybusiness .org/ sites/ default/ files/ LGBT/ information _for _participating_organisations_.pdf (accessed 10 April 2021).

Community Business (2021). *Developments in diversity and inclusion in Asia.* https:// www .communitybusiness .org/ sites/ default/ files/ uploads/ DIAN/ 2021 _dian _brochure.pdf (accessed 28 April 2021).

Dredge, D., & Jamal, T. (2013). Mobilities on the Gold Coast, Australia: Implications for destination governance and sustainable tourism. *Journal of Sustainable Tourism, 21*(4), 557–579.

Edgell, D. L., Allen, M. D., Smith, G., & Swanson, J. R. (2008). *Tourism Policy and Planning: Yesterday, Today and Tomorrow*. Oxford: Butterworth-Heinemann.

Edwards, D., Griffin, T., & Hayllar, B. (2008). Urban tourism research: Developing an agenda. *Annals of Tourism Research, 35*(4), 1032–1052.

Encompass HK (2021). *About us*. http://encompasshk.com/ (accessed 10 April 2021).

Erickson, A. (2017, April 22). Bangkok is about to lose one of the things people love most about it. *The Washington Post*. https://www.washingtonpost.com/news/ worldviews/ wp/ 2017/ 04/ 22/ bangkok-is-about-to-lose-one-of-the-things-people -love-most-about-it/?noredirect=on&utm_term=.0f581ddc2ef9. (accessed 25 April 2021).

Evers, H.-D. (1966). Formation of a social class structure: Urbanisation, bureaucratisation and social mobility in Thailand. *American Sociological Review, 31*(4), 480–488.

France, L. (1998). Local participation in tourism in the West Indian Islands. In E. Laws, B. Faulkner, & G. Moscardo (Eds.), *Embracing and Managing Change in Tourism: International Case Studies* (pp. 222–234). London: Routledge.

Fraser, E. D. (2002). Urban ecology in Bangkok, Thailand: Community participation, urban agriculture and forestry. *Environments, 30*(1), 37–49.

Gay Games 11 Hong Kong 2023 (2023). *Legal Information: Terms and Conditions, Policies Summaries*. https:// www .gghk2023 .com/ terms -and -conditions -expand/ (accessed 29 December 2023).

Giampiccoli, A., & Mtapuri, O. (2012). Community-based tourism: An exploration of the concept(s) from a South African and political perspective. *Tourism Review International, 16*(1), 29–43.

Goodwin, H., & Santilli, R. (2009). Community-based tourism: A success? IRCT Occasional Paper 11. http://www.haroldgoodwin.info/uploads/CBTaSuccessPubpdf .pdf (accessed 29 December 2023).

Gorman-Murray, A., & Nash, C. (2017). Transformations in LGBT consumer landscapes and leisure spaces in the neoliberal city. *Urban Studies, 54*(3), 786–805.

Hillery, G. (1955). Definitions of community: Areas of agreement. *Rural Sociology, 20*(2), 111–123.

Hofferth, S. L., & Iceland, J. (1998). Social capital in rural and urban communities. *Rural Sociology, 63*(4), 574–598.

Hong Kong Free Press (2018, 6 November). The grassroots LGBT+ activists behind the celebrities and headlines. https://hongkongfp.com/2018/11/06/grassroots-lgbt -activists-behind-celebrities-headlines/ (accessed 10 April 2021).

Hong Kong Lesbian and Gay Film Festival (2021). *About us*. https://www.hklgff.hk/?q= about-us (accessed 10 April 2021).

Hong Kong LGBT+ Attorneys Network (2019). *HKGALA: Championing LGBT diversity and inclusion in the legal profession*. https://www.hkgala.com/ (accessed 28 April 2021).

Hong Kong LGBT+ Interbank Forum (2021). *Who we are*. https://www.interbanklgbthk .com/#who-we-are (accessed 28 April 2021).

Hong Kong Pride Parade (2020). *History*. https://hkpride.net/en/history/ (accessed 10 April 2021).

Hong Kong Sex Culture Society (2012). [Xing wen hua ping lun] di yi qi ([Sex culture review] the first issue). http://www.scs.org.hk/comment/Vol_1/201212.php (accessed 28 April 2021).

Hong Kong Special Administrative Region (2014). *Marriage (Amendment) Bill 2014 not passed by Legislative Council.* https://www.info.gov.hk/gia/general/201410/22/P201410220932.htm (accessed 8 April 2021).

Hotel ICON (2020). Icon Pride Package. https://www.hotel-icon.com/offers/icon-pride-package (accessed 27 March 2020).

Hotel ICON (2021). *Leading the way! Hotel ICON hosts diversity and inclusion conference.* https://www.hotel-icon.com/icon-edit/leading-the-way-hotel-icon-hosts-diversity-and-inclusion-conference (accessed 15 April 2021).

Hwang, D., & Stewart, W. P. (2017). Social capital and collective action in rural tourism. *Journal of Travel Research, 56*(1), 81–93.

Idziak, W., Majewski, J., & Zmyslony, P. (2015). Community participation in sustainable rural tourism experience creation: A long-term appraisal and lessons from a thematic villages project in Poland. *Journal of Sustainable Tourism, 23*(8–9), 1341–1362.

Imai, H. (2012). Balancing urban revitalisation, tourism, and development issues in times of crisis: Kawagoe's historical district as a self-sustaining and resilient community. *Contemporary Japan, 24*(2), 149–178.

Ishihara, H., & Pascual, U. (2009). Social capital in community level environmental governance: A critique. *Ecological Economics, 68*, 1549–1562.

Jamieson, W. (2006). Community planning for tourism development. In W. Jamieson (Ed.), *Community Destination Management in Developing Economies* (pp. 63–73). New York: Haworth Press.

Jordan, E. J., Vogt, C. A., Kruger, L. E., & Grewe, N. (2013). The interplay of governance, power and citizen participation in community tourism planning. *Journal of Policy Research in Tourism, Leisure and Events, 5*(3), 270–288.

Kangwanpoom, C. (2014). Importance of participatory process in urban regeneration: Case study of Wat Mangkorn Kammalawat MRT Station's surrounding areas. *Journal of Architectural Research and Studies, 11*(1), 21–36.

Kaothien, U. (1991). Regional and urbanisation policy in Thailand: The tertiary sector as a leading sector in regional development. *Urban Studies, 28*(6), 1027–1043.

Keogh, B. (1990). Public participation in community tourism planning. *Annals of Tourism Research, 17*, 449–465.

Kontogeorgopoulos, N., Churyen, A., & Duangsaeng, V. (2015). Homestay tourism and the commercialisation of the rural home in Thailand. *Asia Pacific Journal of Tourism Research, 20*(1), 29–50.

Lahiri-Dutt, K. (2004). 'I plan, you participate': A southern view of community participation in urban Australia. *Community Development Journal, 39*(1), 13–27.

Lee, D. (2019, 20 May). Cathay Pacific advert showing same-sex couple banned from Hong Kong's MTR and airport. *South China Morning Post.* https://www.scmp.com/news/hong-kong/transport/article/3010825/cathay-pacific-advert-showing-same-sex-couple-banned-hong (accessed 28 April 2021).

Legislative Council of Hong Kong (1991). *Official record of the proceedings of the Legislative Council.* https://www.legco.gov.hk/yr90-91/chinese/lc_sitg/hansard/h910710.pdf (accessed 8 April 2021).

LGBTIQ+ Tourism Asia (2021). *Our products and services.* https://inclusivetourismasia.org/productsandservices/ (accessed 26 April 2021).

Li, W. (2006). Community decision making: Participation in development. *Annals of Tourism Research, 33*(1), 132–143.

Loukissas, P. J. (1983). Public participation in community tourism planning: A gaming simulation approach. *Journal of Travel Research, 22*(1), 18–23.

Luo, C., & Wan, C. (2019, 22 May). MTR's about-turn gay ad. *The Standard*. https:// www .thestandard .com .hk/ section -news/ section/ 11/ 207887/ MTR %27s -about -turnon-gay-ad (accessed 28 April 2021).

Lyon, L., & Driskell, R. (2012). *The Community in Urban Society*, 2nd edition. Long Grove, IL: Waveland Press.

Mahjabeen, Z., Shrestha, K. K., & Dee, J. A. (2009). Rethinking community participation in urban planning: The role of disadvantaged groups in Sydney Metropolitan Strategy. *Australasian Journal of Regional Studies*, 15(1), 45–63.

Marzuki, A., Hay, I., & James, J. (2012). Public participation shortcomings in tourism planning: The case of the Langkawi Islands, Malaysia. *Journal of Sustainable Tourism*, 20(4), 585–602.

Mayaka, M., Croy, W. G., & Cox, J. W. (2018). Participation as motif in community-based tourism: A practice perspective. *Journal of Sustainable Tourism*, 26(3), 416–432.

McGrath, B., Sangawongse, S., Thaikatoo, D., & Barcelloni Corte, M. (2017). The architecture of the metacity: Land use change, patch dynamics and urban form in Chiang Mai, Thailand. *Urban Planning*, 2(1), 53–71.

Moscardo, G. (Ed.) (2008). *Building Community Capacity for Tourism Development*. Wallingford: CABI.

Moser, C. O. N. (1989). Community participation in urban projects in the Third World. *Progress in Planning*, 32, 71–133.

Murphy, P. E. (1983). Tourism as a community industry: An ecological model of tourism development. *Tourism Management*, 4(3), 180–193.

Murphy, P. E., & Murphy, A. E. (2004). *Strategic Management for Tourism Communities: Bridging the Gaps*. Clevedon: Channel View Publications.

Nault, S., & Stapleton, P. (2011). The community participation process in ecotourism development: A case study of the community of Sogoog, Bayan-Ulgii, Mongolia. *Journal of Sustainable Tourism*, 19(6), 695–712.

Noparatnaraporn, C., & King, R. (2007). Memory or nostalgia: The imagining of everyday Bangkok. *SOJOURN: Journal of Social Issues in South East Asia*, 22(1), 57–82.

Nunkoo, R. (2017). Governance and sustainable tourism: What is the role of trust, power and social capital? *Journal of Destination Marketing and Management*, 6, 277–285.

Phuttharak, T., & Dhiravisit, A. (2015). Engaging civil society in urban development: Best practice in Udon Thani, Thailand. *Asian Social Science*, 11(8), 100–107.

Pink Alliance (2021). *Who we are*. https://pinkalliance.hk/about/about-us/ (accessed 10 April 2021).

Pride Lab (2020). 性/別多元培訓 [Gender/diversity training]. https:// www .pridelab .hk/性別多元培訓/ (accessed 28 April 2021).

Rainbow of Hong Kong (2017). *Rainbow of Hong Kong*. http://rainbowhk.org/en-about .html (accessed 12 April 2021).

Reuters (2018). *Hong Kong rejects motion to consider same-sex unions*. https://cn.reuters .com/article/hongkong-lgbt-politics-idUSL8N1XX5IY (accessed 6 April 2021).

Richards, G., & Hall, D. (Eds.) (2000). *Tourism and Sustainable Community Development*. London and New York: Routledge.

Richins, H. (2011). Issues and pressures on achieving effective community destination governance: a typology. In E. Laws, H. Richins, J. Argusa, & Noel Scott (Eds.), *Tourist Destination Governance: Practice, Theory and Issues* (pp. 51–65). Wallingford: CABI.

Simmons, D. G. (1994). Community participation in tourism planning. *Tourism Management*, 15(2), 98–108.

Singh, S., Timothy, D. J., & Dowling, R. K. (2003). *Tourism in Destination Communities*. Wallingford: CABI Publishing.

Sittichok, T. (2018). Mahakan Fort community: The struggle to solve the problem of eviction. *Inthaninthaksin Journal, 13*(1), 9–29.

Sood, J., Lynch, P., & Anastasiadou, C. (2017). Community non-participation in homestays in Kullu, Himachal Pradesh, India. *Tourism Management, 60*, 332–347.

Stone, L. S., & Stone, T. M. (2011). Community-based tourism enterprises: Challenges and prospects for community participation. Khama Rhino Sanctuary Trust, Botswana. *Journal of Sustainable Tourism, 19*(1), 97–114.

Storey, D. (2012). Incompatible partners? Urban poor communities and river systems in Bangkok, Thailand. *International Development Planning Review, 34*(2), 109–128.

Tam, L. (2019, 27 May). Cathay Pacific advert showing same-sex couple holding hands and the reaction by Hong Kong Airport Authority and MTR operator shows how city lags behind on LGBT rights. *South China Morning Post*. https://www.scmp.com/news/hong-kong/society/article/3011969/cathay-pacific-advert-showing-same-sex-couple-holding-hands (accessed 28 April 2021).

Taylor, S. R. (2017). Issues in measuring success in community-based indigenous tourism: Elites, kin groups, social capital, gender dynamics and income flows. *Journal of Sustainable Tourism, 25*(3), 433–449.

Telfer, D. J. (2003). Development issues in destination communities. In S. Singh, D. J. Timothy, & R. K. Dowling (Eds.), *Tourism in Destination Communities* (pp. 155–180). Wallingford: CABI Publishing.

The Law Reform Commission of Hong Kong (1983). *Laws governing homosexual conduct (Topic 2)*. https://www.hkreform.gov.hk/en/docs/rhomosexual-e.pdf (accessed 8 April 2021).

The Law Reform Commission of Hong Kong (2010). *Sexual offences involving children and persons with mental impairment*. https://www.legco.gov.hk/yr16-17/english/panels/ajls/papers/ajls20170227cb4-591-5-e.pdf (accessed 8 April 2021).

The Peninsula Hong Kong (2020). "Stay for love" experience. https://www.peninsula.com/en/hong-kong/special-offers/rooms/stay-for-love-room-offer (accessed 28 April 2021).

Tolkach, D., & King, B. (2015). Strengthening community-based tourism in a new resource-based island nation: Why and how? *Tourism Management, 48*, 386–398.

Tonnies, F. (2001). *Community and Civil Society* (J. Harris & M. Hollis, Trans.). Cambridge: Cambridge University Press (original work published 1887).

Tosun, C. (2000). Limits to community participation in the tourism development process in developing countries. *Tourism Management, 21*, 613–633.

Tosun, C. (2006). Expected nature of community participation in tourism development. *Tourism Management, 27*, 493–504.

Ugur, L. (2017). Mind the gap: Reconceptualising inclusive development in support of integrated urban planning and tourism development. In N. Bellini & C. Pasquinelli (Eds.), *Tourism in the City: Towards an Integrative Approach on Urban Tourism* (pp. 51–66). Cham: Springer.

United Nations World Tourism Organization (2012). *Global Report on City Tourism*. AM reports no. 6. http://historicalcity.eu/wp-content/uploads/2017/12/city-tourism.pdf (accessed 25 April 2021).

United Nations World Tourism Organization (2015). *Tourism and the Sustainable Development Goals*. https://www.e-unwto.org/doi/pdf/10.18111/9789284417254 (accessed 25 April 2021).

Vongvisitsin, T. B., & Wong, A. K. F. (2021). Organisational change towards LGBTQ+ inclusion in hospitality and tourism: Managerial perspectives. *Tourism Management*, 86, 104331.

Walk in Hong Kong (2021). *LGBT in the City*. https://walkin.hk/private-tour/lgbt-in-the-city/ (accessed 15 April 2021).

Wang, H., Yang, Z., Chen, L., Yang, J., & Li, R. (2010). Minority community participation in tourism: A case of Kanas Tuva villages in Xinjiang, China. *Tourism Management*, 31, 759–764.

World Rainbow Hotel (2018). Eaton HK. https://www.worldrainbowhotels.com/asia/hong-kong/kowloon/eaton-hk/ (accessed 14 April 2021).

กรุงเทพมหานคร [Bangkok Metropolitan Administration] (2015). แนวทางในการอนุรักษ์พื้นฟูบริเวณตลาดน้อยและพื้นที่ต่อเนื่อง: คู่มือให้ความรู้ประชาชนเกี่ยวกับมาตรการทางผังเมืองและข้อเสนอแนะแนวทางการปฏิบัติเพื่อส่งเสริมภูมิทัศน์การอนุรักษ์ ฟื้นฟู และพัฒนาย่านตลาดน้อยและพื้นที่ต่อเนื่อง [*Guidelines on conservation and revitalisation of Talad Noi and adjacent areas: Educational handbook for people about urban planning measures and recommendations on landscaping, conservation, revitalisation and development of Talad Noi district and adjacent areas*]. กรุงเทพมหานคร [Bangkok Metropolitan Administration].

กาญจนพงศ์ รินสินธุ์ [Rinsin, K.] (2019, January 10). เดินดูนางเลิ้งเมื่อวัฒนธรรมถูกใช้รองรับการพัฒนา สู่คำถามสิทธิในเมืองที่เท่าเทียม [Looking at Nang Loeng when culture has been used to cater development towards the question about equal rights in the city]. ประชาไท [Prachatai]. Retrieved 25 April 2021 from https://prachathai.com/journal/2019/01/80466.

กาญจนา ตั้งชลทิพย์ [Tangchonlatip, K.] (2007). กรุงเทพมหานคร: เมืองโตเดี่ยวตลอดกาลของประเทศไทย. In วรชัย ทองไทย และสุรีย์พร พันพึ่ง (บรรณาธิการ) [W. Tongthai & S. Panpueng (Eds.)], ประชากรและสังคม 2550 นคราภิวัฒน์และวิถีชีวิตเมือง [*Population and society 2007 urbanisation and urban ways of living*] (pp. 18–35). นครปฐม: สถาบันวิจัยประชากรและสังคม มหาวิทยาลัยมหิดล [Nakhon Pathom: Institute for Population and Social Research, Mahidol University].

ชุลีพร บุตรโคตร [Butkotorn, C.] (2013, 27 March). นางเลิ้งโอด รฟม. ไล่ที่ซุกหัวนอน สงสัยโรงแรมหรู-บริษัทดังไม่โดน จี้รัฐฟื้นชีวิตในมุมมืดข้างทำเนียบ [Nang Loeng complained MRT for expropriating their residences, questioned why luxury hotel or famous company are not affected, pushed the government to revitalise livelihoods in hidden corner next to the parliament]. ศูนย์ข้อมูลและข่าวสืบสวนเพื่อสิทธิพลเมือง [Thai Civil Rights and Investigative Journalism]. Retrieved 25 April 2021 from https://www.tcijthai.com/news/2013/27/scoop/2270.

ฐากร สิทธิโชค [Sitthichok, T.] (2018). ชุมชนป้อมมหากาฬ: การต่อสู้เพื่อแก้ปัญหาการไล่รื้อที่ดิน [Pom Mahakan community: the struggles against expropriation issues]. อินทนิลทักษิณสาร [*Inthaninthaksin Journal*], 13(1), 9–29.

วรี จิระรัตน์พันธ์ [Jiraratanapon, W.] (2007). แนวทางการพัฒนาย่านเสาชิงช้า กรุงเทพมหานคร [Development guidelines for Sao Chingcha District, Bangkok] (Master's thesis). จุฬาลงกรณ์มหาวิทยาลัย [Chulalongkorn University], กรุงเทพมหานคร [Bangkok].

สำนักผังเมือง [Department of City Planning and Urban Development] (2016). ผังเมืองอนุรักษ์และพัฒนาเมืองอย่างยั่งยืน [*Sustainable city conservation plan and urban development*]. กรุงเทพมหานคร [Bangkok].

立法會 [Legislative Council] (2018). 研究制訂讓同志締結伴侶關係的政策的議員議案 [A parliamentary bill to formulate a policy for homosexual couples to enter into the union]. https://www.legco.gov.hk/yr18-19/chinese/counmtg/hansard/cm20181122-translate-c.pdf (accessed 28 April 2021).

香港性文化學會 [Hong Kong Sex Culture Society] (2012). [性文化評論] 第一期 ([Sex culture review] the first issue). http://www.scs.org.hk/comment/Vol_1/201212.php (accessed 28 April 2021).

9 Is local lodging negatively impacting residents' perceptions of tourism in their community?

Patrícia Pinto, Manuela Guerreiro, Ana Renda, Luís Nobre Pereira, Milene Lança and Hio Kuan Lai

1   Introduction

The worldwide relevance of tourism is currently unquestionable, both from economic and social points of view, highlighting the role that this activity plays in the development of territories. Among the various tourist services, the modalities of accommodation have been essential elements due to their importance for tourists. In this context, new forms of accommodation that bring tourists closer to residents (peer-to-peer accommodation) have been a growing trend. Also, the new technologies and the emergence of online reservation platforms such as Airbnb, HomeAway, Home Exchange and CouchSurfing stand out, allowing direct contact between tourists and accommodation owners, whether they are companies or individuals (Gutierrez-Tano et al., 2019; Richards et al., 2020).

On the one hand, local lodging provides greater geographical dissemination and develops sharing economy; on the other hand, placing tourists and residents in contact can lead to changes in residents' quality of life and lifestyles (Suess et al., 2020, 2021). Residents can also perceive the economic, environmental, social, and cultural impacts of tourism differently because of the location and characteristics of this form of accommodation and tourists' profile.

Despite the rapid growth of local accommodation in many destinations, scientific research about residents' perceptions of tourism impacts caused by this kind of accommodation remains undervalued (Guttentag, 2015). Portugal and the Algarve, popular tourism destinations in Europe, are no exception. This research was carried out in the Algarve, by applying 2,004 questionnaires to residents in the low season of tourism activity, in 2020. This chapter focuses on residents' sociocultural perceptions of tourism and it aims to explain how residents' perceptions, attitudes and behaviors can be affected by the daily interaction with tourists.

Results may contribute to the literature in this area and draw the attention of destination management organizations (DMOs) and local actors to the relevance of considering residents' perspective on this growing phenomenon.

2   Literature review

2.1   Local lodging and community residents

The development of information technology encouraged the rise of local lodging (peer-to-peer accommodation), such as Airbnb, HomeAway, Home Exchange and CouchSurfing digital platforms, which simplified the connection between hosts and guests (Gutierrez-Tano et al., 2019; Richards et al., 2020). This kind of accommodation has gained popularity among tourists due to lower pricing, perceived authenticity, and interactions with locals (Guttentag, 2015; Richards et al., 2020; Suess et al., 2020, 2021). As of September 2020, the principal home-sharing platform – Airbnb – was operating in 100,000 cities across 220 countries, offering over 5.6 million accommodation rentals (Airbnb, 2020), more than the five major hotel brands combined globally (Hartmans, 2017).

Local lodging, unlike traditional accommodation, could affect the residential neighborhood (Stergiou & Farmaki, 2020) and cause touristification in the local community (Ioannides et al., 2018). Tussyadiah (2015) pointed out that the interactions between residents and tourists are an inevitable part of the local lodging experience. As more and more tourists stay in local accommodation, residents will be affected at different levels (Suess et al., 2020, 2021). For instance, the increase of noise and pollution (Guttentag, 2015), the rise of housing rent (Stergiou & Farmaki, 2020), the increase in safety concerns by having strangers around (Matarese, 2019), and the loss of sense of community shared among residents (Stergiou & Farmaki, 2020).

Prayag and Ozanne (2018) conducted a systematic review of peer-to-peer accommodation studies. After examining 71 articles published between 2010 and 2016, they identified seven major research topics: conceptual development, regulation, macro-level impacts, regime response, host behavior, guest/

host experience, and marketing issues. Surprisingly, research regarding residents' perceptions about this phenomenon was absent, even though scholars have specifically recommended to examine residents' standpoint in destinations with local lodging presence (Guttentag, 2015).

Suess et al. (2020, 2021) found that residents in the United States with previous experience staying at Airbnb generate more positive emotions towards neighboring tourists and perceive community impacts more positively. Economic benefits and their community attachment influence non-hosting residents' feelings towards tourists. Such emotions affect their sense of feeling safe and overall support for having Airbnb in the community (Suess et al., 2020, 2021). Richards et al. (2020) found in Barcelona that the deterioration consequences derived from the ungoverned development of Airbnb, where residents' aversion spread from tourists staying at Airbnb to all visiting tourists.

Despite the recent growth of research on residents' standpoint about local lodging, the academic research remains minimal (Stergiou & Farmaki, 2020) and mainly focuses on residents' perceptions about the local lodging phenomenon in general. As Richards et al. (2020) revealed, residents' aversion can go beyond the tourists staying at Airbnb to all the tourists. Thus, this study attempts to understand residents' perceptions of aggregated sociocultural impacts of tourism instead of the restrictive effects of the local lodging phenomenon. According to Paulauskaite et al. (2017), local lodging can arouse residents' resentment, ultimately shaping their negative perceptions of this phenomenon. Plausibly, such negative perceptions may extend to tourism impacts as a whole in a destination where local lodging exists.

2.2   Local lodging and sociocultural impacts of tourism

The interactions between residents and tourists can enhance communities' infrastructures, improve residents' standard of living, enhance cultural exchanges, and promote the preservation of cultural resources (Nunkoo & Ramkissoon, 2011; Wan & Li, 2013). Contrarily, tourism can threaten the disappearance of traditions, local and cultural identity, disrupt residents' way of life, and increase the crime rate (Ribeiro et al., 2017; Wan & Li, 2013).

Local lodging creates the opportunity for tourists to experience authentic culture and interact with residents, contributing to tourists' desire to stay in the destination longer and engage in more activities (Tussyadiah & Personen, 2016). However, negative sociocultural impacts are also recognized, particularly in destinations with a high concentration of local lodging, including housing availability, parking issues, noise, and waste management problems, which can ultimately disrupt residents' quality of life (Caldicott et al., 2020). Unquestionably, along with the increase of local lodging, tourists no longer solely remain in the accustomed tourism areas but spread to the residential spaces, resulting in unfavorable resident–tourist interactions (Jordan & Moore, 2018). Hence, not surprisingly, there has been a continuous debate on tourism sustainability in destinations with local lodging presence (Cheng et al., 2022).

Although the impacts of local lodging are not limited to sociocultural, economic, and environmental aspects, Stergiou and Farmaki (2020) emphasize that neighborhood problems occur due to the change in social relations between residents at individual and collective levels. Thus, the current study aims to enhance the literature by exploring whether local lodging may affect residents' perceptions of the sociocultural effects of tourism in the Algarve, a tourism destination with a prominent amount of local accommodation.

3   The Algarve as a tourism destination

The Algarve is the southernmost region of Portugal, surrounded by the Atlantic Ocean at its southern and western coast. Since the opening of Faro Airport in 1965, the region has become one of the most important tourism destinations in Europe, and its economy largely relies on tourism activities (Vargas-Sánchez et al., 2015).

With a land area of around 5,000 km² (5.4 percent of Portugal's total area), the Algarve incorporates 16 municipalities with about 440,000 inhabitants, recording more than 23 million overnight stays (INE, 2021a). Regarding the accommodation units, more than 40 percent are local lodging, surpassing the hotel establishments in the region (INE, 2021b). Indeed, Airbnb in Portugal was claimed to have over €2 billion direct economic impacts in 2018, ranked 10th out of a list of 30 countries that acquired the most significant economic impacts from Airbnb (The Portugal News, 2019).

4   Methodology

4.1   Instrument

This study is part of a major research project about Residents' Attitudes and Behaviors Towards Sustainable Tourism Development in the Algarve

(RESTUR). According to the study's objectives, a questionnaire was designed to collect data from residents aged at least 18 years old in the 16 municipalities of the Algarve. The main questionnaire includes seven parts, but this chapter considers three for the analysis: (1) perceptions of the positive and negative sociocultural impacts of tourism in the community, using a 5-point Likert scale (1 = strongly disagree; 5 = strongly agree); (2) questions about the existence and the support to Airbnb in the neighborhood; and (3) sociodemographic variables (gender, age, marital status, education level, employment situation, municipality of residence, and time of living in the municipality).

4.2   Data collection and sample

The sample was selected using the stratified method proportionally to the number of residents living in the 16 municipalities of the Algarve, gender and age group (INE, 2012). Considering a 95.0 percent confidence level, a 2.0 percent margin of error, and the size of the target population in the region, a sample of 2,400 residents was defined. The COVID-19 pandemic prevented attaining the predefined target subsample for older residents (aged 65 or over). Thus, 2,004 questionnaires were collected and validated (83.5 percent of the predefined sample). The final sampling error was estimated to be less than 2.15 percent for the final sample.

The survey was conducted during the low season of tourism activity in the Algarve in two moments. Between February and March 2020 (before the first lockdown recorded in Portugal – "pre-COVID"), 938 questionnaires were collected and validated, and between October and November 2020 (after the first lifting of lockdown recorded in Portugal – "during-COVID"), 1,066 questionnaires were collected and validated.

The data collection method consisted of self-administered questionnaires, and the research team selected residents to participate following the random route method, with a systematic sampling scheme, conducted in each municipality of the Algarve. Residents were approached randomly in the streets, homes, coffee shops, public parks, and other public places, until the sample defined for each municipality was completed. This sampling method was chosen based upon its good ability to select a representative sample of residents, increase response rates, and observe minority groups that may be left out from other sampling methods (Rada & Martín, 2014).

4.3   Data analysis

Data analysis starts with a descriptive analysis of residents' sociodemographic characteristics and their perceptions about the positive and negative sociocultural impacts of tourism. Non-parametric statistical tests and correlation coefficients were also calculated using the SPSS software.

5   Results

5.1   Residents' profile

Table 9.1 presents the main characteristics of the sample (n = 2,004). The sample matches the target population as to municipality, gender, and age groups and presents similarities in marital status. However, the sample has a larger proportion of residents with a medium and higher education level and employed population. In summary, more than half of the sample is female (52.1 percent), aged between 25 and 64 years old (78.0 percent), married or living together (54.2 percent) and employed (89.3 percent). The largest proportion of respondents have a medium (secondary education or professional training) education level (48.0 percent).

Table 9.2 shows that approximately two-thirds (67.1 percent) of residents have some Airbnb in the neighborhood, but only 6.0 percent own some Airbnb. In relation to residents' support to Airbnb, about half (51.2 percent) of the residents revealed indifference. However, results show that there is a larger proportion of residents that support (33.1 percent) the presence of Airbnb hosts in the neighborhood than oppose it (15.7 percent). Almost three-quarters (73.6 percent) of residents believe that their sense of feeling safe will be the same if the number of tourists increases in the neighborhood. The largest part of the remaining residents (15.6 percent) thinks their sense of feeling safe will be worse if the number of tourists increases in the neighborhood.

5.2   Residents' perceptions about the sociocultural impacts of tourism

This research assessed 20 items measuring the sociocultural impacts of tourism, of which nine are positive impacts and 11 are negative impacts. A reliability coefficient (Cronbach's alpha) was computed for each set of impacts to estimate internal consistency. The Cronbach's coefficients ranged between 0.758 (positive impacts) and 0.897 (negative impacts), showing a good internal consistency level among both sets of items. Thus, it was decided to compute an

Table 9.1   Sample characteristics and comparison with the target population

Sociodemographics (%)	Sample (n = 2,004)	Population of the Algarve* (N = 370,704)
Gender		
Female	52.1	51.8
Male	47.9	48.2
Age group		
18–24	10.5	8.8
25–64	78.0	65.1
65 +	11.5	26.1
Marital status		
Single	33.8	31.8
Married or living together	54.2	50.9
Divorced	9.4	8.6
Widowed	2.6	8.7
Educational level		
Low (less than secondary)	21.6	59.6
Medium (secondary or professional training)	48.0	24.0
High (Bachelor, Master or Doctorate)	30.4	16.4
Employment situation		
Employed	89.3	49.5
Unemployed	1.6	9.1
Retired	5.6	25.7
Student	2.8	4.9
Housekeeper or another situation	0.7	10.8

* **Source:** Own elaboration based on Census 2011 (INE, 2012)

average score of the positive and negative sociocultural impacts of tourism for this data analysis.

Table 9.2   Residents' support, sense of feeling safe, ownership and existence of Airbnb in the neighborhood

Variable	%	Variable	%
Existence of some Airbnb in the neighborhood		*Ownership of some Airbnb*	
Yes	67.1	Yes	6.0
No	32.9	No	94.0
Degree of support for Airbnb hosts in the neighborhood		*Sense of feeling safe if the number of tourists increases in the neighborhood*	
Strongly oppose	4.4	Much worse	2.8
Oppose	11.3	Worse	12.8
Indifferent	51.2	The same	73.6
Support	26.4	Better	8.3
Strongly support	6.7	Much better	2.5

Source: Own elaboration

Results presented in Table 9.3 show that residents have a higher level of agreement with positive sociocultural impacts (global average = 3.29) than with negative ones (global average = 2.80). In terms of the positive impacts, residents mostly agree that "tourism improves residents' hospitality and politeness with tourists"; "tourism contributes to the recognition, prestige and image of their municipality"; and "tourism contributes to stimulating cultural activities, festivals and local traditions". However, they revealed a lower level of agreement when considering that "tourism contributes for improving public services (health centers, sports facilities, police protection, etc.)" and "increasing residents' security". Interestingly, there are significant differences between local lodging owners' perceptions and non-local lodging owners' perceptions with some Airbnb in the neighborhood. Residents who have some Airbnb in the neighborhood revealed a higher level of agreement with statements such as "tourism contributes to the recognition, prestige and image of my municipality" (p-value = 0.026) and "residents in my municipality are hospitable and receive tourists with politeness" (p-value = 0.026), than those who do not have some Airbnb in the neighborhood. In addition, residents that own some Airbnb declared a higher level of agreement than non-owners with the following statements: "tourism contributes to the recognition, prestige and image of my municipality" (p-value = 0.046); "residents in my municipality are hospitable and receive tourists with politeness" (p-value = 0.065); "tourism

Table 9.3 Mean differences of sociocultural impacts by ownership and existence of some Airbnb in the neighborhood

Sociocultural impacts	Existence of some Airbnb in the neighborhood			Ownership of some Airbnb		
	No	Yes	p-value	No	Yes	p-value
Positive impacts	**3.27**	**3.29**	**0.829**	**3.28**	**3.41**	**0.014**
Tourism improves public services (health centers, sports facilities, police protection, etc.)	2.54	2.48	0.146	2.49	2.68	0.027
Tourism stimulates cultural activities, festivals and traditions	3.59	3.60	0.733	3.61	3.53	0.456
Tourism contributes to the preservation of the local culture	3.25	3.25	0.747	3.26	3.26	0.918
Tourism promotes cultural exchange between residents and tourists	3.55	3.58	0.290	3.57	3.59	0.549
Tourism changes the consumption habits of residents (food, clothing, etc.)	2.96	3.00	0.387	2.98	3.09	0.260
Tourism contributes to raising the standard of living of residents	3.00	3.06	0.142	3.02	3.48	<0.001
Tourism contributes to increase security	2.87	2.84	0.484	2.84	3.03	0.050
Tourism contributes to the recognition, prestige and image of my municipality	3.79	3.88	0.026	3.84	3.99	0.046
Residents in my municipality are hospitable and receive tourists with politeness	3.89	4.00	0.026	3.96	4.09	0.065
Negative impacts	**2.83**	**2.78**	**0.198**	**2.80**	**2.71**	**0.154**
Tourism increases drugs and alcohol consumption	3.35	3.36	0.859	3.35	3.41	0.506

Sociocultural impacts	Existence of some Airbnb in the neighborhood			Ownership of some Airbnb		
	No	Yes	p-value	No	Yes	p-value
Tourism increases prostitution and moral degradation	2.78	2.79	0.830	2.79	2.66	0.185
Tourism increases sexual transmitted diseases	2.85	2.86	0.834	2.86	2.83	0.970
Tourism causes more crime and vandalism	2.83	2.79	0.501	2.80	2.77	0.767
Tourism generates loss or change of traditions and cultural identity	2.77	2.76	0.839	2.77	2.75	0.870
Tourism causes loss of tolerance and respect for other cultures	2.53	2.43	0.029	2.46	2.40	0.297
Tourism increases stress and disturb quietness	3.21	3.13	0.119	3.18	2.89	0.009
The increasing number of tourists is likely to result in conflicts with residents	2.69	2.70	0.972	2.68	2.71	0.999
Residents change their behavior in an attempt to mimic tourists	2.57	2.48	0.026	2.50	2.69	0.048
Residents are likely to suffer from living in this tourism destination	2.89	2.81	0.118	2.85	2.57	0.011
My municipality is overcrowded because of tourism	2.71	2.60	0.017	2.64	2.47	0.184

Note: Sociocultural impacts items: 5-point Likert scale (1 = *strongly disagree* to 5 = *strongly agree*). Differences amongst groups were analyzed with the Mann–Whitney U test
Source: Own elaboration

improves public services (health centers, sports facilities, police protection, etc.)" (p-value = 0.027); "tourism contributes to raising residents' standard of living" (p-value<0.001); and "tourism contributes to increase security" (p-value = 0.050).

In what concerns the negative sociocultural impacts, residents neither agree nor disagree with most of the items. However, they agree that "tourism increases drugs and alcohol consumption" and "increases stress". They disagree that "tourism causes a loss of tolerance and respect for other cultures", that "residents change their behavior in an attempt to mimic tourists", and "their municipality is overcrowded because of tourism". A deep analysis of the differences in the negative sociocultural impacts shows that residents having some Airbnb in the neighborhood revealed a significantly higher level of disagreement with the statements: "tourism causes loss of tolerance and respect for other cultures" (p-value = 0.029); "residents change their behavior in an attempt to mimic tourists" (p-value = 0.026); and "my municipality is overcrowded because of tourism" (p-value = 0.017). In addition, residents owning some Airbnb declared a higher level of disagreement than non-owners with the statements: "residents are likely to suffer from living in this tourism destination" (p-value = 0.011) and "tourism increases stress and disturb quietness" (p-value = 0.009). Still, they revealed a lower level of disagreement with the statement: "residents change their behavior in an attempt to mimic tourists" (p-value = 0.048).

Table 9.4 presents residents' perceptions about pros and cons of Airbnb in the neighborhood, along with the correlations with sociocultural impacts. Results show that there is neither a clear agreement nor a disagreement with both advantages and disadvantages of Airbnb. Residents slightly agree that "Airbnb (would) help their neighborhood to face unemployment" (3.36) and "to face current and future economic challenges" (3.21 and 3.22, respectively). Residents agree that "Airbnb (would) generate more noise and disorder" (3.25). Interestingly, residents declared a slight disagreement that "they would personally benefit from more tourists and Airbnb hosts in their neighborhood" (2.97 and 2.80, respectively). In general, residents' perceptions about pros and cons of Airbnb are significantly correlated with the positive and negative sociocultural impacts of tourism. Exceptions are the correlations between the variables "Airbnb (would) generate more garbage and pollution in my neighborhood" and "Airbnb (would) generate more promiscuity in my neighborhood" with the positive impacts. In addition, results indicate a direct correlation between the pros (cons) of Airbnb and positive (negative) impacts and an inverse correlation between the cons (pros) of Airbnb and positive (negative) impacts. Thus, there is empirical evidence that residents reveal

Table 9.4   Correlations between residents' perceptions about pros and cons of Airbnb and sociocultural impacts of tourism

Pros and cons of Airbnb	Mean	SD	Positive impacts		Negative impacts	
			Correl.	p-value	Correl.	p-value
Airbnb (would) help my neighborhood to face current economic challenges	3.21	0.95	0.302	<0.001	-0.141	<0.001
Airbnb (would) help my neighborhood to face future economic challenges	3.22	0.94	0.295	<0.001	-0.129	<0.001
Airbnb (would) help my neighborhood to face unemployment	3.36	0.99	0.256	<0.001	-0.078	0.001
Airbnb (would) generate more garbage and pollution in my neighborhood	3.10	0.94	-0.009	0.715	0.325	<0.001
Airbnb (would) generate more noise and disorder in my neighborhood	3.25	0.94	-0.053	0.023	0.342	<0.001
Airbnb (would) generate more promiscuity in my neighborhood	2.91	0.86	-0.035	0.131	0.386	<0.001
I would personally benefit from more tourists to my neighborhood	2.97	0.96	0.261	<0.001	-0.164	<0.001
I would personally benefit if more Airbnb hosts were in my neighborhood	2.80	0.98	0.258	<0.001	-0.130	<0.001

Note: Residents' perceptions about pros and cons of Airbnb: 5-point Likert scale (1 = *strongly disagree* to 5 = *strongly agree*). SD-Standard deviation. The correlation was measured using the Spearman correlation coefficient
Source: Own elaboration

a higher level of agreement with the advantages of Airbnb and tend to perceive more positive sociocultural impacts of tourism. In addition, residents reveal a lower level of agreement with the disadvantages of Airbnb.

Finally, Table 9.5 shows residents' perceptions about the sociocultural impacts by their degree of support for Airbnb in the neighborhood. Results show that residents supporting Airbnb in the neighborhood have a significantly higher level of agreement with the positive impacts of tourism (3.43). However, it is important to highlight that even residents who oppose Airbnb in the neighborhood slightly agree with the positive sociocultural impacts of tourism (3.09). Residents who oppose Airbnb in the neighborhood stated a significantly higher level of agreement with negative impacts of tourism (3.20). It is also important to note that residents who support Airbnb in the neighborhood revealed disagreement with the negative sociocultural impacts of tourism (2.61).

Table 9.5 Mean differences of sociocultural impacts by residents' degree of support for Airbnb in the neighborhood

Sociocultural impacts	Degree of support for Airbnb hosts			Kruskal-Wallis test	Games-Howell test results
	Oppose	Indifferent	Support	p-value	
Positive impacts	3.09	3.26	3.43	<0.001	O<I; O<S; I<S
Negative impacts	3.20	2.79	2.61	<0.001	O>I; O>S; I>S

Note: Sociocultural impacts items: 5-point Likert scale (1 = *strongly disagree* to 5 = *strongly agree*). Differences amongst groups were analyzed with the Kruskal-Wallis H test. Games-Howell results represent the statistically significant cases
Source: Own elaboration

6   Discussion

Local lodging is a growing phenomenon in the recent decades, following tourists' demand and increasing desire to stay in accommodations with similar characteristics of their own homes and, in this way, to get in touch with the local culture (Tussyadiah, 2015; Tussyadiah & Personen, 2016). Residents who live near a local lodging are very likely to be affected in both positive and negative ways (Suess et al., 2020, 2021). However, in what concerns residents' perceptions about this phenomenon, the academic research has been absent (Guttentag, 2015).

In an attempt to fill this gap, a recent study revealed that residents with previous experience staying at local lodging tend to generate more positive emotions towards neighboring tourists and perceive the impacts of Airbnb in a more positive way (Suess et al., 2020, 2021). This research shows that residents who have some Airbnb in the neighborhood or who own some Airbnb, revealed higher levels of agreement with the positive sociocultural impacts of local lodging and the presence of tourists in the surroundings.

In addition, concerning the negative sociocultural impacts, residents agree that "tourism increases stress", following the results achieved by Caldicott et al. (2020). Residents who have some Airbnb in the neighborhood or own some Airbnb tend to disagree more with the negative sociocultural impacts than residents who are not associated with local lodging. It means that residents related to local lodging tend to appreciate more the positive sociocultural impacts of having tourists and hosts in the neighborhood (Cheng et al., 2022).

Furthermore, results show that residents' perceptions of pros and cons of Airbnb are significantly correlated with the positive and negative perceptions of sociocultural impacts of tourism. Those who perceive the pros of Airbnb in the neighborhood tend to perceive positive sociocultural impacts of tourism, and those who perceive the cons of Airbnb in the neighborhood tend to perceive negative sociocultural impacts of tourism (Jordan & Moore, 2018; Nunkoo & Ramkissoon, 2011; Ribeiro et al., 2017).

Finally, and according to other studies (Matarese, 2019; Richards et al., 2020; Stergiou & Farmaki, 2020; Suess et al., 2020, 2021), results demonstrate that residents supporting Airbnb have higher levels of agreement with the positive sociocultural impacts of tourism.

7   Conclusions and limitations

This study responds to the calls of Guttentag (2015) and Prayag and Ozanne (2018) to broaden the knowledge of local lodging's impacts by incorporating a holistic approach with multiple stakeholders. In this case, residents' perceptions about the sociocultural impacts of tourism were examined in the light of the existence or ownership of local lodging.

Findings reveal that residents affiliated with local lodging, either because they have some Airbnb in the neighborhood or because they own some Airbnb, have higher levels of agreement with the positive sociocultural impacts of tourism, tend to disagree more with the negative sociocultural impacts of tourism, and are more supportive for Airbnb and tourists in their communities.

Taking into account the need for tourism sustainable development and the growing phenomenon of local lodging, this study contributes to the literature and can draw the attention of DMOs and local actors to the importance of analyzing residents' standpoints. Since residents have direct contact with tourists and face the positive and negative impacts of tourism, it is crucial to understand what impacts are perceived and why residents perceive them.

The sample used in this study is representative of residents in the Algarve aged below 65 years old. However, the COVID-19 pandemic prevented attaining the subsample for older residents (aged 65 or over). Thus, it is important to monitor the study over time, including more seniors and other stakeholders. Future research should also explore other residents' perceptions of tourism impacts, specifically the economic and environmental impacts, in the light of local lodging.

References

Airbnb (2020). *News – Fast Facts*. https://news.airbnb.com/about-us.

Caldicott, R., von der Heidt, T., Scherrer, P., Muschter, S., & Canosa, A. (2020). Airbnb: Exploring triple bottom line impacts on community. *International Journal of Cultural, Tourism and Hospitality Research, 14*(2), 205–223.

Cheng, M., Mackenzie, S., & Degarege, G. (2022). Airbnb impacts on host communities in a tourism destination: An exploratory study of stakeholder perspectives in Queenstown, New Zealand. *Journal of Sustainable Tourism, 30*(5), 1122–1140.

Gutierrez-Tano, D., Garau-Vadell, J., & Diaz-Armas, R. (2019). The influence of knowledge on residents' perceptions of the impacts of overtourism in P2P accommodation rental. *Sustainability, 11*(4), 1043.

Guttentag, D. (2015). Airbnb: Disruptive innovation and the rise of an informal tourism accommodation sector. *Current Issues in Tourism, 18*(12), 1192–1217.

Hartmans, A. (2017). Airbnb now has more listings worldwide than the top five hotel brands combined. *Business Insider*, 10 August. https://www.businessinsider.com/airbnb-total-worldwide-listings- 2017-8?r=US&IR=T.

INE (2012). *Census 2011: Final Results for the Algarve Region*. Lisbon: Statistics Portugal.

INE (2021a). *Tourism Statistics 2019*. Lisbon: Statistics Portugal.

INE (2021b). *The Algarve Region in Figures 2019*. Lisbon: Statistics Portugal.

Ioannides, D., Röslmaier, M., & van der Zee, E. (2018). Airbnb as an instigator of "tourism bubble" expansion in Utrecht's Lombok neighbourhood. *Tourism Geographies*, *21*(5), 822–840.

Jordan, E. & Moore, J. (2018). An in-depth exploration of residents' perceived impacts of transient vacation rentals. *Journal of Travel & Tourism Marketing*, *35*, 90–101.

Matarese, J. (2019). Homeowners say Airbnb is replacing neighbors with strangers, changing neighborhood culture. *WCPO*, 18 July. https://www.wcpo.com/money/consumer/dont-waste-your-money/homeowners-say-airbnbis-replacing-neighbors-with-strangers-changing-neighborhood-culture.

Nunkoo, R. & Ramkissoon, H. (2011). Residents' satisfaction with community attributes and support for tourism. *Journal of Hospitality & Tourism Research*, *35*(2), 171–190.

Paulauskaite, D., Powell, R., Coca-Stefaniak, J., & Morrison, A. (2017). Living like a local: Authentic tourism experiences and the sharing economy. *International Journal of Tourism Research*, *9*(6), 619–628.

Prayag, G. & Ozanne, L. (2018). A systematic review of peer-to-peer (P2P) accommodation sharing research from 2010 to 2016: Progress and prospects from the multi-level perspective. *Journal of Hospitality Marketing & Management*, *27*(6), 649–678.

Rada, V. & Martín, V. (2014). Random route and quota sampling: Do they offer any advantage over probably sampling methods? *Open Journal Statistics*, *4*(5), 391–401.

Ribeiro, M., Pinto, P., Silva, J., & Woosnam, K. (2017). Residents' attitudes and the adoption of pro-tourism behaviours: The case of developing island countries. *Tourism Management*, *61*, 523–537.

Richards, S., Brown, L., & Dilettuso, A. (2020). The Airbnb phenomenon: The resident's perspective. *International Journal of Tourism Cities*, *6*(1), 8–26.

Stergiou, D. & Farmaki, A. (2020). Resident perceptions of the impacts of P2P accommodation: Implications for neighbourhoods. *International Journal of Hospitality Management*, *91*, 102411.

Suess, C., Woosnam K., & Erul, E. (2020). Stranger-danger? Understanding the moderating effects of children in the household on non-hosting residents' emotional solidarity with Airbnb visitors, feeling safe, and support for Airbnb. *Tourism Management*, *77*, 103952.

Suess, C., Woosnam, K., Mody, M., Dogru, T., & Turk, E. (2021). Understanding how residents' emotional solidarity with Airbnb visitors influences perceptions of their impact on a community: The moderating role of prior experience staying at an Airbnb. *Journal of Travel Research*, *60*(5), 1039–1060.

The Portugal News (2019, July 5). *Airbnb with €2 billion impact in Portugal*. https://www.theportugalnews.com/news/airbnb-with-2-billion-impact-in-portugal/50215.

Tussyadiah, I. (2015). An exploratory study on drivers and deterrents of collaborative consumption in travel. In I. Tussyadiah & A. Inversini (eds.), *Information and Communication Technologies in Tourism*. Cham: Springer, pp. 817–830.

Tussyadiah, I. & Personen, J. (2016). Impacts of peer-to-peer accommodation use on travel patterns. *Journal of Travel Research*, *55*(8), 1022–1040.

Vargas-Sánchez, A., Valle, P., Mendes, J., & Silva, J. (2015). Residents' attitude and level of destination development. *Tourism Management*, *48*, 199–210.

Wan, Y. & Li, X. (2013). Sustainability of tourism development in Macao, China. *International Journal of Tourism Research*, *15*, 52–65.

10 Governance for sustainable tourism: strong institutions as prerequisites in local tourism development

Miguela M. Mena and Maria Fe Villamejor-Mendoza

Introduction

Tourism has long been considered an effective catalyst of socio-economic development and regeneration locally and globally (UNWTO, 2016; WTTC, 2017). It is one of the world's fastest growing industries and an important source of foreign exchange and employment for many developing countries. Being a people-oriented industry, tourism provides many jobs, which have helped revitalize local economies and culture. However, tourism is especially vulnerable to external shocks and global crises, like the recent COVID-19 pandemic.

In recent decades, the global tourism market has experienced continual growth and deepening diversification making it one of the world's fastest growing economic sectors. The UNWTO estimated that internationally there were just 25 million tourist arrivals in 1950. In January 2020, UNWTO reported that the growth in international tourist arrivals continues to outpace the economy. International tourist arrivals (overnight visitors) worldwide grew by 4 percent, reaching 1.5 billion in 2019. However, a pandemic occurred in 2020 and drastically changed the global travel and tourism industry.

It continues to be a key driver of socio-economic progress through the sector's generation of export revenues, the tourism industry's creation of jobs and enterprises, and infrastructure development to accommodate tourism and non-tourism activities (UNWTO, 2014a, 2014b). It is also credited for its contribution to the diversification and stabilization of the economy, increased tax base for governments, and heightened attraction of tourism-related businesses and organizations seeking amenity locations (Hall & Lew, 2009). Aside from economic gains, tourism is recognized for its impacts on society and culture.

Tourism has been identified as a powerful social force that can achieve important ends when its development is harnessed to meet human development imperatives and the wider public good (Higgins-Desbiolles, 2006).

For many countries, the most compelling reason for pursuing tourism as a development strategy is its alleged positive contribution to the local and national economy. Many of the countries in which tourism is important are among the poorest and least developed in the world. These countries have limited options for economic development and tourism provides the most viable alternative. As tourism has demonstrated its capability of creating wealth and prosperity in a destination, more and more nations directed their tourism plans and programs towards marketing, promotions, and image enhancement to increase the volume and expenditures of international visitors. However, as the industry has grown, it has also become much more diverse and complicated. Destinations realized that economic growth because of tourism development does not necessarily result in poverty reduction. Moreover, like other forms of development, tourism can also cause its share of problems, such as social dislocation, loss of cultural heritage, economic dependence, and ecological degradation. There are also challenges in tourism governance regarding the role of government, the private sector, benefits distribution, and the social and environmental cost of the sector (De Clercq & Belausteguigoitia, 2017; Nunkoo, 2017; Purdy, 2016).

Learning about the impacts of tourism has led many people to seek more responsible holidays. These include various forms of alternative or sustainable tourism such as: "nature-based tourism", "ecotourism" and "cultural tourism". Sustainable tourism is becoming so popular that some say that what we presently call "alternative" will be the "mainstream" in a decade. Sustainable tourism is defined as "tourism that respects both local people and the traveller, cultural heritage and the environment". It seeks to provide people with an exciting and educational holiday that is also of benefit to the people of the host area or country (UNESCO and UNEP, 2016).

Sustainable tourism is considered in paragraph 130 of *The Future We Want* as a significant contributor "to the three dimensions of sustainable development" because of its close linkages to other sectors and its ability to create decent jobs and generate trade opportunities. Therefore, Member States recognize "the need to support sustainable tourism activities and relevant capacity-building that promote environmental awareness, conserve and protect the environment, respect wildlife, flora, biodiversity, ecosystems and cultural diversity, and improve the welfare and livelihoods of local communities" (UN, 2012). McVey (1993) identifies the three core elements of sustainability:

- Economic sustainability, or efforts to maintain growth rates at manageable levels; promoting tourism while keeping an eye on capacities to handle greater demand to avoid consumer dissatisfaction;
- Social sustainability, or society's ability to absorb increasing tourist arrivals without adversely affecting or damaging indigenous culture; and
- Environmental sustainability, which is related to the capacity of the natural and built environment to handle tourism without damage.

The UN Commission for Sustainable Development adds a fourth element – institutional sustainability. The concept of sustainable development attributes a central role to institutions as a tool for its implementation. It is manifested in its commitment to the incorporation of sustainable principles into development planning, partnerships for sustainable development, the use of indicators for monitoring sustainability, presence of monitoring and coordinating bodies for sustainable development, and the enactment of laws that promote sustainable development (Cruz, 2003).

This chapter aims to contribute to the discourse on governance for sustainable tourism and puts forward the argument that strong institutions, which are effective, accountable and transparent, and ensure responsive, inclusive, participatory and representative decision-making at all levels as envisioned in UN Sustainable Development Goal (SDG) 16, are prerequisites in local tourism development. It discusses the current state of knowledge on governance for sustainable tourism and examines the challenges of a small municipality in the Philippines in charting the directions of local tourism planning and development after a devastating earthquake in 2013 and (political) elections in 2016. It uses the Dynamic Governance Theory as a framework that enables the local organizations to look critically at their governance capabilities and the Learning Tourism Destination framework which recognizes the capacity of societies to learn and to develop economic organizations that are relevant to their unique context. As a continuously recovering municipality from socio-economic and environmental damages brought by an earthquake and typhoon and as a locality that consciously utilized tourism as an engine of recovery amidst changing local governance agenda and leadership, it was an ideal area to examine governance for sustainable tourism.

Using an interdisciplinary perspective and mixed-method research design, the local knowledge, processes and perspectives at the individual, organization, community, and destination level were examined. The specific mixed-mode methodology employed in the study incorporates qualitative and quantitative methods such as secondary data analysis, surveys on stakeholder attitudes and perceptions toward tourism development, site immersion and observation, key informant interviews and a series of focus group discussions and workshops. Thematic analysis was done to synthesize the learning from the individuals, organizations, and community's clusters.

The chapter is organized as follows: first, a discussion of the current state of knowledge on governance, tourism governance and sustainable tourism is presented; then a discussion of the tourism development in Maribojoc, Bohol, Philippines including its challenges in charting the directions of local tourism planning and development after a devastating earthquake in 2013 and (political) elections in 2016; a discussion of the Dynamic Governance Theory is subsequently presented; and finally, the conclusion and recommendations.

Governance for sustainable tourism

Although governance remains a popular buzzword in recent times, defining it is not easy (Duran, 2013; Farmaki, 2015; World Bank, 2009). It is generally understood as decentering government and governing and embracing the participation and accountability of other stakeholders in the society, e.g., private sector, civil society organizations and the citizens themselves, to manage public affairs (Cariño et al., 2005). It can promote effective and equitable resources use and development (Duran, 2013), since there are many actors involved and not only government.

The term governance has been defined by several international organizations such as the World Bank, the United Nations Development Programme (UNDP), European Union (EU) and others. The World Bank (2009) stated that "governance consists of the traditions and institutions through which authority is exercised in a country. This includes the process by which governments are elected, overseen and replaced; the government's capacity to effectively formulate and carry out good public policies and the extent to which citizens respect the State and the institutions that govern economic and social interactions".

The UNDP (1999) defined governance as consisting of systems, mechanism, processes, relationships, and institutions through which groups and citizens articulate their interests, perform legal rights, recognize obligations, and resolve differences. The Organisation for Economic Co-operation and

Development (OECD) (1995) defined the term in relation to how societies use and supervise political authority in managing its resources, benefits are distributed, and the nature of relationships between governments and the governed (see Duran, 2013). For the Commission of the European Communities (CEC) (2001), governance entails norms, processes, and behavior in the exercise of powers, especially from a position of openness, participation, accountability, effectiveness, and coherence. It can promote effective and equitable resources use and development (Duran, 2013).

Considering tourism's potential in achieving some of the Sustainable Development Goals (SDGs) and in pursuance of the calls of policymakers, researchers, tourism practitioners and destination managers to pursue and promote good governance in the tourism sector (Amore & Hall, 2016; UNWTO, 2016; Bramwell & Lane, 2011), UNWTO designated 2017 as the International Year of Sustainable Tourism for Development (UNWTO, 2016). It is instructive to note that the SDGs made no explicit reference to tourism; they only make implicit reference to tourism (e.g., Goal 8 which focuses on economic growth and employment; Goal 12 on sustainable consumption and production; Goal 15 on conserve and sustainability of natural resources; and Goal 16 on peace, justice, and institutions which can be helpful in promoting inclusive equitable development). Thus, governance becomes critical for tourism to assist in achieving the SDGs (Siakwah et al., 2020).

The UNWTO (2008, pp. 31–32) defines tourism governance as the "process of managing tourist destinations through synergistic and coordinated efforts by governments, at distinct levels and in different capacities; civil society living in the inbound tourism communities; and the business sector connected with the operation of the tourism system". The UNWTO, however, does not explicitly refer to "local communities" and how they are impacted by tourism. Duran (2013) suggests that while the UNWTO idea on governance represents a considerable advance, tourism governance should be analyzed in terms of "tourism system" and "tourist destination" (UNWTO, 2012). This must account for winners and losers in the sector. According to Duran (2013), governance entails the extent to which institutions (government, the private sector, and other social actors) have the capacity to coordinate, collaborate, and cooperate efficiently to enhance tourism information systems, transform needs into opportunities, and analyze tourism industry sustainability.

Duran (2013, p. 9) defines governance as the emergence of new forms of association and coordination, comprising government and private actors, and civil societies, as well as greater decision-making capacity of non-governmental actors in policymaking. Governance principles have been applied across sectors in economies, including sustainable tourism governance and these sustainability principles in tourism have been both praised and criticized (Farmaki, 2015; Waligo et al., 2013). Stakeholder relations have been identified as a barrier to effective governance and development and this becomes a problem for sustainable tourism (Daphnet et al., 2012; Farmaki, 2015; Leonard, 2018; Waligo et al., 2013). Sustainable tourism entails a limited adverse impact on the environment and local cultures, and strives to improve employment for locals and contribute to national development (Musavengane, 2018; Nunkoo, 2017; Siakwah, 2018).

To reiterate, strong institutions which are *effective, accountable, and transparent; and ensure responsive, inclusive, participatory, and representative decision-making at all levels* are prerequisites to sustainable tourism. "Institutions are the rules of the game in a society ... the humanly devised constraints that shape human interaction. ... They structure incentives in human exchange, whether political, social or economic" (North, 1990, p. 3).

Institutions comprise, for example, contracts and contract enforcement, protection of property rights, the rule of law, government bureaucracies, and financial markets. They also include habits and beliefs, norms, social cleavages, and traditions (so-called informal institutions). Formal institutions typically tend to be the crystallization of informal institutions (North, 1990), as social norms in the realms of gender, class, and caste, for example, determine rules of political participation and representation, methods of economic exchange, and inclusion of different groups in society (Pateman, 1988). The effectiveness of local tourism governance in achieving the goals of its stakeholders depends on the effectiveness of institutional structures and processes, and the relational resources and skill sets available (see e.g. Bell, 2004; Healey, 2006b; White, 2001). Institutional structures are the formal and informal frameworks that create the organization and shape its autonomy, authority, internal coherence and discipline (Beaumont & Dredge, 2010).

Despite the impressive macro contribution of tourism globally, there are varying degrees of governance challenges. These include the disconnect between policies and practices; identity politics; exclusion of minorities; and translating macroeconomic gains into micro benefits (Leonard, 2017a, 2017b; Musavengane, 2018; Nunkoo, 2017). Governance for sustainable tourism can be promoted through multi-stakeholders, including local participation, engagement, and transparency to examine winners and losers (Bramwell, 2004, 2005, 2007, 2010; Qian et al., 2016; Richardson & Connelly, 2002).

The case of Maribojoc, Bohol, Philippines

Tourism has been one of the foundations of economic policy and development in the Philippines since the 1970s (Maguigad, 2013). With the level of activity and the diversity of attractions in the country, it is imperative that tourism should be developed in a sustainable manner (Dela Santa, 2015). But with the plethora of approaches suggested by scholars on attaining sustainable tourism development, implementing this concept in the local economy is still a challenge. The development of tourism policies in the Philippines can be characterized by learning, from lesson drawing in the 1970s and mid-1980s, to technical and conceptual learning in the late 1980s and 1990s, and social learning in the late 1990s and the first decade of the 2000s (Dela Santa, 2015). The use of learning as an approach to tourism development has been institutionalized at the national level but is yet to be promoted in local economies. Autonomy was granted to local governments in developing tourism by Republic Act No. 7160 (The Local Government Code, 1991) and Republic Act No. 9593 (The National Tourism Act of 2009).

On October 11, 2016, President Rodrigo R. Duterte signed Executive Order No. 5, s. 2016 approving and adopting the 25-year long-term vision entitled AmBisyon Natin 2040 as a guide for development planning. Nine priority sectors with the greatest potential to contribute to realizing AmBisyon have been identified (Philippine National Tourism Development Plan, 2016–2022):

- Housing and urban development
- Manufacturing (food processing, housing-related goods and services, transport)
- Connectivity (roads, ports, airports, bridges, communication)
- Education services
- Financial services
- Health services
- Tourism-related services
- Agricultural development
- Countryside development

AmBisyon Natin 2040 provides the anchor for the country's development plans until 2040. Clearly, one of the Philippines' priority sectors is tourism-related services. The Philippines possesses a broad range of natural and cultural heritage tourism assets as well as a growing number of beach and urban leisure and entertainment facilities that are competitive in the region.

Middleton et al. (1993) comment: "Governments have committed themselves to support certain generalized positions which have yet to be fleshed out in myriad local and national campaigns for justice". Strategies are cyclical processes, with capacity building and implementation continuing throughout. The layers of implementation – by different levels of sectors of government and by a wide range of actors outside government – are likely to deepen with each turn of the cycle. National sustainable development strategies are needed to: (1) provide a forum and context for the debate on sustainable development and the articulation of a collective vision of the future; (2) provide a framework for processes of negotiation, mediation, and consensus-building, and to focus them on a common set of priority issues; (3) plan and carry out actions to change or strengthen values, knowledge, technologies and institutions with respect to the priority issues; and (4) develop organizational capacities and other institutions required for sustainable development (Reid et al., 1994). Strategies are needed to overcome the obstacles to sustainable development and make the necessary key changes. Eber (1992) as cited in Bramwell et al. (1996, p. 39) states that tourism can contribute to sustainable development when:

> It operates within natural capacities for the regeneration and future productivity of natural resources; recognizes the contribution that people and communities, customs and lifestyles make to the tourism experience; accepts that these people must have an equitable share in the economic benefits of tourism; and is guided by the wishes of local people and communities in the host areas.

The Philippine National Tourism Development Plan is anchored on improving competitiveness, enhancing development, and pursuing sustainable and inclusive growth, and convergence. It seeks to:

- Develop and market competitive products and destinations
  - Adopt cluster destination concept and product portfolio
  - Raise standards of facilities and services
  - Facilitate investments and lower business cost
  - Safeguard natural and cultural resources, and vulnerable groups
  - Implement marketing and promotions
- Improve market access, connectivity and destination infrastructure
  - Expand capacity of international gateways
  - Expand connectivity between gateways and key growth markets
  - Implement strategic access between international gateways and other clusters
  - Implement destination infrastructure program
- Improve tourism institutional governance and human resources
  - Pursue shared responsibility of national and local governments

- Develop competent, well-motivated and productive work force
- Improve governance relating to safety, security and handling tourists

The Philippines has regional and sub-regional centers that have population sizes, services, natural physical features, and strategic locations that enable them to host certain activities or functions. One of the Philippines' main tourist attractions is Bohol. Bohol is an island province belonging to the Central Visayas region and is classified as a first-class province by the Philippine Department of Finance. It is the 10th largest island in the Philippines. The province has 47 municipalities (30 coastal and 17 inland) and one component city that serves as the provincial capital and its primary gateway. It has a land area of 4,117.26 sq km and has a 261 km coastline. The province is accessible by air and sea transport. Boats operate from the country's capital city and from other ports in Visayas and Mindanao. The region's priority sector includes seaweed/carrageenan, dried mangoes, furniture, IT-BPM, shipbuilding, and tourism.

Bohol is home to beautiful landscapes, coastlines, diversified flora and fauna, religious and historic landmarks and archaeological artifacts, all of which form the foundation of its tourism industry. Starting in 2004, Bohol has experienced a boom in tourism. It has become one of the fastest growing tourist destinations in the country (Bohol Tourism Master Plan, 2003–2005). It had a well-developed tourism industry and boasted a Tourism Master Plan, which is a comprehensive document that details tourism assets, tourism facilities, infrastructure, land zoning, hazards mapping, policies, strategies, and implementation plans. On its website, Bohol is described as mainly one big island with 72 smaller islands (Province of Bohol website). It is being promoted as a major tourist destination by the Department of Tourism (DOT) and as a result had already established a brand known in tourism circles in the Philippines and abroad. Bohol abounds in cultural and natural touristic attractions with its rich culture manifested in the arts and centuries-old churches. Two of the well-known Philippine ecotourism attractions are found in Bohol, namely, the Chocolate Hills, which is a declared geological wonder and its famous fauna, the Philippine Tarsier. It has pristine white beaches (surrounding the entire islands of Bohol and Panglao) and dive sites (Balicasag) as well as inland rivers (Loboc), caves and waterfalls. Tourism is the province's major industry second only to agriculture. Tourism in Bohol generates local revenues, provides employment, and creates local livelihood (Province of Bohol website).

Looking at the list of popular tourist destinations in Bohol, rarely do travel agencies consider the municipality of Maribojoc as part of the itinerary for tours in Bohol. Maribojoc is a 4th class municipality in the province of Bohol with a population of 20,688, a total land area of 6,956 hectares and distributed in 22 barangays. It is 14 km away from the provincial capital and lies on the southwestern coast of Bohol. It has a culturally rich heritage and a vibrant past. It has a sprawling bay, rich in bio-diverse marine life, jagged and ragged panoramic mountain ranges, rolling plains, water resources, and high-grade limestone. Forest products provide an abundant source of raw materials for native handicrafts. Prior to the 2013 earthquake, it hosted a centuries-old church, a museum, the historical Punta Cruz Watch Tower, and an old Spanish cotta stone stair. The research sites were six of the 22 barangays, namely, Agahay, Bayacabac, Poblacion, Punta Cruz, San Vicente, and Toril.

Agriculture is the dominant economic activity and main source of livelihood in the municipality. There are 1,242 farming households or 42.8 percent of total households. Other than agriculture, livestock production and fishing are also another major activity. Despite being a 4th class municipality, Maribojoc has a great potential in terms of tourism. Tourism is vital in the revenue raising of national and local revenues and contributes toward reducing the unfavorable economic condition. Twenty-eight percent of the people were classed as poor as of 2005 (Maribojoc, 2011).

Maribojoc was one of the Bohol municipalities that were severely hit by the 7.2 magnitude earthquake in 2013. The seabed was lifted more than a meter, and as a result, the coastline receded some 50 to 100 meters. A few weeks after the earthquake, the town was partly affected by the landfall of Typhoon Yolanda in the neighboring islands. Cultural heritage sites such as historic churches dating from the Spanish era were demolished in mere seconds of the quake. Roads, bridges, and other infrastructure were also destroyed. The wreckage of each cultural heritage shows how devastating and strong this quake was. The tourism industry was also greatly affected by the earthquake. Much effort has been put into the big tasks of recovery and rehabilitation, particularly of destroyed heritage, tourism, and livelihood sites. Priorities and agendas may also have changed because of the recent change in political leadership.

The terrible disasters not only devastated the lives of families residing in Maribojoc, but also affected most of their tourist spots, significantly decreasing the arrivals in the area. However, the local government though recognizing setbacks in the tourism sector is endeavoring to reconstruct facilities from the rubble of the earthquake. They see windows of opportunity to attract tourists and envision once again having a socially vibrant, economically efficient and ecologically sustainable community. They see tourism as vital in raising revenues for the national and local treasury. Tourism may also reduce the adverse effects of the present unfavorable economic conditions.

Volunteer tourism has provided an opportunity for disaster recovery in Maribojoc. Recognizing the potential role of volunteers in assisting organizations during disasters, volunteer tourism projects were organized to facilitate post-disaster recovery. To facilitate rehabilitation and recovery efforts in Maribojoc, volunteers were invited to be part of volunteer tourism programs in earthquake-hit villages. The voluntourism program was packaged as a series of cultural tourism and immersion activities where both tourist volunteers and members of the local community could share time, labor, and resources to finish the target volunteer work. The program goals were to rebuild communities and to reconnect the host community with the greater Philippine community through volunteering and cultural tourism. These goals were achieved by: (1) construction of traditional houses, (2) revitalizing community sources of living through cultural tourism, and (3) reaching out to local communities through community engagement and attending to the community's health needs. Tourists continue to visit and enjoy the natural and historical sights and cultural performances that Maribojoc has to offer. New activities like firefly watching have become immensely popular. Tourists take the day river tour where they get to see the nipa and mangroves along the river onboard a kayak. Mangrove adventure tours are also conducted. The Punta Cruz Watchtower shares the history of the place when there were still pirates who would attack local communities of Maribojoc. There are also educational tours of an organic demonstration farm which shows vermiculture, herbs and their medicinal uses, and how organic pig, chickens, goats, and cows are raised. Cultural groups continue to showcase the local culture of the place, by providing local homestay facilities and performances such as nipa and basket weaving. Tourists can see the ruins of the San Vicente Ferrer church, as well as the geological changes, specifically the newly uplifted ridges of the fault-lines in Barangay Punta Cruz.

The provincial government identified the following tourism attractions in the town of Maribojoc: Punta Cruz Watchtower in Barangay Punta Cruz; Demonstration Organic Farm in Barangay Bayacabac; San Vicente Mangrove (SAVIMA) forest walk in Barangay San Vicente; Abatan river tour in Barangay Cabawan and Barangay Lincod; socio-cultural activities in Barangay Toril; and church ruins in Barangay Poblacion. After the earthquake, there are also uplifted ridges in Barangay Punta Cruz. Research revealed the following information regarding these key attractions of Maribojoc.

Punta Cruz Watchtower

The Fort of Saint Vincent Ferrer (Fuerte de San Vicente Ferrer) or Punta Cruz Watchtower (Bantayan ng Punta Cruz) is a Spanish colonial era watchtower located at the western tip of the municipality of Maribojoc, Bohol that is located three kilometers away from Maribojoc Church and is known for being the "only perfect isosceles triangle" tower-fort structure in the Philippines. Maribojoc is automatically associated with the Punta Cruz Watchtower because it is their municipal logo, symbolizing the beauty it possesses as well as the functions it served during war, e.g., as a hideout for soldiers and a useful watchtower to detect enemies. Before the earthquake there was a balcony area in front of the watchtower that has a crucifix where people would leave flowers. It is not quite clear what that cross symbolizes but it is special for the people of Maribojoc. Over that balcony was a coral garden where visitors could see the treasures of the ocean without having to dive in because of the clear water. There were also docks that served the fishermen that gave them their main source of livelihood. But after the earthquake, the only thing left was the crucifix on the balcony.

The Punta Cruz Watchtower was seriously damaged based on a technical assessment done by the National Commission for Culture and the Arts after the 2013 Bohol earthquake. The watchtower was rehabilitated in 2016 but was not fully open to tourists. During a visit in 2017, there were several families in the area enjoying the view of the ocean. Some were swimming and simply having fun. There were no activities in the area aside from the tower and it is far away from the market area and people need to bring their own food and must rent the little umbrella tables available. People instead of spending money on the latter would just squat anywhere. Some were enjoying the ocean and swimming and there were no regulations on this activity. There were no restrictions either in waste management or bringing alcohol drinks and smoking. Apart from taking pictures, tourists have nothing to take home because there are no stores near the area.

Underwater Chocolate Hills, Punta Cruz

The underwater Chocolate Hills facility is the first ecotourist dive destination in Bohol. The people of Punta Cruz built the underwater attraction with funding from a German citizen who now manages the diving site. The good thing about this site is that the people plant the corals; they care for them and build a home for the fish. The problem though in this site is that there are no lifeguards, safety measures or rulings on when or when not to dive since there is no provincial regulation. In terms of profit sharing, the Barangay has a share in building and maintaining the man-made diving spot but does not receive an equal share of the profit, which could also give provide them with a livelihood. The main challenge here is how to develop a sustainable livelihood for the people and how to equitably share the profits from tourism activities.

Maribojoc Organic Demonstration farm

The Maribojoc Organic Demonstration farm is a Galing Pook awardee for its program and advocacies. The Galing Pook Awards were launched in 1993 as a pioneering program that searches and recognizes innovative practices by local government units. The local government unit of Maribojoc received one million pesos from this award, and they used the money in expanding the farm, giving free lessons to aspiring farmers and even giving them starter packs for their livelihood. There is an orientation session upon entering the demonstration site of the farm, with a knowledgeable tour guide. Everything – plants and animals and byproducts – on the area is organically grown and produced. They also have conference rooms and catering services that serve organic gourmet meals, including appetizers, desserts, and beverages.

The earthquake caused a lot of problems for the demo farm and many things were damaged. The farm was previously operated by a non-government organization (NGO) where the farm guides conducted seminars to farmers and gave away starter kits like seeds and fertilizers. However, it was transformed into a privatized farm after the 2016 elections but with government personnel from Maribojoc managing the farm. There may be auditing problems here since there was no liquidation of the funding that the NGO received from the government; in addition, there was a question as to how the farm could be privatized when government personnel are the ones managing the farm.

Maribojoc Church

One of Maribojoc's most prized features was the Santa Cruz Parish Church or Holy Cross Parish Church, which is a Roman Catholic Church in the municipality of Maribojoc, under the Roman Catholic Diocese of Tagbilaran. The parish was first established by Jesuits in 1767 or 1768 with Father Juan Soriano, SJ as its first parish priest. The Augustinian Recollects later administered the community until 1898. The once beautiful church was built in 1852 under Father Manuel Plaza and completed in 1872. In 2005, it was designated by the diocese as the Diocesan Shrine of San Vicente Ferrer. It was also declared a National Cultural Treasure by the National Museum of the Philippines and the National Historical Commission of the Philippines. When the earthquake struck in 2013, the entire building crumbled to the ground, leaving only the image of the Sacred Heart of Jesus as well as the statue of Mother Mary standing. The residents believed these survivals were miraculous. According to personal interviews conducted, the residents used to visit the church every week as part of their devotion to Jesus Christ, whose cross's ashes they believe are contained in a box inside the church. After the earthquake, and with the inconvenience of only having tents to cover them from the heat and rain, only a few devotees and tourists were found to be visiting the church.

The local government received funds amounting to 130 billion pesos from the National Museum to reconstruct the church in 2016. The reconstruction of the church is still ongoing.

Firefly watching and kayaking

One of the most visited attractions in Maribojoc is the kayaking activity particularly in Kayak Asia where most of the foreign tourists go. Before the tour starts, there is an orientation on how to paddle and what to expect on the journey. Tourists are advised to put on mosquito repellents and extra clothing. They are given the option to go on their own boat accompanied by an emergency boat or kayak with a guide behind them to help them paddle. Life vests are worn when kayaking and firefly watching and even riding in roofless boats. The research team experienced both kayaking and boating with different providers. While in the boat, there is a student who serves as a tour guide. She knows the tour very well but provides only some information, which is not thoroughly researched and only Google-searched. The kayak experience was tiring but very enjoyable. The facilities were good. They also offered dinner that was a local cuisine like the famous "pusok" which is rice wrapped beautifully in woven coconut leaves.

Several problems are identified particularly in the practice of several people running this kind of business and they have no uniform route. There were no rules/regulations on when and when not to go to the river and the operators relied on whether there were fireflies or not. Aside from getting their livelihood from the river, the tour operators take care of the area. They monitor the changes that occur in the river and try to ensure that there are no motorboats that would destroy the mangrove trees. The company running the motorboat business was one of the Mayor's staff and was given a three-year contract to run this business despite the damage it did to the river and the mangroves. Another concern identified by the Kayak Asia team was that they give the government 150 pesos for every customer that they have and yet they get only sparing help from the government. The latter only helped them once when they funded Kayak Asia's docks years ago. Aside from caring for the river, another advocacy of Kayak Asia is that they send their tour guides to school. Part of the income they generate goes to the education assistance for their team.

Despite promoting ecotourism in Maribojoc, the local government unit lacks a Municipal Environment and Natural Resources Officer (MENRO) which should serve as the implementing arm of the municipal government in the preparation of plans, pursuance of policies and programs for the rehabilitation, protection, maintenance, utilization and development of the municipal environment and resources. Because of the absence of a MENRO, there were several environment-related problems that need immediate attention. Another concern is having a sustainable livelihood and at the same time having an ordinance that ensures the protection and conservation of the environment. There is also a need to establish or revise the rules and regulations for the safety precautions of the tourists as well as establishing the standards and regulations for the industry players.

SAVIMA (San Vicente Mangrove Adventure Tour)

The San Vicente Mangrove Forrest Association (SAVIMA Org), is a community life tour experience focused on sustainable tourism activities such as homestays, livelihood demonstrations like mangrove planting, gathering shells, or catching snapping shrimps, and a one-day ecotourism mangrove adventure package. The 500-meter SAVIMA Mangrove Boardwalk was a community project acquired and applied for from the Department of Environment and Natural Resources in 1999 covering the entire 56.25 hectares of mangrove forest. With financial aid from a US Peace Corps volunteer and funds from the Department of Labor and Employment, Barangay San Vicente was able to construct a 500-meter elevated boardwalk and ecotourism information center. The wooden boardwalk heads straight out towards the shallow part of the sea and through the dense canopy of mangrove trees. After the earthquake, the former Mayor who became the Cabinet Secretary after the elections in 2016 gave the organization one million pesos for the renovation of the boardwalk, and it was repaired and improved. They also used the fund to harvest oysters and constructed public toilets and additional nipa huts. There is an entrance fee and an additional charge for a tour guide, although the language barrier hampers the amount of information provided. Visitors can reach the ocean just below the picnic areas and people can swim anytime on the beach without any regulations. There are changing rooms, public toilets, and nipa huts if the tourists want to stay overnight but there are no stores that could provide people with necessities. Previously, some people would call and ask the members of the SAVIMA to cook for them, but they do not offer that service anymore because it rarely happens. Yet, people still go there to have fun and enjoy the view of the area.

Barangay Toril, Bol-anon cultural trails

Barangay Toril is not different from a typical type of a rural area surrounded by hills or mountains, and rivers. Every household has their own vegetable patch, and they have ranch animals that they can eat or sell that are provided by the government. After the earthquake, volunteer tourists came to the area to help the people rebuild houses. The problem was that the locals were not ready to accommodate some 20 extra people in the area. One local resident invited some guests, acted as a freelance tour organizer and organized cultural activities. Tourists enjoy this area because it has a rustic feel, it is very peaceful, and the people are very hospitable. There are homestays and activities like the cultural trails. Some of the costumes from an independent film were left in the area and tourists can use them for pictures.

Tourism in Toril is increasing and the barangay needs assistance and guidance on how to manage tourism growth and how to generate more livelihood opportunities in the area.

Homestays and resorts

There are several homestays and resorts in Maribojoc. Most of the people that visit the municipality like to be immersed in the rural life and prefer to stay in homes for their accommodation rather than staying in a hotel in the city. A former tourism officer who served for nine years was replaced after a change in leadership in the municipality because of the 2016 elections. The former tourism officer transformed her house into a bed and breakfast to sustain her involvement in tourism and to remain in touch with the community.

Some tourists appreciate this kind of accommodation but there are also problems and concerns. Homestays and resorts are far away from the city, and public transportation is a problem because there are no terminals near the area. You must either rent private vehicles or ask the homestay owners to escort you to certain areas for an additional cost.

Learning tourism destination framework

The tourism industry offers economic opportunities to the municipality of Maribojoc. It contributed greatly to the development of the community. However, in the aftermath of the devastating earthquake in 2013 and the elections in 2016, Maribojoc faces great challenges in development planning and implementation, particularly in local tourism planning. The municipality did not see the urgency to plan the development of their tourism industry.

Environmental issues continue to be a great concern and are prominent in discussions all over the world. The Philippines takes environmental concerns very seriously. The OECD (2016) agrees with Bangko Sentral ng Pilipinas that approximately one third of the population relies on natural resources (i.e., arable land and oceans) for its livelihood. The domestic environment policy is grounded in the 1987 Constitution which provides that the "State shall protect and advance the right of the people to a balanced and healthful ecology in accord with the rhythm and harmony of nation".

Before implementing environmental policies, a thorough assessment is critically important. The Department of Environment and Natural Resources (DENR) will directly regulate the implementation of such policies (Philippine Institute for Development Studies, 2002). In addition, according to the National Economic and Development Authority (2016), the DENR aims to empower its commitment to multilateral environmental agreements through pursuing specific goals and strategies. The Philippine Development Plan mentioned that one of its goals is the "Enhanced resilience of natural systems and improved adaptive capacities of human communities to cope with environmental hazards including climate-related risks". This goal includes the "integration of hazard and climate change vulnerability maps in the updating of the comprehensive land use plans (CLUPs) by the local government units (LGUs) and enforcement of zoning regulations; and encourage more provinces to mainstream disaster risk reduction (DRR) in their plans and build capacities of national and local agencies assigned to lead the effort".

The past decade has seen marked growth in the attention paid by policymakers, development experts, and industry leaders to the contributions made by the tourism sector in many countries, especially in the developing world. However, considering the challenges posed by climate-related risks, natural resource depletion and environmental degradation, tourism impacts cannot be managed in one dimension only. Schianetz et al. (2007) discussed the requirements for building a learning tourism destination (LTD) theoretically, but practical studies supporting the concept are lacking. Accordingly, the LTD framework provided a methodology for pursuing sustainable tourism planning through fostering ongoing group collaboration and collective learning among stakeholders. It is a novel concept of development that advocates collaborative learning and co-creation of knowledge that is based on context-relevant information to formulate policies and strategies that are permissible and feasible among local stakeholders. It is suggested that the LTD framework may serve as a tool for understanding the complexity of local and regional tourism development. The LTD is an approach that recognizes the capacity of societies to learn and to develop economic organizations that are relevant to its unique context. As an alternative to external development models, the LTD is a system where society defines problems based on its perceptions and formulates solutions from its cultural resources to address situations specific to that society.

Butler's (1993, p. 29) definition of sustainable tourism development appears to be a substantial contribution to unify the concept of sustainable tourism development with its parental terms. Butler stated that:

> Sustainable development in the context of tourism could be taken as: tourism which is developed and maintained in an area (community, environment) in such a manner and at such a scale that it remains viable over an indefinite period and does not degrade or alter the environment (human and physical) in which it exists to such a degree that it prohibits the successful development and well-being of other activities and processes. That is not the same as sustainable tourism, which may be thought of as tourism which is in a form which can maintain its viability in an area for an indefinite period of time.

The 2002 World Summit on Sustainable Development (WSSD) suggested the importance of countries undertaking national and subnational strategies as an approach to achieving the goal of sustainable development. Strategies are needed to overcome the obstacles to sustainable development and make the necessary key changes.

In keeping with the ongoing commitment of the Local Government Unit of Maribojoc, it requires the improvement of quality of life but more importantly the attainment of sustainable development in Maribojoc. Tourism development and promotion are among the functions of Local Government Units (LGUs) as mandated by the Local Government Code of 1991 (RA 7160). As local governments shift to more participatory forms of development governance, they are also encouraged to join other stakeholders in local tourism development and promotion. The National Tourism Act of 2009 (RA 9593) encourages LGUs to ensure they prepare and implement a tourism development plan, enforce standards, and collect statistical data for tourism purposes.

The case study was based on previous engagements in the area and the intent was to support the development of a community-based and people-centered tourism in the municipality. Neo and Chen's (2007) Dynamic Governance Theory is used as a framework that will enable these local organizations to look critically at their governance capabilities.

Dynamic governance theory

Several scholars define governance as the interplay among various stakeholders in the public arena. Under the 1987 Constitution, the term governance is conceived as the creation and maintenance of a system of rules that governs a state with the key consideration of "political openness" and "transparency". It is not operated by government agencies alone but also with the active efforts of people in seeking equality, justice, rule of law and people empowerment (Lazo, 2006). About the concept of governance, the subsequent Local Government Code of 1991 made clarifications regarding local governance. Its purpose and design empower residents and elected officials to realize local development goals with the participation of citizens (Local Government Code of the Philippines, 1991).

Moreover, governance is also defined as the ability to coordinate the aggregation of diverging interests to promote policy, projects and programs that credibly represent the public interests. Public involvement, institutional development, transparency of decision-making procedures, interest representation, conflict resolution, limits of authority and leadership accountability are all issues of governance (Frischtak, 1994). To promote good governance, the following are needed: capacity building to improve (1) planning and investment programming systems; (2) absorptive capacity to implement projects; (3) monitoring and evaluation (M&E) systems; and (4) information systems. Effective policy implementation entails deepened citizens' participation in localized decision-making, efficient delivery of social services to the poor, and good central-local fiscal relations. Collaboration among these agencies or departments will serve as a vehicle through which local government sectors provide expanding services. Making public policies more efficient, effective, and equitable are fundamental and arguably have a great impact in civic affairs. Indeed, policies should be carried out proficiently.

Most countries face extreme sustainability challenges with rapid growth, urbanization, industrialization, environmental degradation, resource constraints and dramatic changes in lifestyle. In coping with this reality, countries across the region are tailoring best practices to appropriately bolster sustainable development aspirations. Several governments have established long-term development strategies that inform their national development planning and work towards incorporating the economic, social and environmental protection goals. Sirianni (2009) emphasized that the role of each department within the LGU must be clearly defined so that cooperation and collaboration are promoted. In implementing policies and programs, it is vital to define and implement the collective goals of the state.

Neo and Chen's (2007) Dynamic Governance capabilities include:

1. Thinking ahead – the ability to perceive early signals of future developments that may affect a nation/local government in order to remain relevant to the world/nation;
2. Thinking again – the ability and willingness to rethink and remake currently functioning policies so that they perform better; and
3. Thinking across – the ability and openness to cross boundaries to learn from the experience of others so that new ideas and concepts may be introduced into an institution.

Specifically, this study extracts these worldviews and dynamic governance capacities through:

1. Mapping of the local tourism policies, plans, programs and activities before and after the earthquake;
2. Plotting the roles, major learning and unlearning, major rebuilding, or new ways of doing things, major challenges and difficulties before and after the earthquake;
3. Charting strategic recommendations, coping mechanisms or new approaches undertaken and planned in the future.

Doing these will enable us to understand how local organizations plan (think ahead), rethink or remake after disasters (think again) and collaborate to work together and learn better practices across the country and the globe and make learning tourism destination a reality in the future (think across).

Local tourism development plans should integrate innovations in the national system of standards for tourism enterprises, heritage and environmental protection imperatives in a manner that encourages sustainable tourism development. The plans should also take into consideration disaster risk reduction and climate change adaptation principles. Beyond this, the Tourism

Act emphasizes that tourism development is a shared responsibility of both national and local governments.

It is important to note that different stakeholders (e.g., private sector, people's organizations) involved in the tourism business of Maribojoc are responsible for the implementation of different parts of the principles. Governments, tourism businesses, local communities, NGOs, and the tourists can all contribute to make tourism more sustainable. To achieve the goals of sustainable tourism, the different actors should cooperate and stimulate each other to put the principles into practice.

Healey (1998) suggests that inclusive stakeholder involvement can help people generate mutual learning and produce new ideas, instead of inducing adversarial conflict between fixed interests. Some scholars (Healey, 1998, 2006a; Innes and Booher, 1999) believe that it is important to involve people who live where a project is to be undertaken, because regional and local people have practical knowledge of their areas and can develop ownership through social learning processes. The regional and local power of human beings also ensures that collaborative processes continue through continual critiques and feedback (Innes and Booher, 1999; Healey, 1998).

Dynamic governance brings public and private stakeholders together in collective forums with public agencies. Their motivation drives the extensiveness of public policy and thence engages in consensus-oriented decision-making. It emphasizes the collective goal of various stakeholders together for the purpose of serving as a mechanism in the implementation of policies concerning social issues.

Stakeholders in tourism management planning include:

- Neighbors and residents (local communities)
- Farmers, foresters, hunters, and fishermen
- Tourism providers such as hoteliers, restaurant owners, tourist guides, etc.
- Tour operators and tourism agencies
- Local authorities: local municipalities, local administration
- Local NGOs
- Educational institutions (schools, universities, etc.), research centers
- Visitors
- Media

Through focus group discussions, mini-surveys and analysis of secondary data and materials, the research team was able to draw out what local stakeholders believe could be solutions that could make tourism a viable and sustainable endeavor in the municipality and make Maribojoc not only a strong but also a learning tourism destination. The residents learned that in ensuring a successful tourism plan/program/project, they must consider occurrences like flooding which will prevent them from accommodating tourists because tours are no longer possible. They also learned that generation of funds to sustain the project/program is important. One of the considerations is: what if they earn less and there are fewer tourists coming in? This will affect the quality of operations. If they do not have contingency funds or back-up budget, the operations will surely suffer. One of the interviewees explained that families are being sustained because of their help and because of their own perseverance. Even though the barangay is not involved, they are also helping many families; they have a mutual relationship. They continue to work towards protecting the environment, which is a particularly important component of all this, especially now that the country has unpredictable weather patterns.

Having a clear objective and goal is vital. There must be a common understanding within the community. Doing this will prevent misunderstanding that may derail the program or the project. On the other hand, the residents also learned that to ensure success, common understanding and mutual effort of members and residents of the community is important. They also need to have financial support and capacity building trainings for organizations. Another lesson is that it is important that various groups in the community should participate and give feedback to the project. The residents wanted to emphasize the value of volunteerism. Additionally, it would also help that tourist spots receive help to upgrade their operations. Referrals from different people and previous visitors also help. Training programs and seminars on tourism sustainability are also needed. This will enable knowledge building and sharing. One respondent said that although their tourism is quite slow, he is positive that it can return to the way it was before because many people are more willing to help, especially with the new administration.

The municipality of Maribojoc is listed as one of the destinations in the Religious Heritage Tours, Museum Tours and Thematic Crafts/Handicrafts Tours of Bohol. The themed tours were selected and based on the thematic relevance of the combination of the aesthetic and attractive values found in each heritage/cultural destination as they are grouped together in a package, and the accessibility and proximity of these destinations to each of the sites mentioned in a package. This shows that Maribojoc has the potential to be one of the main tourist attractions in Bohol. The residents and most especially the LGU should conduct programs and projects to improve these tourist sites.

But above all, the LGU of Maribojoc should build effective, accountable, and inclusive institutions.

According to Emerson et al. (2015), the absence of consensus among major political institutions is a serious problem causing a state's future policies to bog down. Too many conflicting voices at the decision-making levels, which cause more confusions and contradictions, contribute nothing to improving a country's system. Therefore, member agencies should bring the state closer to its citizens and by doing so make the state more efficient, democratic, and accountable. Through this the government must organize, coordinate and control complex policy domains. Policies and programs of the LGU should establish mutual understanding instead of mutual mistrust, and mutual interest instead of disregard of others among the citizens.

Dynamic Governance Theory is thus useful in this regard because it looks at the evolving institutional culture in the area and how these learning organizations perceive their roles as well as envision plans, policies, and programs and strategic directions in sustainable tourism development. Institutional culture involves how a group perceives its position in the world, how it articulates its purpose, and how it evolves the values, beliefs, and principles to guide its decision-making and policy choices. In addition, strong organizational capabilities are needed to consider thoroughly major policy issues and take effective action (Neo and Chen, 2007).

For sustainable tourism development, the involvement of LGUs, local stakeholders and the notification targeting the local population is an indispensable element of the planning process. According to Behrens' (2014) study, for every governmental program to be proficiently carried out, extensive government intervention through regulations, representation of inter-industrial interests through associations, efficient distribution of public services and the penetration of society by governmental agencies and activities should be ensured. This study incorporated the concept of collaborative governance in the human services field. LGUs use the direct services or strategic management of resources as instruments of policy implementation, which represents different values that are held with the highest priority in every decision. To date, many services rendered by the government provide quality services directly to the citizens. The aims of Sustainable Development Goals 16.6 and 16.7 are to "promote peaceful and inclusive societies for sustainable development, provide access to justice for all and build effective, accountable and inclusive institutions at all levels". The Maribojoc case suggests that a high level of LGU support will enable the municipality to continue to tackle further issues after the original ones have been dealt with. The SDGs stress that local governments need to take the initiative in dealing with local issues. The importance of cooperation between the local government unit and stakeholders in establishing a shared long-term vision for the region should be agreed through an integrated development plan.

Conclusion and recommendations

There are several opportunities for Maribojoc when it comes to tourism. It just needs several ideas for innovation and studies so that it can execute the project properly prioritizing what the people need. To further address and study organizational culture and relationships among individuals belonging to local people's sectors, entrepreneurs, and tourist groups, a learning organization cluster should be created to capture the organizational views on the environment, community processes, organizations, institutions, and other agents that play a role from the organizational to the destination scale. The LGU of Maribojoc envisions having a socially vibrant, economically efficient and ecologically sustainable community. They see tourism as vital in revenue raising and reducing unfavorable economic conditions.

The Learning Tourism Destination framework recognizes the capacity of societies to learn and to develop economic organizations that are relevant to each unique context. An LTD is any tourism city, town, village, and surrounding that is in the process of achieving agreed upon objectives based on sustainable development:

- Uses lifelong learning as an organizing principle for community, organizations and individuals;
- Promotes collaboration of the tourism, civic, voluntary, and education sectors; and
- Provides an infrastructure to collect new information, disseminate process, and apply gained knowledge.

For Maribojoc to be a learning tourism destination, the following are suggested:

- Enhance the well-being of communities: The municipality of Maribojoc should support and ensure the economic, social and cultural well-being of the communities in which tourism takes place.
- Support the protection of the natural and cultural environment: Allow the use of natural and cultural resources for gaining economic profit while at

the same time guaranteeing that these resources are not deteriorated or destroyed.

- Recognize product quality and tourist satisfaction: The quality of tourism products offered is a key factor for the economic success of tourism. It is not only characterized by material criteria like the quality of transport, accommodation, and food, but also by non-material criteria like hospitality or the quality of experiences.
- Apply adaptive management and monitoring: To ensure that tourism is developed in a way that is ecologically, economically and socially sustainable, adequate management and monitoring must be established, following the basic principles of sustainable use of resources.

Maribojoc is a small player in the tourism industry in the province and the country. In due time, however, if it learns from its past and present, it could be a major player in tourism and in more resilient, livable, and sustainable municipalities.

Sustainable tourism will require collaborating and learning institutions from the government, business sector and civil society organizations. It will also need thinking ahead, thinking again and thinking across, learning from the past and present to get ahead. Ideally, it would also involve the participation of stakeholders beyond and with the government, such as the private sector, NGOs, residents and responsible tourists who are also involved in the definition of development problems and solutions coming from their own perceptions and cultural resources. The journey towards sustainable tourism and stronger institutions is long, evolutionary and may be conflict laden. If not managed well, challenges may not be addressed, and solutions may not be achieved.

Acknowledgment

The authors acknowledge the support from the Office of the Vice President for Academic Affairs of the University of the Philippines for the research funds from the Emerging Inter-Disciplinary Research (EIDR) grants (OVPAA-EIDR-06-18).

References

Amore, A., & Hall, C. M. (2016). From governance to meta-governance in tourism? Re-incorporating politics, interests, and values in the analysis of tourism governance. *Tourism Recreation Research, 41*(2), 109–122.

Beaumont, N., & Dredge, D. (2010). Local tourism governance: A comparison of three network approaches. *Journal of Sustainable Tourism, 18*, 7–28.

Behrens, J. (2014). *Leadership in Collaborative Governance: Understanding the Relationship of Leadership and Collaborative Performance of Local Departments of Social Services Executive.* Richmond, VA. http://scholarscompass.vcu.edu/etd/3341.

Bell, S. (2004). Appropriate policy knowledge, and institutional and governance implications. *Australian Journal of Public Administration, 63*(1), 22–28.

Bohol Tourism Master Plan, 2003–2005. Provincial Planning Development Office. https://ppdo.bohol.gov.ph/plan-reports/development-plans/tourism-master-plan/.

Bramwell, B. (2004). Partnerships, participation, and social science research in tourism planning. In A. Lew, M. Hall, & A. Williams (Eds.), *A Companion to Tourism* (pp. 541–554). Oxford: Blackwell.

Bramwell, B. (2005). Interventions and policy instruments for sustainable tourism. In W. F. Theobald (Ed.), *Global Tourism*, 3rd edition (pp. 406–425). Amsterdam: Elsevier.

Bramwell, B. (2007). Critical and normative responses to sustainable tourism. *Tourism Recreation Research, 32*(3), 76–78.

Bramwell, B. (2010). Participative planning and governance for sustainable tourism. *Tourism Recreation Research, 35*(3), 239–249.

Bramwell, B., Jackson, G., & van der Straaten, J. (1996). *Sustainable Tourism Management: Principles and Practice.* Tilburg: Tilburg University Press.

Bramwell, B., & Lane, B. (2011). Critical research on the governance of tourism and sustainability. *Journal of Sustainable Tourism, 19*(4–5), 411–421.

Butler, R. W. (1993). Tourism: An evolutionary perspective. In J. G. Nelson, R. Butler, & G. Wall (Eds.), *Tourism and Sustainable Development: Monitoring, Planning, Managing* (pp. 27–44). Heritage Resource Center, University of Waterloo.

Cariño, L., Briones, L., Florano, E. R., & Follosco, K. C. (2005). Reinventing Philippine governance for globalization. *Philippine Journal of Public Administration, 49*(1–2).

Commission of the European Communities (CEC) (2001). *European Governance.* White Paper. Brussels.

Cruz, R. (2003). *Towards Sustainable Tourism Development in the Philippines and Other ASEAN Countries: An Examination of Programs and Practices of National Tourism Organizations.* Manila: Philippine APEC Study Center Network.

Daphnet, S., Scott, N., & Ruhanen, L. (2012). Applying diffusion theory to destination stakeholder understanding of sustainable tourism development: A case from Thailand. *Journal of Sustainable Tourism, 20*(8), 110–124.

De Clercq, D., & Belausteguigoitia, I. (2017). Reducing the harmful effect of role ambiguity on turnover intentions: The roles of innovation propensity, goodwill trust, and procedural justice. *Personnel Review, 46*(6), 1046–1069.

Dela Santa, E. (2015). The evolution of Philippine tourism policy implementation from 1973 to 2009. *Tourism Planning and Development, 12*(2), 155–175.

Duran, C. (2013). *Governance for the Tourism Sector and Its Measurement.* UNWTO statistics and TSA issue paper series STSA/IP/2013/01. http://statistics.unwto.org/en/content/papers.

Eber, S. (1992). *Beyond the Green Horizon: A Discussion Paper on Principles for Sustainable Tourism*. Woking: WWF.

Eber, S. (2003). *Integrating Sustainability into the Undergraduate Curriculum: Leisure and Tourism*. Guideline number 10. Guildford: Association of Tourism in Higher Education.

Farmaki, A. (2015). Regional network governance and sustainable tourism. *Tourism Geographies, 17*(3), 385–407.

Frischtak, L. (1994). *Governance Capacity and Economic Reform in Developing Economies*. World Bank Technical Paper No. 254. Washington, DC: World Bank.

Hall, C., & Lew, A. (2009). *Understanding and Managing Tourism Impacts: An Integrated Approach*. Abingdon: Routledge.

Healey, P. (1998). Building institutional capacity through collaborative approaches to urban planning. *Environment and Planning A: Economy and Space, 30*, 1531–1546.

Healey, P. (2006a). *Collaborative Planning: Shaping Places in Fragmented Societies*, 2nd edition. Basingstoke: Macmillan.

Healey, P. (2006b). Transforming governance: Challenges of institutional adaptation and a new politics of space. *European Planning Journal, 14*(3), 299–320.

Higgins-Desbiolles, F. (2006). More than an "industry": The forgotten power of tourism as a social force. *Tourism Management, 27*, 1192–1208.

Innes, J. E., & Booher, D. E. (1999). Consensus building and complex adaptive systems: A framework for evaluating collaborative planning. *Journal of the American Planning Association, 65*(4), 412–423.

Lazo, R. J. (2006). *Philippine Governance and the 1987 Constitution*. Manila: Rex Book Store.

Leonard, L. (2017a). State governance, participation, and mining development: Lessons learned from Dullstroom, Mpumalanga. *Politikon, 44*(2), 327–345.

Leonard, L. (2017b). Environmental impact assessments and public participation: The case of environmental justice and mining development in Dullstroom, Mpumalanga. *Environmental Assessment Policy and Management, 19*(1), 1–25.

Leonard, L. (2018). Examining civil society social capital relations against mining development for local sustainability in Dullstroom, Mpumalanga, South Africa. *Sustainable Development, 27*(12).

Local Government Code of the Philippines (1991). https://www.officialgazette.gov.ph/downloads/1991/10oct/19911010-RA-7160-CCA.pdf.

Maguigad, V. M. (2013). Tourism planning in archipelagic Philippines: A case review. *Tourism Management Perspectives, 7*, 25–33.

Maribojoc (2011). Municipality information and poverty profile. http://www.maribojoc .gov .ph and https:// ppdo .bohol .gov .ph/ profile/ municipal -links/ 1st -district/ maribojoc/.

McVey, M. (1993). *Monitoring Philippine Poverty by Operational Indicators*. Social Weather Stations.

Middleton, N., O'Keefe, P., & Moyo, S. (1993). *Tears of the Crocodile: From Rio to Reality in the Developing World*. London: Pluto Press.

Musavengane, R. (2018). Toward pro-poor local economic development in Zimbabwe: The role of pro-poor tourism. *African Journal of Hospitality, Tourism and Leisure, 7*(1), 1–14.

National Economic and Development Authority (2016). *Philippine Development Plan 2017–2022 Results Matrices*. Pasig: National Economic and Development Authority.

National Tourism Act of 2009 (RA 9593).

Neo, B. S., & Chen, G. (2007). *Dynamic Governance: Embedding Culture, Capabilities and Change in Singapore.* Singapore: World Scientific Publishing.

North, D. (1990). *Institutions, Institutional Change and Economic Performance.* Cambridge: Cambridge University Press.

Nunkoo, R. (2017). Governance and sustainable tourism: What is the role of trust, power and social capital? *Journal of Destination Marketing & Management, 6,* 277–285.

OECD (1995). *Participatory Development and Good Governance.* Paris: OECD Publishing.

OECD (2016). *OECD Investment Policy Reviews: Philippines 2016.* Paris: OECD Publishing.

Pateman, C. (1988). *The Sexual Contract.* Cambridge: Polity Press.

Philippine Institute for Development Studies (2002). *25 Years Journey: Quest for Research-Based Policy Making 2002 Annual Report.* https:// www .pids .gov .ph/ publication/annual-reports/2002-pids-annual-report-25-years-of-journey.

Philippine National Tourism Development Plan 2016–2022. https://visitcentralluzon .com/wp-content/uploads/2018/11/NTDP-2016-2022_Executive-Summary.pdf.

Province of Bohol website. https://www.region2.dti.gov.ph.

Purdy, J. M. (2016). The role of power in collaborative governance. In R. D. Margerum & C. J. Robinson (Eds.), *The Challenge of Collaboration in Environment Governance: Barriers and Responses* (pp. 246–265). Cheltenham, UK and Northampton, MA, USA: Edward Elgar Publishing.

Qian, C., Sasaki, N., Shivakoti, G., & Zhang, Y. (2016). Effective governance in tourism development: An analysis of local perception in the Huangshan mountain area. *Tourism Management Perspectives, 20,* 112–123.

Reid, J., Allen, R., Bass, S., & Clayton, B. (1994). *Strategies for National Sustainable Development.* London: Earthscan.

Richardson, T., & Connelly, S. (2002). *Building Consensus for Rural Development and Planning in Scotland: A Review of Best Practice.* Edinburgh: Scottish Executive Central Research Unit.

Schianetz, K., Kavanagh, L., & Lockington, D. (2007). The learning tourism destination: The potential of a learning organization approach for improving the sustainability of tourism destinations. *Tourism Management, 28,* 1485–1496.

Siakwah, P. (2018). Tourism geographies and spatial distribution of tourist sites in Ghana. *African Journal of Hospitality, Tourism and Leisure, 7*(1), 1–19.

Siakwah, P., Musavengane, R., & Leonard, L. (2020). Tourism governance and attainment of the Sustainable Development Goals in Africa. *Tourism Planning & Development, 17*(4), 355–383.

Sirianni, C. (2009). *Investing in Democracy: Engaging Citizens in Collaborative Governance.* Washington, DC: Brookings Institution Press.

United Nations (2012). *The Future We Want.* Declaration of the UN Conference on Sustainable Development, Rio (2012).

United Nations Development Programme (1999). *Human Development Report.* New York.

United Nations Educational, Scientific and Cultural Organization (UNESCO) and United Nations Environment Programme (UNEP) (2016). *World Heritage and Tourism in a Changing Climate.*

United Nations World Tourism Organization (UNWTO) (2008). *International Recommendations for Tourism Statistics 2008 (IRTS 2008).* Madrid. http://unstats.un .org/unsd/tradeserv/tourism/manual.html.

United Nations World Tourism Organization (UNWTO) (2012). *A Closer Look at Tourism: Sub-National Measurement and Analysis – Towards a Set of UNWTO Guidelines*. Madrid.

United Nations World Tourism Organization (UNWTO) (2014a). *Tourism: An Economic and Social Phenomenon*. Madrid.

United Nations World Tourism Organization (UNWTO) (2014b). *UNWTO Tourism Highlights*. Madrid.

United Nations World Tourism Organization (UNWTO) (2016). *Annual Report 2016*. Madrid.

Waligo, V. M., Clarke, J., & Hawkins, R. (2013). Implementing sustainable tourism: A multi-stakeholder involvement management framework. *Tourism Management*, 36, 342–353.

White, L. (2001). Effective governance through complexity thinking and management science. *System Research and Behavioural Science*, 18(3), 241–257.

World Bank (2009). *The Worldwide Governance Indicators*. Washington, DC: World Bank Group.

World Travel & Tourism Council (WTTC) (2017). *Travel and Tourism Economic Impact 2017 – World*. London.

11 COVID-19 and tourism: a look at the social implications

Gaunette Sinclair-Maragh

Introduction

Coronavirus is a species of the Severe Acute Respiratory Syndrome (SARS) family of viruses. The novel coronavirus SARS-CoV-2 previously 2019-nCoV was epicentred in Hubei Province of the People's Republic of China (Velavan & Meyer, 2020) specifically in Wuhan, China in December 2019 (Ren et al., 2020). This infectious disease subsequently spread across the world (Liu et al., 2020) and was declared a global health emergency by the World Health Organization (WHO) on 30 January 2020 (Velavan & Meyer, 2020). By February to March 2020, the virus entered the mainland of all the regions of the world. It was declared a pandemic by WHO on 11 March 2020 (Bakar & Rosbi, 2020).

To officially name the disease, the coronavirus was abbreviated COVID-19 by the WHO on 11 February 2020. The 'CO' represents corona, 'VI' stands for virus, 'D' for disease and '2019' to mark the year the outbreak began (NCIRD, 2020). Henceforth, COVID-19 will be used in the chapter.

The novel COVID-19 pandemic is regarded as a humanitarian crisis affecting people's lives and triggering economic crises (Vaishar & Šťastná, 2022). The United Nations Department of Economic and Social Affairs (UNDESA, 2020) describes the pandemic as a human, economic and social crisis. A global catastrophe of this severity has not occurred since the onset of the Spanish flu which lasted from 1918 to 1920, and killed over 50 million people worldwide (Medical News Today, 2020).

Previous studies on the virus focused on the psychological and social effects it has had on the general population, principally, children, college students, and health professionals (Saladino et al., 2020). It appears, however, that there have been minimal analyses on the impacts of the pandemic on tourism which the Economic Commission for Latin America and the Caribbean (ECLAC, 2020a) describes as devastating. Additionally, these few studies since the onset of COVID-19 focused mainly on the economic impacts of the virus on tourism (e.g. Ayittey et al., 2020; Bakar & Rosbi, 2020). This is understandable as according to the United Nations World Tourism Organization (UNWTO, n.d.), 100 million direct tourism jobs are at risk as well as the sustainability of the accommodation and food service sectors. These sectors are labour-intensive, employing 144 million workers globally.

The impacts of the virus are most felt in regions such as Latin America and the Caribbean which are highly dependent on tourism (ECLAC, 2020a). These regions are also characterized by inequality, vulnerability, poverty, weak social cohesion and high levels of social discontent (ECLAC, 2020a). UNDESA (2020) reports that the COVID-19 pandemic whilst affecting all segments of the population is particularly detrimental to vulnerable groups such as people living in poverty situations, older persons, persons with disabilities, youth, and indigenous people. In addition, women are most affected by the virus (UNWomen, 2020). They are already among the most at-risk categories of the tourism workforce and therefore, it is likely that COVID-19 could exacerbate their vulnerability.

Small businesses which actually support 80 per cent of global tourism are predominantly vulnerable to the incidence of the pandemic (UNWTO, n.d.). This is further exacerbated in rural communities where there are tourism micro-businesses (Bartlett, 2020). Despite the effects of the pandemic on small tourism businesses in rural areas, the catastrophic scenarios of the decline in tourism are mainly centred on urban destinations (Vaishar & Šťastná, 2022). This suggests that rural community tourism could be further marginalized, being left out of the macro plans for business continuity and recovery.

The virus has resulted not only in illnesses and deaths, but also mental and emotional instability (Cucinotta & Vanelli, 2020). These psychosocial challenges are being experienced by tourism stakeholders from both the demand and supply sides of tourism (Sigala, 2020). The psychosocial impacts of COVID-19 pandemic can be even more detrimental than the direct medical impact (Ayalon, 2020) and therefore, it is important to bring this matter to the fore.

The chapter will examine COVID-19 and its social implications within the context of tourism. It will focus on three social impacts: advanced vulnerability of women employed in the tourism industry, further marginalization of rural tourism communities, and the unusual psychosocial challenges faced by tourism stakeholders. The chapter will also provide recommendations regarding the social adaptation theory as a means of mitigating and driving subsequent changes. The social adaptation theory provides "a neo-Piagetian account of attitudes, values, and other social cognitions, and implies that the adaptive significance of information will determine its impact" (Kahle & Homer, 1985, p. 954). It is an appropriate theory to substantiate the proposed recommendations as social adaptation relates to how an individual or group conforms to the systems of norms and values in a given society, class or social group (Prokhorov, 1979).

Tourism and infectious diseases

Tourism is not new to the impact of infectious diseases. It is a catalyst for infectious diseases as tourists are vectors of infections to destinations that they visit (Vaishar & Šťastná, 2022) and likewise, destinations transmit infections to tourists (CDC, 2021). Tourists have been infected with malaria and yellow fever from their visits to tropical forests, usually without appropriate protection against insect bites or vaccination. Consequently, these diseases are imported to their home country upon their return and transmitted to the local population (Heymann, 2004). In the past, tourists visiting Africa have contracted Ebola and Marburg which are both viral haemorrhagic diseases. Those visiting the Middle Eastern countries have caught the Middle East Respiratory Syndrome / MERS flu (CDC, 2021) and the 2003 severe acute respiratory syndrome / SARS (Wilder-Smith, 2006). These outbreaks have resulted in major prohibition to international travel (Ala'a & Albattat, 2019). There have also been cases of the spread of the influenza infection among people on cruises, airplanes and tour groups (Freedman & Leder, 2005).

Where there is a likely threat of infectious diseases, destinations that are prepared for such crises tend to be in a favourable position as they are more equipped for the impact (Ritchie, 2004). In assessing the impacts of infectious diseases such as SARS and Avian flu on international tourist arrivals in Asian countries, Kuo et al. (2008) found that the number of affected cases has a significant impact on tourist arrivals in SARS-affected countries but not on Avian flu-affected countries. The rationale is that the Avian flu-affected countries were more prepared for the crisis through the thrust of corporate social responsibility (CSR) pre-crisis planning. This is inclusive of tourism businesses; hence the number of visitor arrivals was not severely impacted. The SARS-affected countries were not prepared for such an outbreak and this impacted tourist demand. This is supported by Henderson (2007) who found that the number of international arrivals in Phuket, Thailand decreased by 67.2 per cent (for the first half of 2005) as a result of the tsunami because that country was not prepared to handle a natural disaster of this magnitude.

Impacts of COVID-19 on tourism

The impacts of COVID-19 on the global tourism industry have been real. The onset of the pandemic was unexpected. Unlike the impact of SARS and Avian flu on affected countries, COVID-19 is a global pandemic which according to Orendain and Djalante (2021) is impacting the entire world. It is therefore not contained within specific destinations and was certainly not prepared for. In order to reduce the risk of exposure and curtail the spread of the virus, governments encouraged people to stay home as much as possible (CDC COVID-19 Response Team, 2020). In addition, unprecedented measures were introduced (OECD, 2020a) to include restrictions on travel, business operations and people-to-people interactions (Gaffney & Eeckels, 2020). This resulted in the closure of tourism operations or minimal operations by these entities which according to the OECD (2020a) have brought the tourism economy to a standstill. With the COVID-19 infection being spread by way of international travel (Vaishar & Šťastná, 2022), destinations had no choice other than to close their borders to visitors with many not reopened until July 2020.

The right to travel and to enjoy hospitality and tourism services is curtailed with the various sectors being impacted. For instance, hospitality services were among the first to be impacted by the virus (Gaffney & Eeckels, 2020) as well as amongst the sectors hardest hit by the pandemic (Gursoy & Chi, 2020). Consequently, destinations across the globe have been experiencing serious decline in inbound travel and subsequent tourism revenue (Škare et al., 2021). For some destinations, tourism is a monopolistic economy as it is highly depended on for economic growth and development. This is particularly the case of developing and underdeveloped countries where the impacts of the virus on tourism are most felt. Gaffney and Eeckels (2020, p. 308) declared that the "more a country's economy depends on international tourism as a percentage of GDP, the more quickly and deeply it will be impacted by the cessation of touristic flows".

The imposed travel restrictions and COVID-induced lockdowns to restrain the spread of the virus (Bartik et al., 2020) are unprecedented since the world wars of the twentieth century (Baum & Hai, 2020). Being a service industry which traditionally involves in-person travel to destinations and people-to-people interactions for the ultimate experience, the entire tourism eco-system has felt the full force of the virus, making it an unprecedented crisis for the tourism economy (OECD, 2020a).

The dynamics of the global economy are significantly driven by tourism (Gaffney & Eeckels, 2020). Before the pandemic, the global tourism industry was on a growth trajectory with international tourist arrivals reaching a total of 1.5 billion in 2019, representing an increase of 4 per cent when compared to the previous year (UNWTO, 2020a). A further increase of 3 to 4 per cent was forecasted for 2020, but the ongoing COVID-19 pandemic could result in a decline of 20 to 30 per cent in international tourist arrivals. China, France, Spain, Italy and the USA were the first countries to have manifested the pandemic as well as being most severely impacted (Vaishar & Šťastná, 2022). The USA is a major source of outbound tourists for the majority of destinations and with this country being impacted by the virus and instituting border closure and travel protocols, the impact on outbound travel to destinations around the world has been grave.

Over the past decade, China has joined the USA in being a major source market for international travel and in 2018 was ranked first place as a source of outbound tourists with 10.6 per cent. It also emerged fourth in international tourist arrivals with 4.5 per cent after France, Spain and the USA. China also ranked eleventh in international tourism receipts (2.8 per cent). The start and spread of the virus in China has interrupted outbound travel from this country and impacted the demand-side of tourism for many destinations (Vaishar & Šťastná, 2022).

The pandemic has caused both supply and demand shocks in various sectors (del Rio-Chanona et al., 2020). Tourism is not spared from this shock as between January and June 2020, international tourist arrivals declined by 65 per cent. This represents a substantial decrease of 93 per cent when compared to the same period in 2019 (UNWTO, 2020a). The consequential global decline during the first half of 2020 can be explained from the cumulative decrease in international tourist arrivals in the sub-regions. As indicated in Table 11.1, the decline in arrivals in these sub-regions exceeded 50 per cent. It is important to note that the combined Asia and Pacific region was the first to be infected by the virus, followed by Europe. Both regions at the time of this data gathering topped the list of regional destinations to show a decline in international tourist arrivals. This global decline in international travel demand for the period January to June 2020 resulted in a loss of 440 million international arrivals and approximately US$460 billion in export revenue from international tourism

(TIAC, 2020). There is an estimated loss of $1.3 trillion in export revenue which is five times more in the loss of international receipts when compared to the 2009 global recession (UNWTO, 2021a). The overall decline in tourism for 2020 is exceptional and according to the UNWTO (2021b), it is recorded as the worst year in the history of tourism.

Table 11.1   Figures for the global and sub-regions arrivals between January and June 2020

Regions	Percentage decline in tourist arrivals
Asia and the Pacific	72
Europe	66
Africa	57
Middle East	57
The Americas (including the Caribbean)	55

The pandemic has jeopardized regional economies. The Caribbean region, for example, is impacted because of the globally imposed travel restrictions to curtail the spread of the virus. This region is highly tourism-dependent (Pentelow & Scott, 2011) and with no cruise shipping, limited flights as well as related tourism activities, business operations have been impacted. Since March 2020, tourist arrivals have drastically declined by 11.1 million, representing an over 65 per cent decrease in comparison to the previous year with 32 million arrivals (Turner, 2021). The USA, Canada and Europe are the main source markets for the region and with most airports and seaports closed during 2020, tourism arrivals drastically declined and severely impacted the sub-sectors such as the accommodation sector (ECLAC, 2020a). The pandemic has had a direct negative impact on tourism's contribution to gross domestic product (GDP) growth in the Caribbean and it is projected that for 2020, there will be a decrease of between 6.6 to 8.5 per cent (Bárcena, 2020).

The impact of COVID-19 at the country-level is similar. One primary example is that of Jamaica, a popular destination in the Caribbean region which in 2019 received approximately 4.3 million visitors including stopover arrivals (2.7 million) and cruise passengers (1.6 million) with an overall tourism spend of US$3.64 billion. An increase to 4.6 million visitors was forecasted for the fiscal year 2020 to 2021 with corresponding earnings of US$4.25 billion (Sinclair-Maragh, 2020). This was, however, not realized due to the onset of the pandemic and the corresponding global travel restrictions. This makes it impossible for the industry to maintain the 170,000 direct jobs and contribute its usual 10 per cent to the country's GDP.

Other destinations are likewise affected by the pandemic. Malaysia, for example, has been severely impacted. A major portion of its tourists are from China and not having this source market led to the cancellation of many tours (Foo et al., 2021). The airline industry was the hardest hit when a travel ban was instituted by the Malaysian government and hotel room reservations were also cancelled leading to the displacement of workers (Foo et al., 2021). This situation is mirrored in Australia, with the emerging Chinese and Indian markets no longer travelling (Ghosh, 2020). While a country like Taiwan was able to successfully manage the spread of the infection (Lin et al., 2020), its tourism services were negatively impacted.

The loss to tourism businesses is further exacerbated by recurring costs. Even when tourism businesses such as hotels and attractions are closed they are incurring costs to include security, maintenance, loans and mortgages, thus the urge to restart operations. Although destinations started reopening their borders during the summer months of 2020, the WHO warned that there was "no evidence" that people who have recovered from COVID-19 and have anti-bodies are protected from a second coronavirus infection (UN News, 2020). It was feared that an early reopening of national borders could result in a second wave of the viral infection due to the global transportation network.

By 1 September 2020, 52 per cent of the 217 destinations to include Jamaica, Jordan, Nigeria and Nepal eased their travel restrictions. This facilitated the reopening of tourism businesses in those countries (UNWTO, 2020b). Other destinations prolonged their border control but by the end of 2020, the global tourism industry showed some improvement with 70 per cent of them easing travel restrictions (UNWTO, 2020b). These destinations included Zimbabwe, the Cayman Islands and St. Kitts & Nevis (Sinclair-Maragh, 2020). Countries such as Saudi Arabia did not reopen its borders to international tourists until January 2021.

Although there was a brief recovery during the summer months of 2020, travel restrictions were reintroduced by some destinations at the start of 2021. Some of these destinations are within the European Union (Bonney-Cox, 2021) and extended this health safety measure due to the surge of a new variant of the coronavirus which was deemed more contagious and dangerous. Based on this emergence, there are concerns about tourism's outlook as a return to pre-pandemic levels is not anticipated before 2023 (OECD, 2020b).

Social impacts of COVID-19 on tourism

This section will provide an overview of three categorized impacts of COVID-19 on tourism.

Advanced vulnerability of women employed in the tourism industry

Women are overrepresented in many of the industries that are hardest hit by the virus. These include food service, retail and entertainment. Globally, 40 per cent of all employed women (510 million) actually work in hard-hit sectors. This is higher than the 36.6 per cent men employed in this category (UNWomen, 2020). This is representative of the tourism industry which employs more females than males with 54 per cent of persons employed being women. Ostensibly, this is because tourism offers flexible working hours and part-time job opportunities for women (ECLAC, 2020a). In highly dependent tourism regions such as the Caribbean and Latin America, the accommodation and food service sectors predominantly employ women. In the Caribbean, 13 per cent women compared to the 7.4 per cent men are employed in these sectors and in Latin America, 9.3 per cent women compared to 3.4 per cent men are likewise employed in these activities (ECLAC, 2020a). Overall, women represent approximately 62 per cent of employment in accommodation and food service activities in the Caribbean and 60 per cent in Latin America (ECLAC, 2020a). Table 11.2 shows the percentage of women employed in the accommodation and food service sectors in tourism dependent countries.

Table 11.2   Percentage representation of women employed in the accommodation and food service sectors

Tourism destinations	Percentage women employed
Bolivia	79
Honduras	76
Peru	76
El Salvador	75
Guyana	75
Nicaragua	73
Guatemala	71

Source: ECLAC (2020a)

Although women represent the majority of the tourism workforce they earn less than men and they work in low-level or low-paid employment (Hutchings et al., 2020). The tendency for women to earn less than men shows their precarious economic security. They also face unstable working conditions (ECLAC, 2020a) and are left unprotected with no social protection such as pension, healthcare and unemployment insurance (UNWomen, 2020). Not only are these matters a concern but unpaid care and the burden of domestic work have drastically increased as more women are staying at home due to the pandemic. These situations are likely to cause mental and emotional challenges. Studies have confirmed that women are more likely to be affected by anxiety, depression and distress (Lai et al., 2020).

Despite the gender gaps, Sinclair-Maragh (2017) posits that women are able to take care of their families and communities because by nature they are caring and sensitive. The tourism industry has also been a vehicle to empower and advance women, creating independence for them (Bolles, 2023) although oftentimes they are employed in lower quality jobs (Santero-Sanchez et al., 2015). Nonetheless, some women have advanced to top management positions, therefore changing the tendency of gender inequality. For instance, in Latin America, 51 per cent of tourism businesses are managed by women with Nicaragua and Panama having 70 per cent (World Bank, 2017). Other women have achieved financial independence by owning their own business (Movono & Dahles, 2017).

With tourism businesses being more prone to shut down during the pandemic, employees are further exposed to layoffs and pay cuts (ECLAC, 2020b). Women may be more vulnerable than men as they tend to earn less and have less secure jobs than men. Not being able to obtain a reliable income due to the loss of livelihoods is likely to cause women to be in dire straits. According to UNWomen (2020), they are bearing the brunt of the economic and social fallout of COVID-19. The situation is even worse for women who are poor and marginalized as they face a higher risk of COVID-19 transmission and fatalities (UNWomen, 2020).

Of the 96 million people predicted to experience extreme poverty by 2021, 47 million (49 per cent) will be female, women and girls. This means that more women will be pushed into extreme poverty than their male counterparts, resulting in the widening of the gender-poverty gap. Consequently, the total number of females (women and girls) living on US$1.90 or less will be 435 million (UNWomen, 2020). In terms of age, it is forecasted that women between the ages of 25 and 34 will be most exposed to extreme poverty. This age group is usually at the height of their productive and family formation period.

Further marginalization of rural tourism communities

Tourism is likely to generate a lot of social costs to the local community because of the COVID-19 pandemic (Qiu et al., 2020). This occurred at a time when destinations were looking forward to the celebration of the year 2020 as the one for rural community development with the UNWTO leading the charge. The intended focus was on the role of tourism in providing opportunities to rural communities and preserving the cultural and natural heritage (UNWTO, 2020b).

Rural communities are vulnerable to exclusion, racism, xenophobia, stigmatization and discrimination (Dubey et al., 2020). They are often marginalized from lack of employment opportunities, digital / technology divide, lower income levels and an ageing population (UNWTO, 2020c). Therefore, the aim of the 2020 celebration was to integrate and empower rural communities as well as indigenous people and many other historically marginalized populations in tourism development across the globe.

According to the UNWTO (2020b), rural areas are the hardest hit from the pandemic. The impact is particularly felt among the younger generation who did not migrate from their community because of the opportunities provided by way of tourism activities and corresponding business ventures. Tourism is one of the main sources of employment and income generation for many of these areas. This is because residents take advantage of their agricultural resources as a pull factor for tourists (Vargas & Duarte, 2011). Rural areas are also not equipped with health system capital and are further impacted by the virus because they may not be adjacent to municipal areas where health services are available (OECD, 2020c).

In some forms of tourism such as those that are nature-oriented and community-based, local residents are involved in the delivery of tourism products and services. This allows them to create wealth and improve their well-being (UNWTO, n.d.). The lack of tourism activities resulting from travel restrictions and closure of borders has impacted these residents. Tourism destinations such as those in the Latin America and Caribbean region are known for rural community tourism (Ortiz & Solo, 2009), hence the severity of the impact of COVID-19 on tourism in these areas.

Table 11.3   COVID-19 cases, deaths and mortality in Latin American
countries as of 1 May 2021

Country	Cases	Deaths	Case-fatality (%)	Death/100K /pop.
Argentina	2,977,363	63,865	2.1	142.12
Bolivia	303,732	12,951	4.3	112.49
Brazil	14,659,011	403,781	2.8	192.32
Chile	1,198,245	3,923	1.6	140.77
Colombia	2,859,724	3,720	2.6	146.45
Costa Rica	250,991	3,231	1.3	64.01
El Salvador	69,198	2,124	3.1	32.91
Ecuador	381,862	18,631	4.9	107.24
Guatemala	227,671	7,524	3.3	45.32
Honduras	212,233	5,281	2.5	54.19
Mexico	2,344,755	216,907	9.3	170.02
Nicaragua	6,898	182	2.6	2.70
Panama	364,576	6,232	1.7	146.76
Paraguay	279,077	6,385	2.3	90.64
Peru	1,799,445	61,447	3.4	189.10
Uruguay	198,428	2,616	1.3	82.13
Venezuela	197,683	2,136	1.1	7.49

Source: Johns Hopkins University of Medicine Coronavirus Resource Center (2021)

The Latin America region has been devastated by extremely high rates of
infection and deaths (CRS, 2021). As indicated in Table 11.3, Brazil shows
the highest rate of infection and case fatalities. Tourism in the rural areas of
this country usually provides new opportunities for small farmers as well as
alternative employment and income levels for rural residents (Campagnolla &
da Silva, 1999). In other countries such as Guatemala and Mexico, indigenous
communities are highly visited. Residents usually supply craft items, food and
beverage, as well as provide accommodation facilities. Residents in Colombia
work in the ecotourism areas, providing guide and receptionist services (Ortiz
& Solo, 2009). The loss of income in these rural communities is likely to drive
them into poverty. For the Caribbean region, the rates of infection and deaths

have been low (CHTA, 2021), but the impact of the disease is likewise devastating to the industry.

Approximately 90 per cent of countries closed their World Heritage Sites at the start of the pandemic. Many of these sites are located in tourism-dependent communities (UNWTO, n.d.). By mid-March 2021, 50 per cent of the natural and cultural World Heritage Sites in the 167 countries with properties on the United Nations Educational, Scientific and Cultural Organization (UNESCO) World Heritage List were opened, 22 per cent remained closed and 28 per cent partially opened (UNESCO, 2021). This has impacted the local cottage industries since their market sources have diminished (UNWTO, n.d.).

It is evident that COVID-19 has drastically affected community involvement in tourism, particularly among indigenous and ethnic groups. Human relations are usually generated from the visits of tourists to enjoy their environment, nature, culture, and production among other offerings (Ortiz & Solo, 2009). With the decline in visitors/tourists, the social fabric of the communities is threatened. This is because tourism strengthens the social fabric of rural communities through the provision of economic and socio-cultural benefits. Tourism creates community cohesion and promotes pride among the residents (Reid, 2004). The spike in the infection is also likely to impact plans for rural community tourism development. Sinclair-Maragh (2020) predicts that this is likely to be the case in Jamaica where the government had intended to create a re-imagined tourism that will offer the most authentic Jamaica experiences for visitors.

Unusual psychosocial challenges faced by tourism stakeholders

Heymann (2004) postulates that aside from environmental and economic factors, there are social factors linked to a host of human activities. The challenges for tourism stakeholders as they strive to prevent and control the daily threat of the infectious disease include their response and adherence to the health and safety protocols and disaster risk management legislations that have been implemented by various governments.

Although recommended by the CDC, Simon et al. (2021) postulate that social distancing in itself has resulted in psychological stress. By nature, human beings need socialization or contact with others. This is particularly so for older adults for whom activities serve to preserve their quality of life (Vigolo, 2017). Meeting new people and socialization are among their travel motivators (Hsu et al., 2007). They often treat themselves by taking a vacation and tourism is a means by which this segment of tourists increase their participation in society (Vigolo, 2017). The recreational, nostalgic and educational tourism activities provide pleasurable experiences for them (Fleischer & Pizam, 2002). With the travel restrictions, older adults are unable to travel as they would normally do, and without face-to-face interaction they are more vulnerable to loneliness which in turn impacts their mental, cognitive and social health (Vernooij-Dassen et al., 2020). COVID-19 is therefore causing older people to be more anxious, irritable, angry and to experience undue stress (Lee et al., 2005). Those with cognitive decline may become more anxious, agitated and socially withdrawn (Doraiswamy et al., 2020). In general, human beings experience emotional positives by travelling, meeting new people, and experiencing new and different things.

Social distancing is not only creating negative psychosocial issues but is closely related to an additional economic burden and financial loss which cause further emotional trauma (Sigala, 2020; Dubey et al., 2020). COVID-19 has caused an increase in anxiety and distress across various demographic segments. There is public anxiety regarding illness and death caused by the virus (Cucinotta & Vanelli, 2020) as well as an increase in the fear of viral contamination (Dubey et al., 2020). Females are believed to be at greater risk of the fear of viral contamination than their male counterparts and this has caused severe anxiety and intolerance of uncertainty. Females are also more fearful of social distancing than males and according to Fedorenko et al. (2021), fearing the negative consequences of social distancing can cause distress such as severe depression. Bereaved families and friends are also experiencing psychosocial issues (Dubey et al., 2020). The overall fear of the virus, "coronaphobia", can result in psychiatric health issues which may be more damaging in the long term than the virus itself (Dubey et al., 2020).

The introduction of COVID-19 tests and vaccinations aimed at reducing the effect of COVID-19 has also brought on fears and anxiety on both the demand and supply sides of tourism. In January 2020, the USA instituted a protocol for residents who upon returning to the country test positive for COVID-19. This is likely to cause some anxiety among travellers through the fear of being corona positive (The New Indian Express, 2020). With the USA being a source market for many destinations, this could be a possible barrier to travel.

The COVID-19 infection can be spread by inbound tourism to destinations (Vaishar & Šťastná, 2022). The instituted quarantine measures by destinations require tourists to isolate themselves for a period up to fourteen days to curtail the spread of the disease. This can have an impact on their mental health and well-being resulting in irritability, anger, confusion, frustration, loneliness, boredom, denial, anxiety and depression (Brooks et al., 2020).

With respect to vaccinations, some Americans are hesitant about the vaccine as they have low trust in both the COVID-19 vaccine development and approval processes (Gursoy & Chi, 2021). They are also waiting for society to get back to normal before they travel, dine out or stay at a hotel. Since the duration of the pandemic is unknown, the waiting period can induce anxiety and distress especially with the worry that there could be an upsurge or new variants of the virus. Forty per cent of Americans have already reported symptoms of anxiety and depression, an increase from 10 per cent (Panchal et al., 2020). This is significant as the USA is a main market source for global tourism. The WHO, however, advises that fear emanating from the unpredictable spread of the virus is a natural psychological response to the randomly changing environment (Dubey et al., 2020).

COVID-19 has brought social costs that are borne by residents of tourist destinations. For instance, the lack of employment as a consequence of the pandemic has led to an increase in poaching and looting (UNWTO, n.d.). There is also pressure on the local healthcare system (Qiu et al., 2020) and reduced corporate philanthropy from the industry (Chen et al., 2022). Community events, sporting activities and social gatherings that are likewise attended by visitors are prohibited. Not being able to attend and participate in these activities is likely to result in psychosocial issues.

The resulting death rate from the pandemic has a profound impact on mental health, particularly anxiety and depression (Simon et al., 2020). Table 11.4 illustrates the percentage of declared cases in destinations for November 2020. This will impact internal travel and tourism as China has become one of the leading source markets for global tourism, Italy and France are renowned European destinations, and as a developing country, tourism is important to Chile's economy.

Social adaptation for subsequent changes

Tenets of the social adaptation theory can be employed in mitigating the social impacts of COVID-19 on tourism. This is because social adaptation can be significant when social change affects important aspects of an individual's life (Prokhorov, 1979). These social changes include migration, changes in age, rapid industrial development and major shifts from rural to urban areas. The pandemic can now be added to this list as according to UNDESA (2020), COVID-19 has caused not only human and economic crises but also a social crisis resulting in significant changes to people's lives. The social exchange theory is also applicable to tourism since according to Hospitality Net (2020), tourism in itself has a profound impact on society as it can interfere with the

Table 11.4   Percentage of declared COVID-19 cases in destinations for November 2020

Country	Tourism destinations	Percentage
China	Hubei Province	83.0
Italy	Lombardy	47.0
France	Île-de-France	34.0
	Grand Est	15.0
USA	New York	14.6
	Texas	8.0
Canada	Quebec	61.0
	Ontario	31.0
Chile	Metropolitan Santiago	70.0
Brazil	Sao Paulo	25.0
India	Maharashtra	21.0
Russia	Moscow	24.0

Source: OECD (2020a)

well-being of residents in the tourist destinations by exacerbating public health crises.

This section recommends the application of the social adaptation theory in mitigating the impacts of COVID-19 and driving consequential changes particularly as it relates to the advanced vulnerability of women employed in the industry, further marginalization of rural tourism communities, and the unusual psychosocial challenges faced by tourism stakeholders.

Mitigating the vulnerability of women employed in the tourism industry

Although there are advocacies for women in terms of better lives and well-being as well as equity, these need to be increased and strengthened during the pandemic. Women are known to be sensitive and caring (Cancian & Oliker, 2000). They have a positive attitude towards tourism and will support its development because of the economic benefits to be derived from it (Nunkoo & Gursoy, 2012). The economic benefits gained from employment or entrepreneurial activities help to meet their financial needs (Sinclair-Maragh, 2017). Being displaced from gainful employment due to the pandemic will have an effect on them as women contribute to the socio-economic well-being of their family and community.

The social adaptation theory suggests that an individual can survive in conditions of constant changes in society (Vikhman et al., 2018). With this premise, women should be encouraged and given the required resources as they face the ordeals brought on by the pandemic. Although the governments' resources are stretched from the fight against COVID-19, it is important to strengthen community healthcare programmes with mental health initiatives. These programmes are to provide the required care for women who are facing despondency from the loss of jobs, bereavement and other situations. Government intervention in terms of stimulus or incentive packages will be important for women with entrepreneurial or artisan endeavours. They will have lost their market source and face recurring costs such as loans and rent.

The tourism business entities, in which these women were employed, though facing their own macro situations could also be a part of the survival mechanism for them. Some of these businesses may be operating at low levels but could consider a rotation schedule for staff so that all will benefit. With change being an inherent element in social life and activities (Prastacos et al., 2002), Anderson (1994) points out that although adjustments are difficult, the individual can be "reborn" by the experience. Including women in tourism recovery discussions would contribute to the Sustainable Development Goal (SDG) of achieving gender equality.

Reducing the marginalization of rural tourism communities

Lack of tourism activities in rural communities has resulted in loss of income as well as social costs such as poverty and further marginalization of the community. It is proposed that social adaptation activities can be used to mitigate this situation. Zhao et al. (2014) found that the social adaptation activities of Multinational Corporations (MNCs) had significant positive effects in mitigating public crises. This is because the MNCs paid attention to the social components of their business operation to avoid public crises. It is believed that a balanced approach with economic and social initiatives will avoid both public crises and sustain growth in emerging markets. This finding is crucial in suggesting a social adaptation mitigation strategy for rural community-based tourism operations.

In addition, Vaishar and Šťastná (2022) find that direct restrictions regarding border closure only slightly affected rural tourism in the south Moravian region of Czechia. The restrictions had in fact created opportunities for the development of rural tourism. This is because the local business ventures were mainly supported by domestic tourists for second housing amongst other activities such as cycling and hiking. Of the 246,000 at risk jobs, 5,700 of these are in this region and there was no significant reduction in employment. Although it is unlikely that domestic tourism will compensate for the decline in international tourism flow, especially in destinations that rely heavily on this market (Vaishar & Šťastná, 2022), rural community tourism destinations could mitigate against their situation by attracting the local/domestic market.

There are local residents who due to restrictions are unable to travel overseas. They might still want to get away from their home and work space even for a short stay in bed and breakfast facilities which are least likely to have a large number of visitors. Rural communities that offer ecotourism can also repackage their product to include more family-based engagement and activities with nature. This could be an option for the usually large tour groups and would prevent large numbers of people gathering at the same time. These rural community tourism ventures require the intervention of government and local tourism agencies to help them in restructuring and repositioning their businesses at this time to bolster the micro-economy. This makes it imperative for residents to be included in the recovery strategies (Qiu et al., 2020).

The UNWTO (2021c) supports this view and has partnered with the World Indigenous Tourism Alliance (WINTA) to draw on the cultural diversity and knowledge of indigenous people. This is to create innovative experiences and new business opportunities for tourism destinations and local communities. This initiative under the UNWTO Inclusive Recovery Guide (Issue #4: Indigenous Communities) is the fourth set of guidelines established to address the socio-cultural impacts of COVID-19 placing indigenous communities at the centre of the recovery plans. These solutions are geared towards socio-economic empowerment of indigenous people through tourism, with the intention for them to transition from "assisting to enabling" in areas such as indigenous entrepreneurship and in fostering digital literacy for operating tourism businesses. The initiatives are also geared at strengthening their skills and building capacities as well as acknowledging the relevance of indigenous people by destination authorities and the overall tourism sector.

Alleviating the psychosocial challenges faced by tourism stakeholders

Stakeholders on both the demand and supply side of the business of tourism are being impacted by the COVID-19 pandemic. The travel restrictions, business lockdowns, health and safety protocols and vaccination among other factors are affecting their psychological and social stability.

In general, people are not fully adapting to the protocols and new norms and this is understandable. Social adaptation relates to how an individual or group conforms to the systems of norms and values in a given society, class or social group. It indicates that one may not be socially conformed to the systems of norms because of the controlled environment, for example, social pressure and state regulation (Prokhorov, 1979). It is imperative that all stakeholders have a clear understanding of the virus and its impact on every aspect of life. Each individual has a responsibility in the fight against the spread of the virus so that it can be diminished for return to normalcy as soon as possible. Reassuring the destination's residents on the importance of adhering to the regulations for the pandemic is very important. Public education is an effort to build public trust and will therefore be very important at the destination level.

Although social adaptation is a social process Vikhman et al. (2018) point out that it is closely connected with the technological environment. The use of virtual technology will be a very critical component in tourism delivery and recovery. It is important to reimage tourism with digital technology and "take the experience to the market". Virtual tour packages can be sold through travel intermediaries to the various market segments, particularly to older adults who are among the most vulnerable group to the pandemic. These can include virtual tours to heritage sites, museums and ecotourism sites with nature-based activities by "e-tourers". Nature-based activities are known to promote health and well-being (Iqbal & Mansell, 2021). E-tourers would be able to meet other people on the virtual platform and this would also be very good for the older adult market. This initiative would be in keeping with the proposal by Lloyd-Sherlock et al. (2020) for the needs of older people to be prioritized in response to the pandemic.

The virtual platform could provide hyperlinks to local crafts and produce which e-tourers can purchase for shipment to their location. Local tourism agencies could establish cooperative farming groups to supply their local produce which could be exported to the countries of the source markets. This will increase agricultural production for farmers in rural areas, satisfy the needs of virtual and potential visitors and provide foreign exchange for the destination and country. Social adaptation suggests that an individual can adapt to changes in the environment, despite the economic ills, social control, state regulation and threat of psychosocial manifestations (Prokhorov, 1979).

Conclusion

The purpose of this chapter is to examine the social implications of the coronavirus for tourism by assessing the impacts particularly relating to the further marginalization of rural communities, advanced vulnerability of women and the unusual psychosocial challenges faced by tourism stakeholders. The chapter proposes the use of social adaptation theory to drive subsequent changes during the COVID-19 pandemic. The use of social adaptation theory to mitigate these issues can also be applicable to the sustainable development of tourism after this period, which further studies can address.

It is apparent that COVID-19 is directly impacting tourism, not only in terms of economics but also the social aspects of people's lives as a result of job loss, reduced business operation and subsequent loss of revenue and the instituted health and safety regulations and protocols. It is imperative that tourism destinations reimagine their tourism offerings and recovery strategies during this time so that they will be better able to deliver when the pandemic passes. Data gathering and documentation will be important for the proper mechanisms to be put in place to ameliorate the conditions of rural communities, women and affected tourism stakeholders.

The application of social adaptation theory to mitigate the situation of women employed in the industry, reduce the marginalization of rural tourism communities and alleviate the psychosocial challenges being faced by tourism stakeholders has the potential to assist in transforming tourism needs as per the priorities established by the UNWTO (n.d.), mitigate socio-economic impacts on livelihoods, boost competitiveness and build resilience, advance innovation and digital transformation of tourism, and foster sustainability and green growth. Future studies could empirically analyse these indicators.

Being a new area of study, references had to be drawn from websites as it was difficult to find journal articles with empirical findings on the subject matter. These references are nonetheless useful for this review and analysis. Future research can quantitatively analyse the relationship between the coronavirus and tourism with social indicators as well as economic and cultural measures.

References

Ala'a A., & Albattat A. (2019). Current issues in tourism: Disease transmission as a potential risk for travellers. *Review of Integrative Business and Economics Research*, *8*(4), 103–114.

Anderson, L. E. (1994). A new look at an old construct: Cross-cultural adaptation. *International Journal of Intercultural Relations*, *18*(3), 293–328.

Ayalon, L. (2020). There is nothing new under the sun: Ageism and intergenerational tension in the age of the COVID-19 outbreak. *International Psychogeriatrics*, *1*(4). https://doi.org/10.1017/S1041610220000575.

Ayittey, F. K., Ayittey, M. K., Chiwero, N. B., Kamasah, J. S., & Dzuvor, C. (2020). Economic impacts of Wuhan 2019-nCoV on China and the world. *Journal of Medical Virology*, *92*(5), 473–475.

Bakar, N. A., & Rosbi, S. (2020). Effect of Coronavirus disease (COVID-19) to tourism industry. *International Journal of Advanced Engineering Research and Science*, *7*(4), 189–193.

Bárcena, A. (2020). *The Caribbean Outlook: Toward Recovery and Resilience Building in the Caribbean Post COVID-19*. https://periododesesiones.cepal.org/38/sites/default/files/presentations/201026_final_caribbean_outlook_con_mapa_completo.pdf.

Bartik, A. W., Bertrand, M., Cullen, Z. B., Glaeser, E. L., Luca, M., & Stanton, C. T. (2020). *How Are Small Businesses Adjusting to COVID-19? Early Evidence from a Survey* (No. w26989). National Bureau of Economic Research.

Bartlett, E. (2020). Rural area tourism to provide key opportunities for post COVID-19 economic recovery. *Jamaica Observer*, 7 October. https://www.mot.gov.jm/news-releases/rural-area-tourism-provide-key-opportunities-post-covid-19-economic-recovery-bartlett.

Baum, T., & Hai, N. T. T. (2020). Hospitality, tourism, human rights and the impact of COVID 19. *International Journal of Contemporary Hospitality Management*, *32*(7), 2397–2407.

Bolles, A. L. (2023). Women's work and tourism in Negril, the capital of casual. In F. J. Riemer (Ed.), *Re-centering Women in Tourism: Anti-Colonial Feminist Studies* (pp. 77–88). Lanham, MD: Lexington Books.

Bonney-Cox, S. (2021). European travel restrictions: Nonessential travel curbed. https://www.dw.com/en/european-travel-restrictions-nonessential-travel-curbed/a-56350272.

Brooks, S. K., Webster, R. K., Smith, L. E., Woodland, L., Wessely, S., Greenberg, N., & Rubin, G. J. (2020). The psychological impact of quarantine and how to reduce it: Rapid review of the evidence. *The Lancet*, *395*(10227), 912–920.

Campagnolla, C., & da Silva, J. G. (1999). Tourism in the rural area as a new opportunity for small farmers. *Embrapa Meio Ambiente-Outras publicações científicas (ALICE)*.

Cancian, F. M., & Oliker, S. J. (2000). *Caring and Gender*. Thousand Oaks, CA: Pine Forge Press.

Caribbean Hotel and Tourism Association / CHTA (2021). Health safety vigilance and vaccine key to Caribbean tourism recovery. https://businessviewcaribbean.com/health-safety-diligence-vaccines-key-caribbeans-tourism-recovery/.

CDC COVID-19 Response Team (2020). Severe outcomes among patients with coronavirus disease 2019 (COVID-19) United States, February 12–March 16, 2020. *Morbidity and Mortality Weekly Report*, *69*(12), 343–346.

Centers for Disease Control and Prevention / CDC (2021). *Ebola and Marburg. Travelers' Health.* https://wwwnc.cdc.gov/travel/diseases/ebola.

Chen, H., Liu, S., Liu, X., & Yang, D. (2022). Adversity tries friends: A multilevel analysis of corporate philanthropic response to the local spread of COVID-19 in China. *Journal of Business Ethics, 177,* 585–612.

Congressional Research Service (CRS) (2021). *Global Economic Effects of Covid-19.* CRS Report R46270. Washington, DC: Congressional Research Service. https://sgp.fas.org/crs/row/R46270.pdf.

Cucinotta, D., & Vanelli, M. (2020). WHO declares COVID-19 a pandemic. *Acta Bio Medica: Atenei Parmensis, 91*(1), 157.

del Rio-Chanona, R. M., Mealy, P., Pichler, A., Lafond, F., & Farmer, J. D. (2020). Supply and demand shocks in the COVID-19 pandemic: An industry and occupation perspective. *Oxford Review of Economic Policy, 36*(Supplement_1), S94–S137.

Doraiswamy, S., Cheema, S., & Mamtani, R. (2020). Older people and epidemics: A call for empathy. *Age and Ageing, 49*(3), 493.

Dubey, S., Biswas, P., Ghosh, R., Chatterjee, S., Dubey, M. J., Chatterjee, S., Lahiri, D., & Lavie, C. J. (2020). Psychosocial impact of COVID-19. *Diabetes & Metabolic Syndrome, 14*(5), 779–788.

Economic Commission for Latin America and the Caribbean / ECLAC (2020a). *The Impact of the COVID-19 Pandemic on the Tourism Sector in Latin America and the Caribbean and Options for a Sustainable and Resilient Recovery.* International Trade Series No. 157. Santiago: ECLAC.

Economic Commission for Latin America and the Caribbean / ECLAC (2020b). *The Social Challenge in Times of COVID-19.* Santiago: ECLAC.

Fedorenko, E. J., Kibbey, M. M., Contrada, R. J., & Farris, S. G. (2021). Psychosocial predictors of virus and social distancing fears in undergraduate students living in a US COVID-19 "hotspot". *Cognitive Behaviour Therapy, 50*(3), 217–233.

Fleischer, A., & Pizam, A. (2002). Tourism constraints among Israeli seniors. *Annals of Tourism Research, 29*(1), 106–123.

Foo, L. P., Chin, M. Y., Tan, K. L., & Phuah, K. T. (2020). The impact of COVID-19 on tourism industry in Malaysia. *Current Issues in Tourism, 24*(19), 2735–2739.

Freedman, D. O., & Leder, K. (2005). Influenza: Changing approaches to prevention and treatment in travelers. *Journal of Travel Medicine, 12*(1), 36–44.

Gaffney, C., & Eeckels, B. (2020). COVID-19 and tourism risk in the Americas. *Journal of Latin American Geography, 19*(3), 308–313.

Ghosh, S. (2020). Asymmetric impact of COVID-19 induced uncertainty on inbound Chinese tourists in Australia: Insights from nonlinear ARDL model. *Quantitative Finance and Economics, 4*(2), 343–364.

Gursoy, D., & Chi, C. (2020). Effects of COVID-19 pandemic on hospitality industry: Review of the current situations and a research agenda. *Journal of Hospitality Marketing & Management, 29*(5), 527–529.

Gursoy, D., & Chi, C. (2021). Celebrating 30 years of excellence amid the COVID-19 pandemic: An update on the effects of COVID-19 pandemic and COVID-19 vaccines on hospitality industry. Overview of the current situation and a research agenda. *Journal of Hospitality Marketing & Management, 30*(3), 277–281.

Henderson, J. C. (2007). Corporate social responsibility and tourism: Hotel companies in Phuket, Thailand, after the Indian Ocean tsunami. *International Journal of Hospitality Management, 26*(1), 228–239.

Heymann, D. L. (2004). Effects of social, environmental and economic factors on current and future patterns of infectious diseases. *Interactions Between Global Change and Human Health (Scripta Varia), 106,* 290–303.

Hospitality Net (2020). Counting the social costs of tourism in the COVID-19 era in Asia. https://www.hospitalitynet.org/news/4100143.html.

Hsu, C. H., Cai, L. A., & Wong, K. K. (2007). A model of senior tourism motivations Anecdotes from Beijing and Shanghai. *Tourism Management, 28*(5), 1262–1273.

Hutchings, K., Moyle, C. L., Chai, A., Garofano, N., & Moore, S. (2020). Segregation of women in tourism employment in the APEC region. *Tourism Management Perspectives, 34,* 100655.

Iqbal, A., & Mansell, W. (2021). A thematic analysis of multiple pathways between nature engagement activities and well-being. *Frontiers in Psychology, 12,* 862.

Johns Hopkins University of Medicine Coronavirus Resource Center (2021). *Mortality Analyses.* https://coronavirus.jhu.edu/data/mortality.

Kahle, L. R., & Homer, P. M. (1985). Physical attractiveness of the celebrity endorser: A social adaptation perspective. *Journal of Consumer Research, 11*(4), 954–961.

Kuo, H. I., Chen, C. C., Tseng, W. C., Ju, L. F., & Huang, B. W. (2008). Assessing impacts of SARS and Avian Flu on international tourism demand to Asia. *Tourism Management, 29*(5), 917–928.

Lai, J., Ma, S., Wang, Y., Cai, Z., Hu, J., Wei, N., & Hu, S. (2020). Factors associated with mental health outcomes among health care workers exposed to coronavirus disease 2019. *JAMA Network Open, 3*(3), e203976.

Lee, S., Chan, L. Y., Chau, A. M., Kwok, K. P., & Kleinman, A. (2005). The experience of SARS-related stigma at Amoy Gardens. *Social Science & Medicine, 61*(9), 2038–2046.

Lin, C., Braund, W. E., Auerbach, J., Chou, J. H., Teng, J. H., Tu, P., & Mullen, J. (2020). Policy decisions and use of information technology to fight coronavirus disease, Taiwan. *Emerging Infectious Diseases, 26*(7), 1506.

Liu, M., Gao, Y., Yuan, Y., Yang, K., Shi, S., Zhang, J., & Tian, J. (2020). Efficacy and safety of integrated traditional Chinese and Western medicine for corona virus disease 2019 (COVID-19): A systematic review and meta-analysis. *Pharmacological Research, 158,* 104896.

Lloyd-Sherlock, P. G., Kalache, A., McKee, M., Derbyshire, J., Geffen, L., Casas, F. G. O., & Gutierrez, L. M. (2020). WHO must prioritise the needs of older people in its response to the Covid-19 pandemic. *BMJ, 368.*

Medical News Today (2020). Comparing COVID-19 with previous pandemics. https:// www .medicalnewstoday .com/ articles/ comparing -covid -19 -with -previous -pandemics.

Movono, A., & Dahles, H. (2017). Female empowerment and tourism: A focus on busi-nesses in a Fijian village. *Asia Pacific Journal of Tourism Research, 22*(6), 681–692.

National Center for Immunization and Respiratory Diseases (NCIRD), Division of Viral Diseases In Centers for Disease Control and Prevention (CDCP) (2020). *About COVID-19.* https://www.cdc.gov/coronavirus/2019-ncov/cdcresponse/about -COVID19.html.

Nunkoo, R., & Gursoy, D. (2012). Residents' support for tourism. *Annals of Tourism Research, 39,* 243–268.

Orendain, D. J. A., & Djalante, R. (2021). Ignored and invisible: Internally displaced persons (IDPs) in the face of COVID-19 pandemic. *Sustainability Science, 16*(1), 337–340.

Organisation for Economic Co-operation and Development / OECD (2020a). *Tourism Policy Responses to the Coronavirus (COVID-19).* 2 June. https:// www .oecd .org/

coronavirus/policy-responses/tourism-policy%20responses-to-the%20coronavirus-covid-19-6466aa20/.

Organisation for Economic Co-operation and Development / OECD (2020b). *Rebuilding Tourism for the Future: COVID 19 Policy Responses and Recovery.* https://www.oecd-ilibrary.org/social-issues-migration-health/rebuilding-tourism-for-the-future-covid-19-policy-responses-and-recovery_bced9859-en.

Organisation for Economic Co-operation and Development / OECD (2020c). *The Territorial Impact of COVID-19: Managing the Crisis across Levels of Government.* https://www.oecd-ilibrary.org/social-issues-migration-health/the-territorial-impact-of-covid-19-managing-the-crisis-and-recovery-across-levels-of-government_a2c6abaf-en.

Ortiz, D., & Solo, T. V. (2009). *Responsible and Sustainable Tourism: Lessons from Latin America and the Caribbean.* World Bank Responsible Tourism Series 142. Washington, DC: World Bank.

Panchal, N., Kamal, R., Orgera, K., Cox, C., Garfield, R., Hamel, L., & Chidambaram, P. (2020). *The Implications of COVID-19 for Mental Health and Substance Use.* San Francisco: Kaiser Family Foundation.

Pentelow, L., & Scott, D. J. (2011). Aviation's inclusion in international climate policy regimes: Implications for the Caribbean tourism industry. *Journal of Air Transport Management, 17*(3), 199–205.

Prastacos, G., Söderquist, K., Spanos, Y., & Van Wassenhove, L. (2002). An integrated framework for managing change in the new competitive landscape. *European Management Journal, 20*(1), 55–71.

Prokhorov, A. M. (1979). *Great Soviet Encyclopedia, Vol. 23.* London: Macmillan.

Qiu, R. T., Park, J., Li, S., & Song, H. (2020). Social costs of tourism during the COVID-19 pandemic. *Annals of Tourism Research, 84*, 102994.

Reid, S. (2004). The social consequences of rural events: The Inglewood Olive Festival. Conference paper. CAUTHE 2004: Creating Tourism Knowledge, 607.

Ren, S. Y., Gao, R. D., & Chen, Y. L. (2020). Fear can be more harmful than the severe acute respiratory syndrome coronavirus 2 in controlling the corona virus disease 2019 epidemic. *World Journal of Clinical Cases, 8*(4), 652.

Ritchie, B. W. (2004). Chaos, crises and disasters: A strategic approach to crisis management in the tourism industry. *Tourism Management, 25*(6), 669–683.

Saladino, A., Algeri, D., & Auriemma, V. (2020). The psychological and social impact of Covid 19: New perspectives of well-being. *Frontiers in Psychology.* https://doi.org/10.3389/fpsyg.2020.577684.

Santero-Sanchez, R., Segovia-Pérez, M., Castro-Nuñez, B., Figueroa-Domecq, C., & Talón Ballestero, P. (2015). Gender differences in the hospitality industry: A job quality index. *Tourism Management, 51*, 234–246.

Sigala, M. (2020). Tourism and COVID-19: Impacts and implications for advancing and resetting industry and research. *Journal of Business Research, 117*, 312–321.

Simon, N. M., Saxe, G. N., & Marmar, C. R. (2020). Mental health disorders related to COVID 19-related deaths. *JAMA, 324*(15), 1493–1494.

Sinclair-Maragh, G. (2017). Demographic analysis of residents' support for tourism development in Jamaica. *Journal of Destination Marketing & Management, 6*(1), 5–12.

Sinclair-Maragh, G. (2020). Tourism today. *Public Opinion.* http://publicopinion.news/author/gsinclair-maragh-phd/.

Škare, M., Soriano, D. R., & Porada-Rochoń, M. (2021). Impact of COVID-19 on the travel and tourism industry. *Technological Forecasting and Social Change, 163*, 120469.

The New Indian Express (2020). Coronavirus: The pandemic fear. https:// www .newindianexpress .com/ magazine/ 2020/ mar/ 29/ coronavirus -the -pandemic -of fear-2121950.html.

Tourism Industry Association of Canada / TIAC (2020). *State of Tourism in Canada during COVID-19 Dashboard 2.0. Elevating Canadian Experiences.* https://tiaaitc.ca/ _Library/Coronavirus_2020/State_of_Tourism_in_Canada_Dashboard_2_0_Oct ber_2020_EN.pdf.

Turner, M. (2021). Stats: Tourist arrivals to Caribbean dropped 65% in 2020. Caribbean. https:// www .travelagentcentral .com/ caribbean/ stats -tourist -arrivals -to -caribbean -dropped-65-2020.

United Nations Department of Economic and Social Affairs / UNDESA (2020). *Social Impact of COVID-19.* https://www.un.org/ development/ desa/ dspd/ 2020/ 04/ social -impact-of-covid-19/.

United Nations Educational, Scientific and Cultural Organization / UNESCO (2021). *Monitoring World Heritage Site Closures.* https://whc.unesco.org/en/news/2103.

United Nations News / UN News (2020). "No evidence" that recovered COVID-19 patients cannot be reinfected, says WHO. https:// news .un .org/ en/ story/ 2020/ 04/ 1062612.

United Nations World Tourism Organization / UNWTO (n.d.). Tourism and COVID-19: Unprecedented economic impacts. https:// www .unwto .org/ tourism -and-covid-19-unprecedented-economic-impacts.

United Nations World Tourism Organization / UNWTO (2020a). *World Tourism Barometer* No. 18.

United Nations World Tourism Organization / UNWTO (2020b). 70% of destinations have lifted travel restrictions, but global gap emerging. Eighth edition of the UNWTO Travel Restrictions Report. Madrid, Spain, 2 December.

United Nations World Tourism Organization / UNWTO (2020c). *Impact Assessment of the Covid-19 Outbreak on International Tourism.* Updated December 2020. https:// www .unwto .org/ impact -assessment -of -the -covid -19 -outbreak -on -international -tourism.

United Nations World Tourism Organization / UNWTO (2021a). Tourist arrivals down 87% in January 2021 as UNWTO calls for stronger coordination to restart tourism. https:// www .unwto .org/ news/ tourist -arrivals -down -87 -in -january -2021 -as-unwto-calls-for-stronger-coordination-to-restart-tourism.

United Nations World Tourism Organization / UNWTO (2021b). 2020: Worst year in tourism history with 1 billion fewer international arrivals. 28 January. https:// www .unwto .org/ news/ 2020 -worst -year -in -tourism -history -with -1 -billion -fewer -international-arrivals.

United Nations World Tourism Organization / UNWTO (2021c). *Empowering Indigenous Communities to Drive Tourism's Recovery.* Madrid, 21 May.

UNWomen (2020). COVID-19 and its economic toll on women: The story behind the numbers. https://www.unwomen.org/en/news/stories/2020/9/feature-covid-19 -economic-impacts-on-women.

Vaishar A., & Šťastná, M. (2022). Impact of the COVID-19 pandemic on rural tourism in Czechia: Preliminary considerations. *Current Issues in Tourism, 25*(2), 187–191.

Vargas, J. C., & Duarte, A. (2011). Potential for rural tourism in company Paso Jhú of the Piribebuy district, Department of Cordillera, Paraguay. *Investigación Agraria*, *13*, 113–117.

Velavan, T. P., & Meyer, C. G. (2020). The COVID-19 epidemic. *Tropical Medicine & International Health*, *25*(3), 278–280.

Vernooij-Dassen, M., Verhey, F., & Lapid, M. (2020). The risks of social distancing for older adults: A call to balance. *International Psychogeriatrics*, *32*(10), 1235–1237.

Vigolo, V. (2017). Older tourists' travel planning behavior. In *Older Tourist Behavior and Marketing Tools* (pp. 63–84). Cham: Springer.

Vikhman, V. V., Romm, M. V., & Vilberger, M. E. (2018, April). Phenomenon of social adaptation in modern socio-economic changes in society. *International Conference on Actual Issues of Mechanical Engineering (AIME 2018)* (pp. 612–617). Amsterdam: Atlantis Press.

Wilder-Smith, A. (2006). The severe acute respiratory syndrome: Impact on travel and tourism. *Travel Medicine and Infectious Disease*, *4*(2), 53–60.

World Bank (2017). *Tourism for Development: Women and Tourism Designing for Inclusion*. https:// documents1 .worldbank .org/ curated/ en/ 401321508245393514/ pdf/ 120477 -WP -PUBLIC -Weds -oct -18 -9am -ADD -SERIES -36p -IFCWomenandTourismfinal.pdf.

Zhao, M., Park, S. H., & Zhou, N. (2014). MNC strategy and social adaptation in emerging markets. *Journal of International Business Studies*, *45*(7), 842–861.

12 The contagious effect of COVID-19 on residents' perceptions about the sociocultural impacts of tourism

Manuela Guerreiro, Patrícia Pinto, Célia Ramos, João Filipe Marques, Milene Lança and Hio Kuan Lai

1 Introduction

The global pandemic crisis induced by COVID-19 took the planet by surprise. The pandemic dramatically affected tourism flows worldwide, even for well-established destinations such as the Algarve, in Portugal. During 2020, this region saw its tourist flows reduced to a minimum with all the evident economic and social effects. This situation affected not only the hospitality sector, which is experiencing an unprecedented economic crisis, but also local communities (Uğur & Akbıyık, 2020).

The pandemic also brought important challenges to tourism research and the way it relates to social and cultural life. Predictably, its impacts started to be studied immediately, namely the tourists' perspectives about the situation. Recent studies also confirm that, despite being aware of the risks arising from the presence of tourists in the communities (Qiu et al., 2020), residents tend to develop positive feelings regarding their return as their economic and sociocultural impacts are still considered positive (Farmaki et al., 2020). However, further research is needed to clarify residents' perceptions about tourism impacts before and during the COVID-19 pandemic (Joo et al., 2021).

Therefore, this study aims to explore and analyze residents' perceptions about the sociocultural impacts of tourism on a region strongly dependent on this activity, before and during the COVID-19 pandemic. Main results point out that the differences between "pre-COVID" (before the pandemic) and "during-COVID" (during the pandemic) perceptions about the positive and the negative sociocultural impacts of tourism are significant. These results can assist destination management organizations to monitor a recovery and design future pro-tourism decisions, allowing tourists to continue traveling and interacting with residents in tourism destinations such as the Algarve (Yang et al., 2021; UNWTO, 2020).

2   Literature review

2.1   The importance of analyzing residents' perceptions of tourism impacts to achieve sustainable tourism development

Tourism is a global industry with significant impacts on residents and their communities (Ap, 1992). The various impacts of tourism have been addressed in academic research since the beginning of the 1960s, including residents' perceptions about the economic, environmental and sociocultural dimensions. The examination of residents' perceptions of tourism impacts are heterogeneous and started from the positive tourism impacts in the early 1960s, then shifting the focus to the negative impacts in the 1970s. From the 1980s, a more balanced approach was established (Andereck & Vogt, 2000).

Residents' perceptions of tourism impacts (Sharpley, 2014) are crucial since residents are key stakeholders in achieving sustainable tourism development (Lundberg, 2017). Nevertheless, what the scientific literature lacks are studies on differential rates of tourism growth and its effects on host communities (Dioko, 2017). In an attempt to overcome this limitation, recent studies show that sustainable tourism development can only be reached through the incorporation of residents' perceptions of tourism impacts, especially the sociocultural impacts on local communities (Ribeiro et al., 2017) and, as Krippendorf (1987) argues, these impacts are so significant that they should be studied before anything else.

2.2   Residents' perceptions about the sociocultural impacts of tourism

Tourism is a social phenomenon that involves people moving away from their regular residence and temporarily staying in another place, where they interact with other people (Sharpley, 2014). In Graburn's (1989) view, it means that people move from the "ordinary/profane life" (daily life routines) to the "nonordinary/sacred life", provided by tourism. This liminal space-time allows tourists to behave in a completely different way (Thomassen, 2014). Such experiences induce situations of akrasia, during which moral values are suspended and behaviors change in an unjustified way, even for those who practice them (Fennell, 2015). It may affect not only tourists' behaviors, but also community residents, through their interactions with tourists (Sharpley, 2014).

Tourism may cause the disappearance of traditions, local and cultural identity, increase the crime rate, vandalism, prostitution, consumption of alcohol and narcotics, increase stress and conflicts between residents and visitors, causing disruption to residents' way of life. Therefore, residents may suffer from living in a tourism destination (Ribeiro et al., 2017). Nevertheless, tourism may also enhance festivals, activities and local traditions, improve residents' standard of living, enhance cultural exchanges, promote the preservation of cultural resources and residents' sense of security, and improve the destination's recognition, prestige and image (Ribeiro et al., 2017; Šegota et al., 2017). More recently, some authors highlight the rise of residents' social capital due to the contact with tourists (Zhang et al., 2021).

Residents' perceptions about the sociocultural impacts, like other tourism impacts, affect different dimensions, such as residents' perceptions of quality of life (QoL), residents' emotional solidarity with tourists, residents' involvement and dependence on the tourism sector, residents' attitudes towards tourism development and residents' support for tourism development (Moghavvemi et al., 2017; Ribeiro et al., 2018; Ribeiro et al., 2013; Uysal et al., 2016; Woo et al., 2015; Woosnam & Norman, 2010). These reasons justify the importance of analyzing residents' perceptions about the sociocultural impacts of tourism in their communities.

2.3 The effects of COVID-19 on residents' perceptions about the sociocultural impacts of tourism

The impacts of the COVID-19 pandemic on tourism and hospitality are unprecedented, wrecking the tourism industry all over the globe (Pham et al., 2021; Škare et al., 2021; Zhang et al., 2021), and probably changing the tourist psyche in the years to come (Kock et al., 2020). In fact, this pandemic is affecting not only tourists who are unable or restricted to travel at the moment (and may change fundamentally their behavior after the COVID era), but also local communities reliant on tourism as a way of survival (Uğur & Akbıyık, 2020).

As stated by Haywood (2020), whereas in pre-COVID times many communities demonstrated a "love-hate relationship" with tourism, considering its benefits and costs, now many people are calling for a more profound reassessment since economic revival has to be a top priority. However, it does not mean residents are not concerned about the health risks that may accompany tourists (Joo et al., 2021; Qiu et al., 2020), but many residents, especially those affiliated with tourism, still describe the social benefits of interacting with visitors and the enjoyment of hosting foreign people as a main personal gratification (Farmaki et al., 2020). In addition, Joo et al. (2021) found that the positive relationship between residents' emotional solidarity towards tourists and residents' support for tourism development also holds in an unstable and troubled situation like this pandemic. Although residents are aware of the current risks enhanced by tourism and perceive health and social negative impacts, which justify the practice of social distancing, they continue to support tourism in their communities due to the perception of the economic and sociocultural positive impacts.

Finally, some authors emphasize that the effects of COVID-19 on tourism risk perceptions and destinations' marketing will be long-lasting even after the pandemic is controlled (Ying et al., 2021), calling for the attention of policymakers to monitor a recovery which allows tourists to continue traveling and interacting with local people (Yang et al., 2021). Collins-Kreiner and Ram (2020) also highlight the challenge of "evidence-based policy" in order to mitigate the socio-economic impacts of COVID-19 and accelerate recovery through travel and tourism (UNWTO, 2020). To this end, further research is required, particularly on residents' perceptions about tourism impacts during and after the COVID era (Joo et al., 2021), keeping in mind that this crisis can be seen as a positive transformative moment (Higgins-Desbiolles, 2020). Governments, local communities and the tourism industry will benefit from this information in assisting future pro-tourism decisions.

3   Methodology

3.1   Context

The Algarve is the southern region of Portugal, bounded to the north by the Alentejo region and to the east by the Spanish province of Huelva. Its area comprises just over 5,000 km^2, perfectly coinciding with the district of Faro, where about 440,000 residents live, spread over 16 municipalities (INE, 2018a). In 2017, the Algarve contributed 4.6 percent to the national GDP, around 20.0 million euros (INE, 2018a). Tourism is the main activity in the Algarve, representing about 66.0 percent of the regional GDP and employing more than 60.0 percent of the workforce (RTA, 2012). In 2017, the region registered around 4.5 million guests in tourist accommodation establishments, continuing to be the leading tourism destination in Portugal (30.9 percent of total overnight stays) (INE, 2018b). In 2020, due to the effects of COVID-19, the Algarve suffered tourism losses of around 60.0 percent, with a decrease of 60.6 percent in the number of guests and 62.1 percent in the total revenue (TravelBI, 2021).

3.2   Instruments

To achieve the objectives of the study, a questionnaire was drawn up to collect data from residents, aged at least 18, which was applied in the 16 municipalities of the Algarve, based on a stratified sample by municipality, gender and age group, proportional to the resident population in each municipality (INE, 2018a).

The questionnaire is composed of 46 questions with the aim of understanding residents' attitudes and behaviors towards sustainable tourism development in the Algarve. This chapter analyzes two groups of questions, regarding residents' perceptions of the current state of tourism development and residents' perceptions of the sociocultural impacts of tourism. The questions were evaluated using a Likert scale ranging from 1 (strongly disagree) to 5 (strongly agree). In addition, questions related to sociodemographic characteristics will be examined.

3.3   Data collection and sample

During the study preparation phase, it was planned to observe 2,400 residents in the low season of tourism activity (February / March and October / November 2020), based on a sample size calculated for 95.0 percent confidence level and 2.0 percent margin of error. However, due to COVID-19, it was not possible to complete the quota foreseen for senior residents (aged 65 or over) since they are the most vulnerable to the disease and the more resistant to collaborating in an onsite survey. This situation resulted in an 83.5 percent data collection execution for this age group. For the other age groups, the quotas were fully accomplished.

Residents were personally approached by the survey team, who followed the itinerary method with pre-defined selection rules, at random in the streets, residences, coffee shops, stores, gardens, public parks, etc., until the sample calculated for each municipality was completed. The questionnaires were self-administered, i.e., filled out individually by residents. In total, 2,004 questionnaires were collected and validated during the low season of tourist activity in the Algarve, allowing a maximum sampling error of 2.15 percent for a confidence level of 95.0 percent. The first set of 938 questionnaires were collected between February and March 2020 (pre-COVID) and the second set of 1,066 questionnaires were collected between October and November 2020 (during-COVID).

3.4 Data analysis

Data analysis begins with a descriptive statistical analysis of residents' sociodemographic characteristics. Then, the study uses an exploratory factor analysis (EFA) on the questions assessing residents' perceptions about the sociocultural impacts of tourism. This multivariate technique allows the reduction of a set of variables into a smaller set of new variables or factors. EFA was preceded by two analyses to determine if data were adequate for the method: the computation of the Kaiser-Meyer-Olkin (KMO) measure of sampling adequacy and the Bartlett's test. Both analyses indicated the suitability of the variables for EFA. The number of factors to be retained was determined using the Kaiser criterion, which states that only factors with an eigenvalue higher than one should be kept (Costello & Osborne, 2005). Based on the new variables calculated using the EFA results, multivariate analysis of variance (MANOVA) and t-tests for independent samples were conducted to assess the effect of data collection periods, "pre-COVID" (before the pandemic) and "during-COVID" (during the pandemic), on residents' perceptions about the sociocultural impacts of tourism in the Algarve.

4 Results

4.1 Profile of respondents

The sample is composed of 2,004 residents evenly distributed according to gender, although with a slight predominance of females (52.1 percent). Most are aged between 25 and 64 years old (77.9 percent), with young people, aged between 18 and 24 years old, being less represented (10.6 percent), as well as seniors, with ages equal to or above 65 years old (11.5 percent). The average age corresponds to 43.8 years old (min. 18 | max. 88 | SD = 14.6). Most of the respondents are married or are living together (53.2 percent), but many are single (33.2 percent). Residents have mainly academic qualifications at the level of high school (47.6 percent) or higher education (Bachelor) (24.7 percent), although some have the maximum of nine years of schooling (13.4 percent). Most are employed (87.5 percent), some are students (2.7 percent), and others are retired (5.5 percent). The majority have a long-term residence in the Algarve, i.e., they have lived in the region for at least 16 years (70.8 percent).

4.2 Residents' perceptions about the sociocultural impacts of tourism

This study assesses 20 items measuring the sociocultural impacts of tourism. In order to reduce the data dimension and facilitate further interpretations, EFA technique was first applied using the principal factoring extraction method and varimax rotation. The KMO value and of the Bartlett's test show the adequacy of EFA to the data (KMO = 0.89; Bartlett's test: $p = 0.00$). The Kaiser's criterion suggests that five factors should be retained. Together, these factors explain 62.29 percent of the total variance of the original set of items. Attempts were made to retain a factor solution that explains a higher percentage of explained variance conduct to unclear interpretation solutions. The items measuring the sociocultural impacts and the factors produced by EFA are presented in Table 12.1. Table 12.1 also shows some descriptive statistics for the items, i.e., the mean and standard deviation.

Considering the meaning of the items with higher loadings in each factor, they were labeled *Hostility and acculturation, Anomie and violence, Local culture and collective identity, Quality of life and public policies* and *Residents' hospitality*. Factors 1 and 2 are related to negative impacts of tourism, whereas Factors 3 and 4 capture positive impacts. Factor 5 has a neutral meaning.

Factor 1, *Hostility and acculturation*, is especially related to the feeling that tourism can be a source of social perturbation and loss of cultural identity, especially due to overcrowding resulting from an excessive number of tourists visiting the municipalities. In most cases, the means for the items in this factor are lower than 3, meaning that residents disagree that tourism affects their municipality negatively at this level. The overall average for the items included in Factor 1 is 2.73, clearly supporting this conclusion. The item reporting a higher agreement value is "Tourism increases stress and disturbs quietness" (mean = 3.15; level of agreement = 42.9 percent).

Factor 2, *Anomie and violence*, captures another set of possible negative sociocultural impacts from tourism, more related to criminal and deviant behaviors, including drug and alcohol consumption or sexual promiscuity. As with Factor 1, most items in this factor report mean values lower than 3, which suggests that residents do not agree that tourism negatively affects their municipality at this level. As before, the low overall mean (2.94) validates this conclusion. The item with a higher agreement level is "Tourism increases drugs and alcohol consumption" (mean = 3.35; level of agreement = 47.7 percent).

Factor 3, *Local culture and collective identity*, puts forward the tourism potential in preserving the local culture and the municipality's image. For most items, the mean exceeds 3.5, meaning that residents show some agreement with them. These results are in accordance with the overall average for the factor, 3.56. The exception is for the item "Tourism stimulates cultural activities, festivals and traditions" that reported a slightly lower average (3.26). The item reporting the highest agreement value is "Tourism contributes to the recognition, prestige and image of my municipality" (mean = 3.84; level of agreement = 76.5 percent).

Factor 4, *Quality of life and public policies*, joins the items measuring perceptions that tourism can improve the standard of living, including the public services provided at the municipality and security among residents. Residents perceive these potential positive impacts less favorably than those included in Factor 3, with the mean values reasonably close to 3, meaning neither agree nor disagree. The average value for the scale is at the same level (2.84). The item reporting the highest agreement value is "Tourism contributes to raising the standard of living of residents" (mean = 3.04; level of agreement = 37.2 percent).

Lastly, Factor 5, *Residents' hospitality*, has a single item, "Residents in my municipality are hospitable and receive tourists with politeness". It reports the highest mean agreement level on the scale (3.96), with 77.3 percent of respondents agreeing that residents warmly welcome tourists in the Algarve.

4.3   The effect of COVID-19 on residents' perceptions about the sociocultural impacts of tourism

In order to assess the effects of COVID-19 on residents' perceptions about the sociocultural impacts of tourism, five new variables were created by computing the average score of the items included in each factor. The new variables were labeled using the corresponding factor names. As for the original items, these new variables also range from 1 to 5. Their means and standard deviations are in Table 12.1. The analysis proceeded by testing whether these variables reported significant differences between the two periods under review: "pre-COVID" (938 responses) and "during-COVID" (1,066 responses).

Multivariate analysis of variance (MANOVA) was conducted to compare the five variables between the two data collection periods. The MANOVA results

Table 12.1   Descriptive statistics and results from EFA

Factors and Items	Loadings	% Explained variance/ Cronbach alpha	Mean (SD)	% Agreement[a]
F1. Hostility and acculturation		28.72% / 0.855	2.73 (0.76)	
Residents are likely to suffer from living in this tourism destination	0.781		2.84 (1.13)	29.4
My municipality is overcrowded because of tourism	0.755		2.63 (1.08)	22.4
The increasing number of tourists is likely to result in conflicts with residents	0.743		2.69 (0.99)	21.0
Tourism increases stress and disturbs quietness	0.683		3.15 (1.10)	42.9
Residents change their behavior in an attempt to mimic tourists	0.581		2.50 (0.92)	25.1
Tourism causes loss of tolerance and respect for other cultures	0.556		2.46 (0.90)	12.9
Tourism generates loss or change of traditions and cultural identity	0.548		2.76 (0.99)	15.0
F2. Anomie and violence		15.73% / 0.883	2.94 (0.88)	
Tourism increases prostitution and moral degradation	0.866		2.79 (1.03)	22.0
Tourism increases sexual transmitted diseases	0.857		2.85 (0.99)	22.2
Tourism causes more crime and vandalism	0.774		2.80 (1.02)	23.4
Tourism increases drugs and alcohol consumption	0.767		3.35 (1.07)	47.7
F3. Local culture and collective identity		6.90% / 0.742	3.56 (0.67)	
Tourism stimulates cultural activities, festivals and traditions	0.828		3.26 (0.96)	66.9

Factors and Items	Loadings	% Explained variance/ Cronbach alpha	Mean (SD)	% Agreement[a]
Tourism promotes cultural exchange between residents and tourists	0.813		3.84 (0.81)	63.0
Tourism contributes to the preservation of the local culture	0.645		3.58 (0.88)	46.6
Tourism contributes to the recognition, prestige and image of my municipality	0.489		3.84 (0.81)	76.5
F4. Quality of life and public policies		5.88% / 0.624	2.84 (0.66)	
Tourism contributes to increase security	0.642		2.84 (0.98)	27.2
Tourism contributes to raising the standard of living of residents	0.633		3.04 (1.03)	37.2
Tourism changes the consumption habits of residents (food, clothing, etc.)	0.615		2.99 (1.04	34.4
Tourism improves public services (health centers, sports, police protection, etc.)	0.526		2.50 (0.96)	16.2
F5. Residents' hospitality		5.07%	3.96 (0.83)	
Residents in my municipality are hospitable and receive tourists with politeness	0.885		3.96 (0.83)	77.3

Note: [a] Sum of responses in the categories 4 (agree) and 5 (totally agree) of the scale
Source: Own elaboration

indicate a significant main effect for the collection period (Pillai's Trace value of 0.01, $F = 4.81$, $p = 0.00$). Thus, MANOVA results reveal the effect of data collection periods on residents' perceptions about the sociocultural impacts of tourism in the region. The univariate tests further indicate that there are significant differences on two variables, one related to the negative impacts of tourism, *Hostility and acculturation* ($F = 11.90$, $p = 0.001$), and another related to the positive impacts of tourism, *Quality of life and public policies* ($F = 7.29$, $p = 0.007$). Further *t*-tests for independent samples show similar results: *Hostility and acculturation* ($t = 3.40$, $p = 0.001$); *Quality of life and public policies* ($t = -2.86$, $p = 0.004$). No significant effects are found on the other three variables (all $p > 0.10$).

Figure 12.1 compares the means of the five variables in the two data collection periods. Before the pandemic situation and the first lockdown in Portugal (pre-COVID), residents were significantly more sensible/critical about the excess of tourism in the Algarve and its consequences in disturbing communities' way of life and the loss of cultural identity (*Hostility and acculturation*), than in the subsequent phase. In turn, in the second data collection period, after the first general unlockdown in Portugal (during-COVID), residents

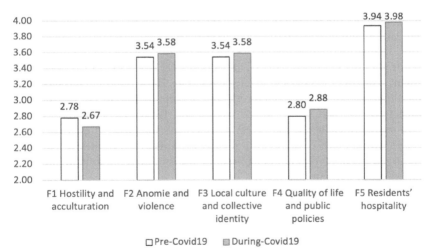

Note: 1 – strongly disagree; 2 – disagree; 3 – neither agree nor disagree; 4 – agree; 5 – strongly agree
Source: Own elaboration

Figure 12.1   Overall perceptions about the sociocultural impacts of tourism: a pre and during COVID-19 means comparison

were significantly more favorable to the positive impacts of tourism on *Quality of life and public policies*. Residents' perceptions are most likely affected by the severe socio-economic outcomes caused by tourism decline during the pandemic. This situation may explain the increasing support for the activity in the current context, due to the understanding of the fundamental role that tourism plays in the Algarve.

5   Discussion

In the quest to achieve sustainable tourism development, policy makers are more interested in listening to residents and considering their contribution in the design of more accurate strategies (Ribeiro et al., 2017), especially in terms of their aim to work towards the United Nations Sustainable Development Goals (Boluk et al., 2019).

Social perturbation and loss of cultural identity are identified as main negative impacts of tourism in local communities. These findings are aligned with the results obtained in other tourism destinations (Ribeiro et al., 2017; Šegota et al., 2017). In the same way, positive impacts, namely the contribution of tourism to preserve the local culture, destination image and to improve residents' standard of living revealed to be aligned with literature.

In line with the widely recognized impacts of COVID-19 on the tourism sector (Pham et al., 2021; Škare et al., 2021; Zhang et al., 2021), findings also recognize that the pandemic is influencing residents' perceptions about the sociocultural impacts of tourism (Uğur & Akbıyık, 2020). Before COVID-19, residents were more critical about the excess of tourists in the place where they live as well as with the loss of their cultural identity. During the pandemic, residents expressed more favorable perceptions about the effect of tourism on their quality of life and public policies.

6   Conclusions

A sample of 2,004 residents participated in a survey with the aim of understanding the effects of COVID-19 on their perceptions about the sociocultural impacts of tourism in their own communities.

The results identify two groups of negative impacts, namely *Hostility and acculturation* plus *Anomie and violence*, two groups of positive impacts, namely *Local culture and collective identity* plus *Quality of life and public policies*, as well as a neutral one, *Residents' hospitality*. The effects of COVID-19 were confirmed, particularly on *Hospitality and acculturation* (negative impacts) and *Quality of life and public policies* (positive impacts). Residents were more critical about the excess of tourism in the Algarve before the COVID-19 pandemic.

Considering the effects of COVID-19 on societies, especially on the tourism sector, and considering the fragile situation of mature mass tourism destinations such as the Algarve, this study sheds light on residents' perceptions of tourism impacts in the current pandemic context. Although residents perceive the health risks associated with tourism flows, they are more tolerant to tourists since they are aware of the positive economic impacts.

Monitoring residents' perceptions about tourism impacts, especially about the sociocultural impacts and how they are influenced by the COVID-19 pandemic, will allow governments, local communities and the tourism industry to design more sustainable and pro-tourism policies. Facing this crisis as a positive transformative opportunity, findings will assist regions in their efforts to align the policies with the United Nations Sustainable Development Goals.

Future studies should deepen the knowledge on residents' perceptions about tourism impacts, as well as explore its relationship with other relevant constructs under the effect of COVID-19.

References

Andereck, K., & Vogt, C. (2000). The relationship between residents' attitudes toward tourism and tourism development options. *Journal of Travel Research, 39*, 27–36.

Ap, J. (1992). Residents' perceptions on tourism impacts. *Annals of Tourism Research, 19*(4), 665–690.

Boluk, K., Cavaliere, C., & Higgins-Desbiolles, F. (2019). A critical framework for interrogating the United Nations Sustainable Development Goals 2030 Agenda in tourism. *Journal of Sustainable Tourism, 27*(7), 847–864.

Collins-Kreiner, N., & Ram, Y. (2020). National tourism strategies during Covid-19 pandemic. *Annals of Tourism Research, 89*(1), 103076.

Costello, A., & Osborne, J. (2005). Best practices in exploratory factor analysis: Four recommendations for getting the most from your analysis. *Practical Assessment: Research & Evaluation, 10*, 1–9.

Dioko, L. (2017). The problem of rapid tourism growth: An overview of the strategic question. *Worldwide Hospitality and Tourism Themes, 9*(3), 252–259.

Farmaki, A., Miguel, C., Drotarova, M., Aleksić, A., Časni, A., & Efthymiadou, F. (2020). Impacts of Covid-19 on peer-to-peer accommodation platforms: Host perceptions and responses. *International Journal of Hospitality Management*, *91*, 1–10.

Fennell, D. (2015). Akrasia and tourism: Why we sometimes act against our better judgement. *Tourism Recreation Research*, *40*(1), 95–106.

Graburn, N. (1989). Tourism: The sacred journey. In V. L. Smith (Ed.), *Hosts and Guests: The Anthropology of Tourism*, 2nd edition (pp. 21–36). Philadelphia: University of Pennsylvania Press.

Haywood, K. (2020). A post COVID-19 future: Tourism re-imagined and re-enabled. *Tourism Geographies*, *22*(3), 599–609.

Higgins-Desbiolles, F. (2020). The "war over tourism": Challenges to sustainable tourism in the tourism academy after COVID-19. *Journal of Sustainable Tourism*, *29*(4), 551–569.

INE (2018a). *Anuário Estatístico da Região do Algarve 2017*. Lisbon: Instituto Nacional de Estatística, I.P.

INE (2018b). *Estatísticas do Turismo 2017*. Lisbon: Instituto Nacional de Estatística, I.P.

Joo, D., Xu, W., Lee, J., Lee, C., & Woosnam, K. (2021). Residents' perceived risk, emotional solidarity, and support for tourism amidst the COVID-19 pandemic. *Journal of Destination Marketing & Management*, *19*, 1–11.

Kock, F., Nørfelt, A., Josiassen, A., Assaf, A., & Tsionas, M. (2020). Understanding the COVID-19 tourist psyche: The evolutionary tourism paradigm. *Annals of Tourism Research*, *85*, 1–13.

Krippendorf, J. (1987). *The Holiday Makers. Understanding the Impact of Leisure and Travel*. Oxford: Butterworth Heinemann.

Lundberg, E. (2017). The importance of tourism impacts for different local resident groups: A case study of a Swedish seaside destination. *Journal of Destination Marketing & Management*, *6*, 46–55.

Moghavvemi, S., Woosnam, K., Paramanathan, T., Musa, G., & Hamzah, A. (2017). The effect of residents' personality, emotional solidarity, and community commitment on support for tourism development. *Tourism Management*, *63*, 242–254.

Pham, T., Dwyer, L., Su, J., & Ngo, T. (2021). COVID-19 impacts of inbound tourism on Australian economy. *Annals of Tourism Research*, *88*, 2–14.

Qiu, R. T., Park, J., Li, S., & Song, H. (2020). Social costs of tourism during the COVID-19 pandemic. *Annals of Tourism Research*, *84*, 102994.

Ribeiro, M., Pinto, P., Silva, J., & Woosnam, K. (2017). Residents' attitudes and the adoption of pro-tourism behaviours: The case of developing island countries. *Tourism Management*, *61*, 523–537.

Ribeiro, M., Valle, P., & Silva, J. (2013). Residents' attitudes toward tourism development in Cape Verde Islands. *Tourism Geographies*, *15*(4), 654–679.

Ribeiro, M., Woosnam, K., Pinto, P., & Silva, J. A. (2018). Tourists' destination loyalty through emotional solidarity with residents: An integrative moderated mediation model. *Journal of Travel Research*, *57*(3), 279–295.

RTA (2012). *Demografia e Geografia do Algarve*. Faro: Região de Turismo do Algarve.

Šegota, T., Mihalič, T., & Kuščer, K. (2017). The impact of residents' informedness and involvement on their perceptions of tourism impacts: The case of Bled. *Journal of Destination Marketing & Management*, *6*(3), 196–206.

Sharpley, R. (2014). Host perceptions of tourism: A review of the research. *Tourism Management*, *42*, 37–49.

Škare, M., Soriano, D., & Porada-Rochoń, M. (2021). Impact of COVID-19 on the travel and tourism industry. *Technological Forecasting & Social Change*, *163*, 1–14.

Thomassen, B. (2014). *Liminality and the Modern: Living Through the In-Between.* Farnham: Ashgate Publishing.

TravelBI (2021). Proveitos. TravelBI by Turismo de Portugal. https:// travelbi .turismodeportugal.pt/.

Uğur, N., & Akbıyık, A. (2020). Impacts of COVID-19 on global tourism industry: A cross-regional comparison. *Tourism Management Perspectives, 36,* 1–13.

UNWTO (2020). *Supporting jobs and economies through travel & tourism: A call for action to mitigate the socio-economic impact of Covid-19 and accelerate recovery.* https://www.e-unwto.org/doi/book/10.18111/9789284421633.

Uysal, M., Sirgy, M., Woo, E., & Kim, H. (2016). Quality of life (QoL) and well-being research in tourism. *Tourism Management, 53,* 244–261.

Woo, E., Kim, H., & Uysal, M. (2015). Life satisfaction and support for tourism development. *Annals of Tourism Research, 50,* 84–97.

Woosnam, K., & Norman, W. (2010). Measuring residents' emotional solidarity with tourists: Scale development of Durkheim's theoretical constructs. *Journal of Travel Research, 49*(3), 365–380.

Yang, Y., Altschuler, B., Liang, Z., & Li, X. (2021). Monitoring the global COVID-19 impact on tourism: The COVID 19 tourism index. *Annals of Tourism Research, 90,* 103120.

Ying, T., Wang, K., Liu, X., Wen, J., & Goh, E. (2021). Rethinking game consumption in tourism: A case of the 2019 novel coronavirus pneumonia outbreak in China. *Tourism Recreation Research, 46*(2), 304–309.

Zhang, H., Song, H., Wen, L., & Liu, C. (2021). Forecasting tourism recovery amid COVID-19. *Annals of Tourism Research, 87,* 1–16.

13 The future of cultural urban tourism amidst calls for social inclusivity during the COVID-19 pandemic

Zaheer Allam and David S. Jones

Introduction

As the world continues to experience a sustained population increase and rapid urbanization, cities are seen to be gaining in popularity. Such popularity is prompted by factors like the spirited use of technologies to bolster economic activities and the increasing attention to soft and hard green and blue infrastructure development (Allam & Dhunny, 2019; Allam & Newman, 2018). In addition, cities have been seen to be shifting their attention to place marketing, where they capitalize on their cultural heritage as a strength and tool to attract visitors, investors, and tourists.

The strategy to exploit cultural heritage, as a marketing tool is indeed effective as it allows urban managers to showcase and express the uniqueness and authenticity of their cities (Allam, 2020a, 2020b). Such echoes the intent of ICOMOS's *NARA Document on Authenticity* (1984) and its 'Washington Charter' (or the *Charter for the Conservation of Historic Towns and Urban Areas*, 1987).

The need for such marketing strategies, as noted by Richards (2018), is to align cities with changing tourism trends. The shift is often instigated by an emerging group of non-government-related people and/or organizations who are becoming cultural enthusiasts and who are willing to travel far and wide in search of particular and unique cultural products and marvels that address their penchants. Richards also credits these increasing activities, in promoting culture, to the advancement in technologies that are helping in conserving, showcasing, and promoting tangible and intangible cultural products and artefacts, and events and activities, to a wide array of audiences. According to Wang et al. (2018), championing cities as cultural heritage destinations is also seen to be paying off economically and intellectually, especially in terms of job creation, attracting new investors and opening opportunities for new business opportunities.

While those strategies have greatly helped cities in place identity, the recent emergence of the Black Lives Matter (BLM) movement in the USA, and its cascade internationally, have been seen to highlight a global unfolding of events whose participants have sought to question and discredit the mainstream perception of social inclusivity of contemporary 'cultural agendas' in urban arenas often aided by social media digital platforms. This shifting discourse is based upon a number of factors including the erection of a sizeable number of symbols, statues, monuments and (place/street/road/park/etc.) names amongst others that represent/narrate the cultural identity of a place but which are not authentic because they enshrine narratives belonging to foreigners whose ideologies barely reflect the traditions and values of locals today.

Fundamentally, these artefacts and nomenclature-epithets are symbols representative and expressive of the legacy of human inequalities and unfairness in cities. This is especially so where they are linked to the historical cultural heritage of Black citizens, and Indigenous and First Nation peoples, as being disregarded and down-trodden in favour of a foreign culture, or a dominant political and/or social colonizer, or gender controller (Heathwood, 2019). With such, Black and Indigenous citizens are socially and [*his*]tory-narratively discriminated against in almost all aspects, especially in matters of urban leadership and management, in securing job opportunities, in receiving access to and services in sectors like education, justice systems, the health sectors and in the economic sectors to name a few (Markwick et al., 2019; Katz & Braly, 1935). The treatment of Black and Indigenous citizens in an unfair manner, and in historically mis-narrated stories that have been exposed by the events of BLM, goes beyond the ability to simply showcase their heritage, and equalize their narratives. This is because such a de-narration, or generic de-colonization process, involves both tangible and intangible artefacts, stories and values that have been under-represented in our urban cultural heritage inventories and histories. In some urban areas there is not even a single aspect of an Indigenous heritage being highlighted or recognized (Pendleton, 2019). Instead, those cities that have amassed colonial histories, legacies and monuments celebrating individuals and institutions have often been in the forefront in undermining the dignity, presence, and contribution of Indigenous populations.

This BLM tension is palpable. But it also reflects generational tensions that have bubbled to the surface over many centuries. Witness Scottish and Welsh pride and assertiveness of their own values and languages to the dismay of the

English fearful of dismantling their own island-based 'Empire'. Witness the long running tensions in Australia about the *terra nullius* myth and Aboriginal self-determination, 'land rights', and their 'Stolen Generation'. Witness the tensions about slavery within the former Confederate states of the USA. Witness Québécois pride in the mosaic of Canada, and the bubbling tensions in India about British and East India Company exploitation and colonization legacies.

In response to the above, this chapter explores and discusses the consequences of promoting tourism based upon colonial historical narratives whilst openly overlooking, negating and disrespecting the rich and unique multi-culturalism and legacies of Indigenous peoples and 'transported' peoples. In so doing, the authors will also make some recommendations focusing upon the classification of culture as an evolving and dynamic feature of nature.

The economics of cultural urban tourism

The economic contribution of cultural identity and heritage is not disputed in cities. In fact, there is sufficient evidence that it is amongst the sectors that are (pre-COVID-19) keenly contributing substantially to the growth of urban economies in the promotion of social cohesion and environmental sustainability (Nocca, 2017). For instance, in a report by the UK National Commission for UNESCO, it was established that UNESCO projects helped Scotland generate over £10.8 million between 2014 and 2015 (UNESCO, 2020). In England, the engagement with cultural heritage contributed over £31 billion in 2019, and contributed directly to the employment of over 464,000 people (Historic England, 2019). In the USA, the arts and cultural sector contributed over US$804.2 billion; equivalent to 4.3 per cent of the USA's national GDP in 2016 (NEA, 2019). This exploitation of and engagement with culture was also seen to have unprecedented economic impacts in the Asian region, especially in promoting tourism, where it was reported that the region experienced a 4.2 per cent increase in GDP growth due to tourism activities, with over 324 million tourists recorded to have visited the region in 2017 (Thomson & Newman, 2018).

Such economic figures, emanating from the cultural and art sectors, are promising as these are expected to continue growing in parallel with advancements in technologies that are clearly increasingly bolstering and supporting this sector, and use cities as their 'theatres' for experiences. With urbanization, it is expected that more cultural products will emerge, noting that technology is helping to regenerate, preserve and conserve existing ones, and that technology is additionally becoming a cultural heritage artefact in its own right (e.g. telephone technologies, etc.). Such advancements and evolutionary innovations help in generating more job opportunities, attracting more domestic and international tourists, increasing foreign direct investment (FDI) revenues, and eventually leading to the upgrading of urban infrastructure and systems to render the sector even more attractive and accessible.

Such an emphasis is pronounced in countries that rely heavily on tourism, particularly Small Island Developing States (SIDS), and others with heavy colonial pasts who do not have large manufacturing industrial economic backbones. This conclusion is affirmed in a report by United Nations World Tourism Organization (UNWTO, 2020) that highlights that regions like the Middle East were leading in terms of tourism activities in 2019, with the sector growing by over 8 per cent from the previous record. There was also some positive growth in African countries which recorded over 4 per cent growth. Tourism is also still valued in developed economies (often in art and cultural expositions and experiential activities, etc.), with substantial activities observed in Europe in 2019, where the region recorded an increase in arrivals of at least 4 per cent translating to 743 million international tourists.

Before the world woke to the reality of COVID-19 in 2020, the World Tourism Organization (UNWTO, 2020) had predicted that global tourism activities would record an average increase of at least 4 per cent from the previous record of 1.5 billion tourism travels recorded in 2019. However, after COVID-19, and the subsequent containment measures that include severe restrictions on travel, border/state movement restrictions, the grounding of airlines and other forms of transportation, and the overall consequential lockdowns, it will not be tenable to achieve this 4 per cent increase. The OECD (2020) reports that already, at the time of writing, the coronavirus pandemic has led to a 60 per cent decline in tourism activities globally and that this would rise to an over 80 per cent decline if reopenings of major destinations and air flight accessibility is delayed until December 2020. But, as of 2020, countries are slowly reopening their economies, and the International Airline Travel Association (IATA, 2020) reported that global airline activities may resume before the end of that year; thus sparking some elements of hope in this sector. Coupling this with government direct interventions in the sector in terms of recovery stimulus programmes and financial support mechanisms may see the sector resume, albeit at a slow rate, but it is without doubt one that has potential to spur some growth in economies that are already struggling.

Reassessing cultural urban identity amidst the Black Lives Matter movement

The momentum gained from the BLM protests as a result of the killing of George Floyd by police officers in Minneapolis in the USA on 25 May 2020 (Furber et al., 2020), sparked a series of protests, both in the USA and beyond. Amidst the violence of these protests, the destruction and rifling of some businesses and establishments were observed. Perhaps the most notable impact has been, from a cultural tourism perspective, at the time of writing, and which has been witnessed across the globe, is the toppling of statues of notable historical figures. On this, it is worth noting that outside the USA, there is largely no report of destruction of properties or businesses except for statues and monuments. The accusations levelled against those whose statues and monuments were and have been defaced, destroyed, toppled or moved, include their participation in racial discrimination, and that they abetted or celebrated violence against minority groups and Indigenous peoples during their lives re-positioned against contemporary values.

All the mayhem, and spirited efforts to bring down the statues happened amidst lockdowns and containment measures warranted by the spread of COVID-19. During this period, most cities across the globe were still hurting, especially economically due to the negative impacts that COVID-19 had caused on almost all economic sectors. Even at such low economic moments, the costs of moving the statues that were at risk of being destroyed, or those that had already been defaced was shouldered by cities. Such costs were an economic burden, as most cities did not have money planned for such eventualities, especially with most of them relying upon local governments for financial support. To put this in perspective, in the USA, the City of New Orleans incurred an estimated US$2.1 million to move four Confederate statues. Initially, as reported by LeBlanc (2017), the mayor of the city, Mitch Landrieu, estimated that it would only cost approximately US$170,000, but other unseen costs including litigations and safety concerns pushed the final price to a much higher margin.

From a purist perspective, those statues were part-and-parcel of that city's urban fabric and had served as attraction centres that branded the city in a unique way. Thus, they served as attractors for tourism and earned that city some or substantial direct and indirect revenue. But, from an ethical, moral, and psychological standpoint, such statues, despite their economic, design and aesthetic values, served as symbols of discrimination, inequality and inequity that minority groups and Indigenous peoples had long endured. Their presence in cities thus served and increased the pain that those discriminated felt, and the BLM protests and agitation for their removal made this vividly and emotionally clear.

Before the Floyd protests, a series of brutal and racially discriminatory policies and/or incidents had been witnessed, in the USA and beyond. For instance, during this period when the world is battling COVID-19, Black Africans were reported to have been racially discriminated against in China (CBS, 2020). In the UK (Alexander, 2018), Italy (Giuffrida, 2018) and Germany (DW, 2020), Black communities have been marginalized, and this is even reflected in the sporting world (football) where those peoples have quietly endured sustained and prolonged abuse and racial stereotyping from their White counterparts (van Sterkenburg et al., 2019). In Australia, Bodkin-Andrews and Carlson (2016) describe how Aboriginals have endured marginalization including in securing jobs and in the education sector to name a few. In the USA, similar incidents of police brutality had, like that of Floyd, been prevalent including the notable killing of Rodney King in 1992 leading to nation-wide protests (Sams, 2020). The repeated incidents of brutality against the Black community rekindled the pains and agony that Indigenous peoples and people of 'colour' had endured at different times and in different countries at the hands of racists and under the harsh rule of colonialism.

While representations of those difficult pasts were openly celebrated in public spaces, the BLM protests underlined the urgent need for a re-evaluation of how historical culture is to be celebrated and inviting retrospection and thought on its impact upon emerging populations for building inclusive communities. For this reason, many city halls around the world have considered removing statues and monuments of controversial historical figures, and also renaming streets, institutions and buildings (Wright, 2020). While, amidst the looming health dangers brought about by the coronavirus pandemic, some of those were quickly rejected by the general public, this is an important stride to ensure that the cultural heritage being used to market urban place identity is factual and forward-looking. Thus, a shift that seeks to cater for all past, present and future generations, and relates well with both residents and tourists. This is important as both residents and tourists play critical roles in marketing cities as the prime consumers of its cultural products, and they are particularly active in sharing information and images to their peers across the globe especially in this dispensation of social media platforms which are now increasingly popular in driving tourism agendas and economies (Cotirlea, 2014). It therefore beholds city managers, from both a social and economic perspective, to ensure that everyone feels represented in cities.

On the unhealthy relationship of colonization and heritage regulations

From a wide range of contemporary literature, cultural heritage conservation has been hailed for its role in defining, promoting and conserving the identity of different places. This has led to increased investments in the cultural heritage sector including the establishment of financial resources like the World Heritage Fund and World Heritage publications. Such resources are not only meant to promote conservation but also to help in protecting world cultural heritage sites. But, to avoid similar scenarios like those of the BLM protests, where some cultural heritage has had to be pulled down, the conservation, protection and presentation of heritage needs to reflect the true identity of the place, by taking into account the historical dynamics associated with a particular place. Hence the unbiasing of heritage 'evaluative assessments' that informed statements of significance. This argument aligns well with that of Lewis et al. (2018) who argue that conservation pursuits should respect, recognize and incorporate different factors including the diversity of heritage of a given place. That is, the conservation should not be seen to be biased in favour of one cultural heritage at the expense of others, such as observed in former colonies where the cultures of invaders (colonialists) have been given more attention than those of the Indigenous peoples, 'transported peoples' and the local communities themselves (Chirikure et al., 2010).

Allowing such skewedness in culture translation and narrative making attracts numerous challenges including the destruction of heritage of locals or Indigenous peoples, which in essence may have been in existence many years before the emergence of the culture being given precedence. For instance, in Casco Viejo, San Felipe, Panama, it is reported that the decision to regenerate the town that had become dilapidated resulted in the eviction of poor locals, and the destruction of their rich heritage. Their place was instead gentrified and taken over by wealthy foreigners who were attracted by the aesthetic transformation of the town, and these gentrifiers arrived with their own cultures (Hollmann, 2010). Pwiti and Ndoro (1999) explain that when a particular culture is elevated more than others, especially those that came before it, the locals, and those whose culture is being overlooked, may retaliate as they try to save their culture. In this process, those retaliating peoples may be reminded of their generational pain and losses they may have endured, especially in cases of colonial heritage. Such feelings may sometime degenerate to violence, graffitied expressions, hate and disharmony between different groups, and in the long run, create a place where such negatives may never achieve social inclusivity which is amongst the prerequisites in our urban liveability and Sustainable

Development Goals (SDGs) policy pursuits. Another challenge, that would be experienced, is of illegal acquisition, removal and display of cultural heritage of a given group by another. For instance, Starrenburg (2018) highlights how different cultural objects and artefacts were looted from different colonies and were relocated and positioned in some European museums, or hidden inside their deep vaulted archives. Such actions have caused UNESCO to be criticized by different groups including by academics and Indigenous communities for failing to protect those cultural objects or at least initiating processes that would see those items, artefacts and body parts repatriated. For this reason, some local communities have already sought legal redress seeking repatriation of their cultural objects.

There have been attempts by many Indigenous communities to repatriate ancestral body parts, skulls, and funeral artefacts from the bowels of European and post-[independent]-colonized nations' museums and archives over the last 20 years (Liddle, 2013). As expressed by Wadawurrung Elder Bryon Powell over the repatriation of the ancestral remains of four Wadawurrung people from the Museum of Victoria, 'Sorrow that it has taken so long, sorrow that our ancestors have been sitting in cardboard boxes in museum shelves and now they're coming home.' And there are continuing debates about the *c*.447–438 BCE-era Parthenon Marbles, or 'Elgin Marbles', that were removed in 1801–1812 from Athens by the 7th Earl of Elgin to England where they are now on display in the purpose-built Duveen Gallery within the British Museum (Sanchez, 2017).

The third challenge that may arise from skewed recognition of cultural heritage is the unprecedented violence and destructions, like those happening in different parts of the world, as a result of the BLM protests.

A sizeable number of targeted statues and monuments are in one way or another presently erected in areas that the locals or protesters argue that they do not represent the cultural vibrancy of communities and positive heritage thereof. For instance, the statue of Cecil Rhodes, which was toppled in Cape Town, South Africa in 2019, had always attracted controversy as the locals, especially students did not in any way think it represented South African culture, and that in its place there could have been erected a statue of one of their legends or heroes (Stiem, 2018). Another Rhodes statue erected in Oxford, outside Oriel College, was recently brought down in protest at the racism and colonial policies he oversaw in South Africa (Race & Briant, 2020). The statue of Rhodes in South Africa is representative of numerous other such statues in different parts of the world that colonialists systematically and deliberately erected while overlooking colonized countries' heritage, and deliberately classified their own as the contextual heritage of the place. Similar trends persist even after colonialism, with Caust and Vecco (2017) attributing this penchant to politics, greed, and economic interests, where the managers of a place assume that they will attract tourists (and thus dollars) by having such 'heritage'.

However, the current BLM protests have shown that associating the wrong heritage to a place will eventually have negative consequences both socially and economically. This is very evident when protesters charge to remove the representation of a 'foreign culture' or 'slavery' through the toppling of statues in different urban areas across the world like the demise of the statue of seventeenth-century slave trader Edward Colston (1636–1721) (an English merchant, philanthropist, and Tory Member of Parliament who was involved in the Atlantic slave trade) in Bristol (Landler, 2020). As Landler (2020) wrote:

> Bristol is, for all intents and purposes, the town that Edward Colston built. Tearing down his statue has reopened a painful reckoning with the past – one that has long divided this port city of 460,000, laying bare its contradictions. It is multicultural but segregated, festive but given to spasms of unrest, liberal but enriched by the lucre of slavery. After the protesters toppled Colston, they dumped him in Bristol Harbor, a theatrical touch that recalled the rebellious British subjects in colonial Boston. But this protest was inspired by the Black Lives Matter movement, not the Boston Tea Party, and it poses a nettlesome challenge to Bristol, similar to that faced by cities across the American South, where statues of Confederate generals are teetering.

Statue defacement and removal over April–July 2020 has been a prevalent trend internationally and has relevance to cultural heritage due to the arte-fact as well as the personality and/or process 'celebrated' in the artefact. Statue defacement and removal incidents have been prevalent in England and Scotland, across many of the southern and eastern states of the USA often linked to Confederate leaders and/or slave owners, across all states in Australia linked to Aboriginal colonization and human rights as well as social advancement and to a lesser degree slave ownership associations, and scattered incidents across southern Asia also linked to colonization and slave ownership and transportation. All incidents are linked to the BLM and or as a response to symbols of 'colonization' and 'forced transportation'. These incidents echo similar social tensions across the globe in the late 1960s and early 1970s as a response to social equity and rights outcries in many nations but also responses to changes in colonized nations to independence or shifts between communist and non-communist regimes or similar. The incidents affected small cultural heritage artefacts but also several sites included on the World Heritage List. Many of the latter human movements have been prompted by a conscious desire to rewrite national histories and to re-narrate national stories through a non-colonized lens.

The majority of these incidents are associated with a broader understanding of the discourse about colonization and decolonization, as echoed in Shashi Tharoor's Oxford Union talk (News18), wherein he stated:

> It's been pointed out that for the example dehumanisation of Africans in the Caribbean, the massive psychological damage that has been done, the undermining of social traditions, of the property rights, of the authority structures of the societies – all in the interest of British colonialism and the fact remains that many of today's problems in these countries including the persistence and in some cases the creation of racial, of ethnic, of religious tensions were the direct result of colonialism. So there is a moral debt that needs to be paid. … there have been incidents of racial violence, of loot, of massacres, of bloodshed, of transportation and in India's case even one of our last Mughal emperors. Yes, may be today's Britains are not responsible for some of these reparations but the same speakers have pointed with pride to their foreign aid – you are not responsible for the people starving in Somalia but you give them aid surely the principle of reparation for what is the wrongs that have done cannot be denied. It's been pointed out that for the example dehumanisation of Africans in the Caribbean, the massive psychological damage that has been done, the undermining of social traditions, of the property rights, of the authority structures of the societies – all in the interest of British colonialism and the fact remains that many of today's problems in these countries including the persistence and in some cases the creation of racial, of ethnic, of religious tensions were the direct result of colonialism.

The fourth challenge resides in story telling or narrating 'history' in an equitable and decolonized manner, language, and lens. For example, in 1884 in the main street of the former gold mining city of Ballarat in Australia, Wadawurrung Elder noted that:

> King Billy [Mullawallah] … was in Ballarat the other day, and … delivered a short lecture on the land question from his point of view. He said that the ground he then stood on was rightfully his property, of which he had been robbed by the white man, and it was the duty of the invaders, therefore, to pay him rent as long as he and his fellow blackfellows lived, at any rate. (Anon., 1844)

Despite this oration, the notion of recognition of Aboriginal 'ownership' of Australia only gained respectful recognition in the 1990s in Australia. Thus, a truthful story by Mullawallah was disregarded as an untruth by colonial and subsequently post-federation Australia, until overturned by the Australian High Court's determination *Mabo v. Queensland (No. 2)* known as the Mabo decision (1992). In this sense, stories, narratives, explanations, text, song, story, voice and meaning 'narrate' whether in an oral or non-oral mode(s) or via voice or non-voice that is transferred to Western language and text (Nicholson et al., 2020).

Narratives embody a responsive relationship and engagement between place + human + animal + time. Landscape designs, or master plans, textual histories, etc., are all dependent upon a 'reading' of place and its resources, its contextualization. Thus, as humans, whether Western (or Wadawurrung, or Indian, or etc.) or Eastern, colonizers or Indigenous, male or female, we 'write' narratives (whether fiction or non-fiction), stories, songs, myths, and we use these narratives to locate ourselves at a certain point in time, place, community and meaning (Nicholson et al., 2020). Potteiger and Purinton (1998) established a set of narrative typologies (when discussing landscape) determining that 'The narratives of the world are numberless'. They can be

> carried by articulated language, spoken or written, fixed or moving images, gestures, and the ordered mixture of all these substances; narrative is present in myth, legend, fable, tale, novella, epic, history, tragedy, drama, comedy, mime, painting, stained glass windows, cinema, comics, news item, conversations, and cultural backgrounds. Caring nothing for the division between good and bad literature, narrative is international, transhistorical, transcultural: it is simply there, like life itself. (Potteiger and Purinton, 1998, p. 5)

Thus, story writing – which is a cultural construction in its own right as alluded to by Barthes and Duisit (1975) – can be skewed and biased in a colonial lens, which is what both Sharoor's and Mullawallah's above quotes echo and demonstrate. As an example, the controversy over Maya Lin's winning design for the Vietnam Veterans Memorial (1981–1982) in Washington DC, which provoked social outrage over her ethnicity as the competition winner, her innovative use of the metaphor of the 'deep wound', but more importantly the competition jury awarding the commission to a non-conventional memorial has resulted in an additional 'mainstream' memorial being erected immediately nearby under foliage. Thus, we are talking not just about the nature and structure of the story, but also the representational form and nuances of the artefact (Berdahl, 1994).

The skewedness in representation of cultural heritage is thus counter-productive both in terms of social inclusivity, and also in economic pursuit, especially in the modern day when the availability of technology is aiding easy access to information and thus its re-casting in influencing alternate information. In particular, as noted by De Bernardi (2019), representing colonial heritage to replace the heritage of First Nations peoples would not attract tourism activities but would instead be repulsive, especially to locals, who also form part of the potential tourist catchment and are concerned with 'authenticity' through their eyes and values (Di Pietro et al., 2018). Therefore, as discussed by Heathwood (2019), heritage certification bodies like UNESCO should fast-track pending proposals by locals to have their heritage listed with the world cultural heritage regime, thus helping in the conservation of those places and also allowing locals to benefit from the associated business opportunities, employment opportunities and other such benefits that cultural heritage attracts, while allowing for increased flexibility for the repurposing of classified heritage structures to encourage 'positive' legacies over 'negative' ones.

Discussion and conclusion

Culture is becoming one of the major contributors to different urban dimensions like economy, society, and environment, and well as a city's identity, place-making and narration. As noted above, in the quest for gaining a competitive advantage, many cities have turned to the exploitation of cultural heritage as a tool for place branding through place identity making which ultimately has contributed to fuelling tourism activities. In return, such cities, as noted by Richards (2018), have benefited from the increasing number of cultural tourists seeking diverse and unique cultural products. Thereby, some economic frontiers, like new startup businesses fashioned to satisfy tourism demands, have emerged, promoting not only revenue bases for urban citizens, but also for municipalities, and creating new job opportunities. Dimelli (2019) notes that in the course of regenerating and conserving different cultural heritage, like historical sites, statues, buildings and landscapes, there is increased environmental awareness and conversations about cultural agendas and policies.

While those benefits are apparent, there remain some areas that need to be strengthened in order to cater for the evolving nature of culture in particular locations and times. In the past, as noted by Heathwood (2019), agencies like UNESCO have been criticized for their approach taken in the certification of heritage sites listed as world heritage. Many critics have argued that there has been unfairness and inequality with heritage related to colonialism, attracting more attention than those of the Indigenous and local communities, as echoed in Jokilehto et al.'s *Filling the Gaps – An Action Plan for the Future* (2005), despite those having been present long before colonial ones. It is for such reasons that Ndoro (1994) was prompted to conclude that in some instances, it is the available institutionalized legislations that allow (and require) the responsible bodies to portray ignorance or indifference when listing the historical heritage, thus highlighting the need for those to be revised.

The aftermaths of such skewed approaches in treating culture have prompted unprecedented upheavals like the recent BLM protests, following the murder of Floyd, but later escalating to targeting statues representing or symbolizing the culture of racism and inequality against minority groups. Such protests could have been avoided if the available conservation regulations were flexible and pragmatic, especially to accommodate the changing urban demographic composition in which people are seen to be enthusiastic about culture. But, as it stands, most cultural conservation regulations are still very strict and non-flexible, and to some extent, have been seen to freeze development – freezing a story like in a preserved museum context – and to reflect a version of the past that does not sit well with those seeking unique cultural experiences. On this, De Bernardi (2019) notes that most new urban populations – both residents and visitors – are interested in authentic cultural products; hence, the available regulations should strive to ensure that the original and authentic heritage that identifies a given place is strengthened, even if this negates inclusivity among the broader population.

One way to ensure that conservation regulations are relaxed to match the modern demands is to ensure that international bodies mandated to draft those regulations and control the conservation and listing of different heritage are not crowded by former colonial empires, as is the case today. With those accused of discrediting local culture in favour of their own still holding the reins of leadership of those bodies, it will take time before the diverse cultures of locals are recognized and allowed to thrive in their own geographies. The current situation will continue to prompt protests like those organized by BLM, and as noted above, such will continue to result in disruptions and social media-informed revolts that are counter-productive to urban resilience, liveability and economic growth.

Based on the above, though there are different approaches and strategies that could be adopted to rectify the shortcomings in regulations, this chapter proposes the pursuit of a balanced equitable viewpoint where cultural heritage, forming a mix of culture and identities, is given an equal platform to thrive. That is, allowing historical heritages to effectively represent and reflect the past of different communities, while also allowing such to be repurposed for new uses that benefit and empower local populations. This includes allowing different communities to exploit their culture as tools for their economic empowerment and as tools for their identity. Doing this will allow cities to eventually break from purist perspectives of heritage conservation where discrimination against other cultures by one that is deemed superior has been the norm. Adopting such a viewpoint would help conserve the already existing culture. Hence, the richness and uniqueness of a built environment would not be compromised, even if this involves some renovations as has been the case with the toppling of select statues and monuments. Through this, culture heritage will be complemented by others before or after their position on historical timelines and their narrative text and imagery. In summary, through this, cities could better manage to brand themselves, and could manage to attract even more economic opportunities, through enhanced tourism activities. There will also be increased social inclusivity as everyone will form part-and-parcel of the overall urban community, unlike today where some are perceived as minorities and have to endure different types of discriminations and inequalities.

References

Alexander, C. (2018). Breaking black: The death of ethnic and racial studies in Britain. *Ethnic and Racial Studies*, *41*, 1034–1054.

Allam, Z. (2020a). Digital urban networks and social media. In Z. Allam (ed.), *Cities and the Digital Revolution: Aligning Technology and Humanity*. Cham: Springer, pp. 61–83.

Allam, Z. (2020b). On culture, technology and global cities. In Z. Allam (ed.), *Cities and the Digital Revolution: Aligning Technology and Humanity*. Cham: Springer, pp. 107–124.

Allam, Z., & Dhunny, Z. A. (2019). On big data, artificial intelligence and smart cities. *Cities*, *89*, 80–91.

Allam, Z., & Newman, P. (2018). Redefining the smart city: Culture, metabolism and governance. *Smart Cities*, *1*, 4–25.

Anon. (1884). The land tenure question. *Kerang Times and Swan Hill Gazette*, 3 June.

Barthes, R., & Duisit, L. (1975). An introduction to the structural analysis of narrative. *New Literary History*, *6*, 237–272.

Berdahl, D. (1994). Voices at the wall: Discourses of self, history and national identity at the Vietnam veterans memorial. *History and Memory*, *6*, 88–124.

Bodkin-Andrews, G., & Carlson, B. (2016). The legacy of racism and indigenous Australian identity within education. *Race Ethnicity and Education*, *19*, 784–807.

Caust, J., & Vecco, M. (2017). Is UNESCO world heritage recognition a blessing or burden? Evidence from developing Asian countries. *Journal of Cultural Heritage*, *27*, 1–9.

CBS (2020). Racist incidents against Africans in China amid coronavirus crackdown spark outcry. https://www.cbsnews.com/news/coronavirus-racism-africans-china/.

Chirikure, S., Manyanga, M., Ndoro, W., & Pwiti, G. (2010). Unfulfilled promises? Heritage management and community participation at some of Africa's cultural heritage sites. *International Journal of Heritage Studies*, *16*, 30–44.

Cotirlea, D. (2014). From place marketing to place branding within the nation branding process: A literature review. Ovidius University Annals: Economic Sciences Series, *14*.

De Bernardi, C. (2019). Authenticity as a compromise: A critical discourse analysis of Sámi tourism websites. *Journal of Heritage Tourism*, *14*, 249–262.

Di Pietro, L., Guglielmetti Mugion, R., & Renzi, M. F. (2018). Heritage and identity: Technology, values and visitor experiences. *Journal of Heritage Tourism, 13*, 97–103.

Dimelli, D. (2019). Modern conservation principles and their application in Mediterranean historic centers: The case of Valletta. *Heritage, 2*, 787–796.

DW (2020). Anti-racism protests spread to Berlin and London. https://www.dw.com/en/anti-racism-protests-spread-to-berlin-and-london/a-53643710.

Furber, M., Burch, A. D. S., & Robles, F. (2020). What happened in the chaotic moments before George Floyd died. https://www.nytimes.com/2020/05/29/us/derek-chauvin-george-floyd-worked-together.html.

Giuffrida, A. (2018). Italy used to be a tolerant country, but now racism is rising. https://www.theguardian.com/world/2018/feb/18/italy-used-to-be-a-tolerant-country-but-now-racism-is-rising.

Heathwood, A. (2019). The unintended consequences of UNESCO world heritage listing. https://theconversation.com/the-unintended-consequences-of-unesco-world-heritage-listing-71047.

Historic England (2019). *Heritage and the Economy 2019*. Historic Environment Forum, November.

Hollmann, C. (2010). The case of inclusive gentrification in Casco Viejo: When long-term investment and community interests aligns. Northeastern University, Boston, Massachusetts, 2010.

IATA (2020). Covid-19 puts over half of 2020 passenger revenues at risk. https://www.iata.org/en/pressroom/pr/2020-04-14-01/.

ICOMOS (1987). *Charter for the Conservation of Historic Towns and Urban Areas*.

ICOMOS (1994). *The Nara Document on Authenticity*. https://www.icomos.org/en/charters-and-texts/179-articles-en-francais/ressources/charters-and-standards/386-the-nara-document-on-authenticity-1994.

Jokilehto, J., Cleere, H., Denyer, S., & Petzet, M. (2005). *The World Heritage List: Filling the Gaps – An Action Plan for the Future*. ICOMOS.

Katz, D., & Braly, K. W. (1935). Racial prejudice and racial stereotypes. *The Journal of Abnormal and Social Psychology, 30*, 175–193.

Landler, M. (2020). In an English city, an early benefactor is now 'a toxic brand'. https://www.nytimes.com/2020/06/14/world/europe/Bristol-Colston-statue-slavery.html.

LeBlanc, P. (2017). Cost of removing confederate monuments in New Orleans: $2.1 million. https://edition.cnn.com/2017/06/12/us/new-orleans-confederate-monument-removal-price-trnd/index.html.

Lewis, R., Arthurs, K., Berker, M., Bishop, A., Louis, T., Slack, J., Stennings, S., Thomas, H., & Thomas, I. (2018). *Cultural Heritage for Inclusive Growth*. London: British Council.

Liddle, C. (2013). Indigenous remains returned home to Wadawurrung people. https://www.sbs.com.au/nitv/article/2013/11/04/indigenous-remains-returned-home-wadawurrung-people.

Mabo v. Queensland (no. 2). AHC, Australian High Court: 1992; Vol. HCS 23.

Markwick, A., Ansari, Z., Clinch, D., & McNeil, J. (2019). Experiences of racism among aboriginal and Torres Strait islander adults living in the Australian state of Victoria: A cross-sectional population-based study. *BMC Public Health, 19*, 309.

Ndoro, W. (1994). The preservation and presentation of great Zimbabwe. *Antiquity, 68*.

NEA (2019). Latest data shows increase to US economy from arts and cultural sector. https://www.arts.gov/news/2019/latest-data-shows-increase-us-economy-arts-and-cultural-sector.

News18 (2020). Read: Shashi Tharoor's full speech asking UK to pay India for 200 years of its colonial rule. https://www.news18.com/news/india/read-shashi-tharoors-full -speech-asking-uk-to-pay-india-for-200-years-of-its-colonial-rule-1024821.html.

Nicholson, M., Romanis, G., Paton, I., Jones, D. S., Gerritsen, K., & Powell, G. (2020). 'Unnamed as yet': Putting Wadawurrung meaning into the north gardens landscape of Ballarat. *UNESCO Observatory E-Journal Multi-disciplinary Research in the Arts*, 6.

Nocca, F. (2017). The role of cultural heritage in sustainable development: Multidimensional indicators as decision-making tool. *Sustainability, 9*, 1–28.

OECD (2020). Tourism policy responses to the coronavirus (Covid-19). https://read .oecd-ilibrary.org/view/?ref=124_124984-7uf8nm95se&title=Covid-19_Tourism _Policy_Responses.

Pendleton, M. B. (2019). Memorializing men of the lost cause: Public opinion of confederate monuments in Virginia 1900–present. Master's thesis, James Madison University.

Potteiger, M., & Purinton, J. (1998). *Landscape Narratives: Design Practices for Telling Stories*. Hoboken, NJ: Wiley.

Pwiti, G., & Ndoro, W. (1999). The legacy of colonialism: Perceptions of the cultural heritage in southern Africa, with special reference to Zimbabwe. *The African Archaeological Review, 16*, 143–153.

Race, M., & Briant, N. (2020). Cecil Rhodes: Protesters demand Oxford statue removal. https://www.bbc.com/news/uk-england-oxfordshire-52975687.

Richards, G. (2018). Cultural tourism: A review of recent research and trends. *Journal of Hospitality and Tourism Management, 36*, 12–21.

Sams, J. (2020). Riots in wake of Floyd's death could become mostly civil disorder for insurers. https://www.insurancejournal.com/news/national/2020/06/03/570824 .htm.

Sanchez, J. P. (2017). How the Parthenon lost its marbles. https:// www .nationalgeographic .com/ history/ magazine/ 2017/ 03 -04/ parthenon -sculptures -british-museum-controversy/.

Starrenburg, S. (2018). Cultural heritage protection: A truly 'global' legal problem? *Völkerrechtsblog*.

Stiem, T. (2018). Statue wars: What should we do with troublesome monuments. https://www.theguardian.com/cities/2018/sep/26/statue-wars-what-should-we-do -with-troublesome-monuments.

Thomson, G., & Newman, P. (2018). Urban fabrics and urban metabolism: From sustainable to regenerative cities. *Resources, Conservation and Recycling, 132*, 218–229.

UNESCO (2020). Socio-economic impacts of world heritage listing. https://whc.unesco .org/en/socio-economic-impacts.

UNWTO (2020). International tourism growth continues to outpace the global economy. https:// www .unwto .org/ international -tourism -growth -continues -to -outpace-the-economy.

van Sterkenburg, J., Peeters, R., & van Amsterdam, N. (2019). Everyday racism and con- structions of racial/ethnic difference in and through football talk. *European Journal of Cultural Studies, 22*, 195–212.

Wang, B., Dane, G. Z., & de Vries, B. (2018). Increasing awareness for urban cul- tural heritage based on 3D narrative system. *The International Archives of the Photogrammetry, Remote Sensing and Spatial Information Science*, Vol. XLII-4/W10, pp. 215–221. Delft, The Netherlands.

Wright, W. (2020). Cities want to remove toxic monuments. But who will take them? https://www.nytimes.com/2020/06/18/us/confederate-statues-monuments-removal .html.

14 Toward a new tourism paradigm

Geoffrey Godbey and Galen Godbey

The end of endless tourism

Tourism defined as anyone going anywhere at any time to do anything they want during leisure has been rendered obsolete. The World Tourism Organization, in 2019, blithely predicted the growth of world tourism would continue at 4 percent in 2020:

> 1.5 billion international tourist arrivals were recorded in 2019, globally. A 4% increase on the previous year which is also forecast for 2020, confirming tourism as a leading and resilient economic sector, especially in view of current uncertainties. By the same token, this calls for such growth to be managed responsibly so as to best seize the opportunities tourism can generate for communities around the world. (WTO, 2019)

Such predictions no longer make sense. Why? The world is heating up, drying out, burning up and drowning at rapidly increasing rates. It was over 100 degrees Fahrenheit in Siberia in 2020, the hottest temperature ever recorded. The year 2023 was the hottest since records began. A worldwide pandemic, COVID-19, has produced bans on public gatherings, the massive shutdown of bars and restaurants, and major constraints to visiting most tourism sites. The two countries which generate the most outbound international tourists, China and the United States, were hit the hardest. In effect, tourism, in which a large number of strangers from diverse locations travel to a destination in the confined spaces of planes, cars, trains, and buses, stay in densely populated living quarters, travel in confined spaces while at the destination, dine and drink in cramped conditions and see tourist sites in which they are often literally shoulder to shoulder, is the perfect vector to promote COVID-19 and many other communicable diseases. Even in remote wilderness sites, people huddle together in a small fraction of the area. In cities, tourist districts such as Amsterdam's red-light district (whose future is the subject of growing controversy; Holligan, 2023) or Hangzhou's West Lake area draw huge numbers of tourists to densely populated areas. Epidemiologists make it clear that more epidemics will follow, often from animal–human interactions as humans invade the space in which wild animals live. The internationally known strategic consultant, Ian Bremmer, in his 2022 book *The Power of Crisis* discusses "The Next Pandemic" as a given that governments and corporations need to prepare for – but may not: COVID "wasn't by itself frightening enough to make us forge a new system of international cooperation or, even at home, force Republicans and Democrats to work together" (Bremmer, 2022, p. 73).

It is not only the virus which is reshaping and limiting tourism: rapidly intensifying global warming and climate change have caused limitations and uncertainties for tourism. Drought and heat are increasingly putting an end to current sites for snow-skiing, wine-making and winery tours, outdoor tennis tournaments, and a host of festivals. Many water-based tourist attractions have either insufficient or no water. Some tourist areas, such as Miami Florida, have water in the streets from King Tides, even on sunny days. Coastal waters in many countries are so hot that beachgoers cannot even lie on the sand and the water is like taking a bath.

Additionally, increasing conflict, ranging from the Russian invasion of Ukraine to the fears of a Chinese assault on Taiwan (chip maker to the world), and anti-Muslim riots and the subversion of democracy in India by the BJP pro-Hindu government discourage people from traveling in those regions.

In light of the mammoth problems of environment and disease, and increasingly unstable governments and public safety in many countries, tourism may be forced to move, as its ideal, from "sustainable" to "regenerative." A key feature of regenerative tourism is that it defines growth and success differently from traditional models.

> Regenerative tourism defines success as *more net benefit* (after costs have been accounted for, all waste eliminated, and all damage restored), and more personal and institutional capacity to adapt, be resilient, creative, collaborative etc., while providing a greater and richer sense of meaning for guests and hosts. (Pollock, 2019)

There can be no such thing as a sustainable business within a system which is, itself, unsustainable. Tourism, along with many other composite industries, does not recognize the externalities (unintended consequences) of its existence. Thus, for example, the operation of cruise lines rarely recognizes or deals with the consequences of emptying their garbage at sea and using fuel that is a horrible pollutant.

Any movement toward regenerative tourism will need to throw its political weight behind governmental and corporate efforts to find solutions to energy issues.

Sustainable travel, let alone regenerative travel, will still have to find solutions to the carbon emissions produced by air travel. Until the economy recovers, there's likely to be less travel, more local travel, or slower travel by car, train, bike or foot. This moment of reflection, say proponents, is where regeneration begins (Christoff, 2020). For example, the US economy has come back strongly from the COVID period, and consumer demand for travel has exploded in 2023. These developments unfortunately have contributed to increased, rather than reduced, emissions during 2022.

Technological change and the speed with which it occurs will be pivotal in shaping tourism, a form of behavior which always involves moving bodies through space.

More contingent tourism

The previously described factors mean tourism will become less certain, unable to be planned with certainty far in advance, although contingent plans will be made from a greater information base. The golf tournament trip will happen if the course does not become so hot that spectators can't be outside. The visit to the city square in Krakow, Poland will happen if there is not torrential rain. Visits to a Spanish winery may depend on fire and heat conditions, whether a pandemic is keeping the tasting rooms closed, or whether grapes can still be grown in the area. The tourist and those who serve tourists will need to become much more flexible, taking a kind of "if this, then that" attitude and policy. Cancellation policies of airlines, hotels and tourist attractions will become even more important. Travel insurance will also become more important – if it remains available.

More contingent tourism may also affect the kind of tourist experience one has. While MacCannell (1973) saw tourism as a progression, for many, from visiting the "front region" of a tourist area, which was staged to look like the authentic site but was not, to slowly seeking the "back region" where the authentic site was revealed. This process, however, generally took several visits and stability to happen. When tourism opportunities become less predictable, the opportunities for getting out of the front region may be less and less. A first trip to Great Britain is usually to London, seeing the Tower of London,

Buckingham Palace, etc. If one could go back several times on a predictable basis, one might end up in villages in the Yorkshire Dales or Liverpool. Desire to see the back region, however, is increasing, and many tourists try to experience it on their first visit.

A key issue in the future of tourism is whether "mass" tourism can return as the most common and profitable form of tourism. Paid holidays, increasing leisure time and the development of railroads and standardized time keeping helped bring about "mass tourism" (Bramwell, 2004). More recently, mass tourism has also increasingly depended on auto travel, airlines, online booking, chain hotels and motels, and the development of segregated tourism districts within cities and countryside alike. It has also become dependent on the development of tourist "attractions" such as Disney World, which exist only to attract tourists. As previously mentioned, MacCannell (1973) and others have observed that such developments serve as the "front region" of tourism which, in many ways, keep tourists from understanding the "back region" of an area where different ways of living unfold.

All "mass" tourism has one thing in common – large numbers of tourists traveling in close proximity, eating together, visiting sites crowded with other tourists, and behaving in common ways. This form of tourism accounts for most of the tourism revenue in the world!

> It is inarguably the most popular form of tourism. But most responsible travel experts consider it a shallow, exploitative, and unsustainable form of travel, consuming huge amounts of resources while giving little back to the local community. (Bramwell, p. 3)

Mass tourism also likely contributes more to environmental problems and is least likely to be functional in periods of epidemics or pandemics. Where mass tourism is no longer possible or functional, much of the profit may be sucked out of tourism.

Uncertainty could produce travel itineraries with fewer places on the list and longer stays. Rather than risking going from a main arrival destination to many other areas, tourists may stay hunkered down in the area in which they originally arrived. They may also stay longer if their hotel, motel, camper van or Airbnb lodging is secure. In many tourism cities, local government is re-claiming apartments used by tourists, now empty, to deal with a housing shortage. Capacity for tourist lodging may diminish. Also, if cruise liners, which have been extremely popular, continue to exist, they may have to change the practice of stopping at many ports for short periods of time.

Uncertainty may also drive a final nail in the coffin of "time sharing." A time-share is a vacation property arrangement that lets you share the property cost with others in order to guarantee time at the property, usually for many years. As the environment becomes less predictable, committing to a long-term arrangement at the same property, perhaps on a beach or in a desert area, may become riskier, and, therefore, less attractive.

Vacation home ownership and the cycle of involvement with them may also become more contingent. If the vacation home is in an area that is relatively stable from the standpoint of climate and disease, such homeowners may be tempted to move to them full time. If it is in an area which becomes riskier, the temptation to sell immediately may increase. Some older research shows that vacation homes are used by families with children and as the children grow up and lose interest in accompanying their parents to such places, the parents either sell the vacation home or begin to think about it becoming their primary residence or using it more frequently as they near retirement (Godbey and Bevins, 1987). This long-term cycle of involvement may be shortened by disease, climate issues or migration as a result of climate issues.

More complex tourism

Tourism will become more complex, requiring more information gathered by the would-be traveler, and more monitoring in real time: Have dust storms become more severe? Is there an outbreak of a disease? Is there enough water in the lake for our boat? Are there food riots or other civil disturbances created by the widespread hunger climate crisis or wars (e.g., Ukraine)?

Part of the increased complexity may be the preparation necessary for most tourism experiences. Part of that preparation will be the increased need for insurance. Insurance that an international flight will fly. Insurance for vacation homes in wooded areas, on the ocean front, or in areas experiencing more extreme heat. Insurance that an ocean cruise will take place or that a conference scheduled to be held in New Orleans or Shanghai will take place, if these cities are not largely under water within a decade or two. Such insurance has become both costlier and, sometimes, simply unavailable.

Similarly, the tourist experience will become more complex as would-be tourists are forced to document their health status, undergo vaccinations reflecting the needs of the tourist destination, and otherwise submit to forms of screening not previously undertaken. Entrance of tourists into many countries has become more highly regulated and complex.

Some of this complexity will be mitigated by the use of face and fingerprint recognition. Companies will form to smooth the way for more complex travel and may lead to a kind of reinvention of travel agents. Such agents will basically be selling insider knowledge rather than airline or train tickets. These agents may be human or AI.

More customized tourism

One aspect of more customized tourism is to divide the "mass" tourism experience into individual parts. In regard to travel, for example, self-driving automobiles, smart cars, more sophisticated GPS devices, passenger "pods" for buses, trains and maybe even airplanes, high speed trains and other innovations may be used to transport tourists as well as recreation vans (RVs). Closer to home, tourist trips are already the norm and these travel trends make such short-haul tourism more easily individualized.

In many countries), high speed trains are replacing air travel for shorter hauls. There is increasing evidence that tourists find flying to be a painful, difficult and unpredictable experience. In one survey, only 10 percent of respondents said they would miss flying on an airplane! (Robinson, 2020).

Urban outdoor areas may become more popular as city streets are "customized" for walking, bicycling and outdoor dining and entertainment. Reclaiming streets for tourism purposes, such as festivals, dining and drinking, and entertainment is occurring in many countries. Reclaiming the streets will allow not only for social distancing but is a potentially effective way to decrease the density of tourists in a given area. This will require, in many cases, benches and chairs for sitting, the creation of shade, and outdoor bathrooms and water sources. Streets may be increasingly categorized as follows:

- Laneways –very narrow and limited to 4 mph. Pedestrians would feel comfortable strolling or lingering here.
- Accessways – slightly wider and have a speed limit of 14 mph; here, cyclists can travel naturally, without being hemmed into "safe zones," since most of the space on that type of street is dedicated to cyclists' use.
- Transitways – wider still. They allow for all modes, except cars, and always give priority to public transit through dedicated lanes and signal priority.

- Boulevards – consistent with "complete streets" principles, these streets allow for all modes of transportation, including cars. They include barriers and have a speed limit of 25 mph (Ng, 2019).

The pandemic afforded an opportunity to see what life is like without crowds, and many tourism experts wonder if it will lead to durable changes. This may involve figuring out how to travel while the pandemic exists, visiting fewer locations for longer periods of time, choosing destinations closer to home, booking entire houses via Airbnb, rather than hotel rooms (to limit viral exposure), and putting premiums on nature and space. More tourists are opting to travel to coastal, rural and mountain destinations, given that remoteness means less risk.

Tourists will likely take fewer trips, but for longer periods of time. The customization of tourism may also increase from different financial costs depending on what risks the tourist is willing to take. Want your hotel room super disinfected? Twenty percent surcharge. Willing to visit a portion of Egypt which has higher levels of drought and disease? Save 50 percent.

Finally, the fate of tourism may be customized among nations and regions, with some having a thriving industry and others excluded.

> Airlines and hoteliers hope nascent "travel bubbles" – small groups of countries reopening borders only among themselves – and "green lanes" for pre-screened travelers, such as those with antibodies showing immunity to COVID-19, will allow a gradual reopening. They also hope that roughly normal travel will then resume next year. More likely is that a new system of interlocking safe zones will operate for the foreseeable future, or at least until a vaccine is widely deployed. Travel will normalize more quickly in safe zones that coped well with COVID-19, such as South Korea, or between Germany and Greece. But in poorer developing countries struggling to manage the pandemic, such as India or Indonesia, any recovery will be painfully slow. (Fallows et al., 2020)

The unfolding future of tourism

As the preceding text has indicated, the tourism industry proved highly vulnerable to the COVID pandemic and the general economic havoc that the virus wreaked upon national economies. At the start of the pandemic, the World Travel and Tourism Council projected that well over 100 million jobs and revenues approximating $3.4 trillion would be lost from the pandemic. In the US, airlines and other parts of the industry received help from national governments and private sources. Carnival Cruise Line took eight of its ships out of service. In many tourist destinations, vaccine distribution for new varieties of disease may be slow – if available at all.

While pent up demand is providing airlines with huge numbers of passengers at present, airlines should consider their economic and political positions very carefully for the future. A few transportation and tourism companies may be successful in securing bailout capital when future pandemics hit, but this is no long-term solution. Indeed, airlines that take government loans could become targets for takeovers as they struggle with higher operating costs, lower demand due to lingering worries about the virus, and the need to repay the loans. Outside the US, the situation was worse in many countries: Avianca and Aero Mexico declared bankruptcies early in the COVID crisis (Sorkin, 2020). To the extent that government money is involved, there could be pressure to spend it on domestic tourism rather than international. If tourism retreats to serving elites primarily (especially older wealthy people), serious social resentment against international tourism may develop.

A new paradigm

Our argument, once again, is that the key descriptors of the tourist experience for the next five to ten years will be contingent, customized, costly, complex, and rarer. The industry has had a tremendous shock, to be sure; however, the truly crucial question is what happens after COVID? The COVID crisis staggered the industry; however, the potential knockout blow could be administered by the climate crisis, if the industry does not respond with foresight and active participation in the regenerative coalition that is already forming within the industry and outside it.

The following paragraphs are highly speculative. We assume, optimistically, that humans will try to save themselves by saving their heretofore nurturing planet, and that governments and business sectors can develop discipline and focus on this vital issue. We argue a scenario and a strategy aimed at placing the tourism industry in the center of the broad political coalition of organizations that will be necessary, not only to save tourism through its transformation, but, far more importantly, to slow down and begin to reverse the climate crisis that threatens the viability of current and future generations. The tourist industry, big as it is, is not strong enough by itself to restore the old "normal." It needs partners to secure the help it needs to redefine itself into a regenerative force for nature and part of the glue that can hold our increasingly fragile and interdependent world together.

Shaping a new model for the industry

Markets are not naturally occurring phenomena. Governments create markets and make and enforce the rules. Especially in times of crisis, governments play a critical, often determinative role in outcomes: traditional industry lobbying loses its effectiveness when confronted by radically dangerous situations.

It should be abundantly clear by now that we are moving into a long period of increasingly dangerous climate catastrophes. The scale of the threat will render traditional lobbying techniques less effective. The selection of political leaders and government office holders will assume the greatest possible importance; indeed, the election of Joe Biden in the 2020 US Presidential election advanced American policy toward climate and environment, as well as COVID-19. Most governments have provisions for states of emergency, and we are likely to see such provisions activated as climate refugees around the world begin to be counted in the tens of millions instead of tens of thousands. Great mischief can be perpetrated under the guise of managing emergencies; nonetheless, the relatively slow pace of study commissions and legislative activity suggests that emergency declarations will become more common. To support a habitable environment, governments will have to struggle with the costs and politics of redesigning whole economies, including agriculture and manufacturing; devising new systems for managing natural resources, especially water, and for relocating significant portions of their populations. Given the gigantic scale of these problems and processes, helping tourism finishes last, even with its labor intensiveness.

The sobering reality is that most of the governments of the world have not yet found the courage to tax and mobilize themselves and their people at a scale likely to stop and begin to reverse the crisis. The climate issue is in doubt, and there are no guarantees that Homo sapiens, this heretofore stupendously successful species, will save itself.

The earth does not need us.

In short, tourism has a *limited* future unless there are places worth going to and unless people have confidence that the opportunity cost of travel is not too great. It is an industry in need of a new paradigm, one that will permit the rebranding of tourism as an asset in the fight for a world worth seeing and experiencing and contributing to. The tourist industry can contribute much, even in our weakened state, to the previously mentioned coalition that is beginning to form in response to the climate crisis. The goal, of course, is not to get back to what was an unsustainable industry model: it must be to invent a new model which places us squarely on the side of reducing, not contributing to, this emergent, existential threat.

Industry leaders, in concert with governments, NGOs, and private investors, must use the next few years to rethink the assumptions behind and effects of current industry practices. We must face up to the fact that an industry which employs millions of people across the globe and until very recently entailed approximately 10 percent of global GDP, will not be regarded as economically or politically essential, as the brutal effects of climate crisis become unavoidably obvious.

Never have foresight, leadership, and finding new ways to manage organizations and their processes and external relationships been more important. The long-term, most fundamental problem for the tourism industry, as threatening as COVID is, is not the virus. While we may experience more deadly pandemics in the future, the existential threat to the industry, and to civilization itself, is the climate crisis. Pandemics, as terrible as they are, eventually are brought under control or die out.

As merciless as the pandemic has been so far, the campaign to reverse global warming and other environmental depredations will require not just bailouts and "fixes." There is no Band-Aid big enough to solve the problems that lie ahead. It will require a whole new paradigm for tourism, one that goes beyond "sustainable" tourism.

Sustainable tourism is a low bar, and inadequate for the potential extinctions and mortal scale of climate crisis. Sustainable tourism is to climate crisis and the maintenance of biodiversity what "corporate social responsibility" is to the behavior of business corporations: more than lip service, but grossly inadequate for the future. The undeniable reality is that the tourist industry is, and is seen to be, one of the sources of climate crisis. Just as there is growing consensus that the American business corporation, with its Milton Friedman ideology of shareholder capitalism and exploitation of workers, must be, and is beginning to be, reinvented (think B Corporations); just as regenerative agriculture is beginning the hard journey from margin to mainstream, the tourism industry must think and act anew – quickly.

The goal must be to rapidly and radically reduce CO_2 and methane emissions and to leave tourist destinations – including the people who live there – better than we found them. As governments, corporations, and other organizations mobilize to deal with the climate crisis, tourism must show that it is an asset in the fight for a livable planet. In the upcoming long and apocalyptic struggle to slow and then reverse the climate crisis, the tourist industry must prove itself worthy of a favorable regulatory environment and investment by both the private sector and governments. We must show that tourism can help the earth regenerate itself. This is not an option: it is the only strategy available for the long-term future of the industry.

Inventing the new paradigm

Bill Reed, an architect and principal of Regenesis Group, a design firm in Massachusetts and New Mexico that has been practicing regenerative design, including tourism projects, since 1995, is an advocate for regenerative tourism. He views efforts like increasing fuel efficiency and reducing energy use as helpful, but by no means adequate to the scale of the issues involved: they simply offer "a slower way to die." He explains that "Regeneration is about restoring and then regenerating the capability to live in a new relationship (with nature) in an ongoing way" (Christoff, 2020).

Intrepid Travel, which leads small tour group itineraries, has been carbon neutral for the past decade, and seeks to cover more than 100 percent of its carbon footprint. If the industry as a whole can help reverse the poisoning of our environment, it will create a basis for blending tourism with economic development, foreign policy and diplomatic goals, and job creation – all things that will improve the industry's standing in the halls of power, both corporate and public (Christoff, 2020).

Regenerative tourism certainly does seek to reduce the carbon involved in tourism-related transportation, housing, interactions of tourists with local people, and at tourist sites themselves; however, its advocates see it as a broader, values-based orientation toward life, and as a way of promoting international relationships that support both cultural understanding and environmental vigor. It attracts architects and designers from the world of LEED and green design; from the world of bottom-up economic and social development; from individuals and firms who want to create "an economy of meaning," and not just increase numbers of dollars and visitors; from people who are fighting to relieve saturated tourist sites and promote less well known, but wonderful places; from people who favor stakeholder economies, rather than shareholder economies; and from the growing number of economists and social critics who refuse to use GDP as a proxy measure for national well-being (Pilling, 2018). From an organizational point of view, regenerative strategies and practices can be applied by both for-profit and non-profit organizations, and they are wholly consistent with the increasingly relevant "B corporation" concept of making profits to achieve well-defined societal or global goals.

Leading organizations through a transformative process will be an unprecedented challenge. There is strong resistance from those who cling to the belief that the virus has gone away (not true!) and that we can now return to pre-pandemic normalcy. Changing and getting stakeholder buy-in on organizational visions, missions, cultures, policies and recruitment practices is difficult and time-consuming. Great foresight, different leadership qualities, and new ways of managing resources will be required. There will be disruption and setbacks as the new model emerges and is adapted to specific contexts. Patience and resiliency will be necessary as we finish moving through the long stage of denial and into the shorter period of ambiguity, ambivalence, and experimentation, a process that can yield "critical incidents" that display the logic of a new model and accelerate its adoption.

Collaboration and inclusiveness will become the new bywords for people at all levels and in all roles of tourism companies – collaboration with other tourism organizations and representatives of other industries that are beginning to pursue regenerative models. Major efforts need to be made to engage the people who live near tourist sites, as the "foreign compound model" of tourist resorts is replaced by a model of collaboration, revenue-sharing, and joint planning with local leaders and everyday people. Several years ago, One Seed Expeditions started giving 10 percent of its revenue to local NGOs, which in turn give the money to local entrepreneurs in the form of micro loans (Christoff, 2020).

Tourists themselves will need to be encouraged to see the new model as a good and necessary thing – without such buy-in, the industry will be lost. On the other hand, tourism that reduces carbon and improves relations with other countries could radically improve support from policy makers and from those financial institutions that see the need for pursuing a circular economy that seriously reduces waste and carbon release. Moreover, regenerative strategies can add a sense of purpose and meaning for those who see their tourist adventures as creating hope for the planet's future.

Foresight, leadership and management

It is encouraging to see important tourism companies and associations beginning to work together to flesh out and propagate the regenerative model. Six non-profits combined several years ago to form the Future of Tourism Coalition. These players have agreed to thirteen principles of regenerative travel, and numerous travel groups have already embraced these principles. The Regenerative Travel booking agency vets prospective member tourist organizations on carbon usage, employee well-being, using food from local sources, and connecting visitors with locals (Christoff, 2020). Thus far, 45 organizations have passed muster.

National tourist board and agencies are rethinking the purposes, value and goals of tourism: Hawaii, now struggling to recover from devastating fires caused by climate change, has historically been overrun with surf and sun worshippers. Prior to the start of the pandemic, support was growing within the islands' tourist circles to connect visitors with Hawaii's history, traditions, and culture. Tourism New Zealand has reconsidered its indicators of success, realizing that economic impact is not enough: social impact, public health, and the natural environment deserve more attention.

These are modest beginnings; however, the spirit behind these initial steps is consistent with emerging forces in the wider world. More and more economists and political leaders are seeking supplements to or replacements for GDP as a way of measuring an economy. As David Pilling of London's *Financial Times* puts it, "If GDP were a person, it would be indifferent, blind even, to morality. It measures production of whatever kind, good or bad. GDP likes pollution, particularly if you have to spend money cleaning it up" (Pilling, 2018, p. 3).

GDP has a bias for growth, but all growth is not progress toward a better world. Again, Pilling: "If environmentalists are right, the pursuit of growth without end could even threaten the very existence of humanity, ransacking our biodiversity and driving us to unsustainable levels of consumption and CO_2 emission that wreck the very planet on which our wealth depends. Only in economics is endless expansion seen as a virtue. In biology, it is called cancer" (Pilling, 2018, p. 13).

Tourism in Hawaii, Greece and other areas of the world raked in huge amounts of revenue pre-COVID, contributing much to state and national GDP. But there is a revolt brewing against the tourist industry in that state, and one can only wonder how August 2023's firestorm will affect thinking about the islands' future in general and touristic strategies in particular. Native Hawaiians increasingly believe that the state is being run for the tourist industry and that the industry has contributed to the weakening of native culture and values. There is pressure to refocus tourism to take culture and environment more seriously (Christoff, 2020). Purpose, values, and meaning are just as important to the future of the industry as are revenues. Indeed, there will be less revenue unless all stakeholders – workers, people who neighbor tourist sites, investors (both private and governmental) – can derive satisfaction from tourist activities that leave the long-abused earth and the people of host states or nations better off.

Simon Sinek, in his book *Start with Why*, shows a strong link between productivity and workers' understanding of the vision, mission, and strategies of their organization – why they are doing what they are doing. The more inspiring the goals, the greater the productivity (Sinek, 2009, p. 15). Daniel Pink, in his book *Drive*, has shown that workers need more than good wages to be productive (Pink, 2009, pp. 85–152). Obviously, compensation matters to worker behavior; however, as workers get any kind of financial security or even just predictability, additional money does not increase productivity. In addition to fair wages, workers want three things: a sense of mastery in their work – they want training so that they can be good at what they do; they want autonomy, or at least a voice in deciding what gets done, when it gets done, how it gets done; and they want a sense of purpose – what difference does their job or their company make in the wider world?

Regenerative tourism, even in its tender beginnings, seems to understand these insights and embody these values. Yes, it is about CO_2 reduction, but that goal is wrapped inside a humanistic and biological complex of insight and values that matter greatly: stopping the poisoning of the environment, while debasing and demoralizing humanity, would be a partial victory, at best.

Regenerative tourism as a strategy requires a huge commitment to collaborative leadership models and power sharing with workers, other tourist organizations, and people who live in or near tourist sites. It will also require what Simon Sinek calls an "infinite mindset." Sinek's book *The Infinite Game* (2019) is a critique of Milton Friedman's view that companies, while subject to law, have no responsibility except to their shareholders: other individuals and organizations with a substantial, even compelling interest in the success of the firm simply should not count in the decisions of the CEO and Board. This view has contributed to profit maximization, short-term thinking, and social dislocation in virtually all industries and society at large during the past forty years (Stiglitz, 2019, pp. 314–315).

Sinek sees this as a fundamental misunderstanding of how business works. Although sports and military metaphors are often applied to business competition, business is not like a game. It has no beginning and end, and rules are much more limited and ambiguous. If your company has outplayed its competition for ten years, OK. But the point is not to win a decade: it is to develop an infinite mindset and stay in business for as long as you can. Or, as Warren Buffett puts it, invest in companies that are built to last (Sinek, 2019, p. 208).

Sinek captures the business realities that contribute to environmental degradation that will constrain, if not preclude, the reinvention of tourism: "This is the great irony. The defenders of finite-minded capitalism act in a way that actually imperils the survival of the very companies from which they aim to profit. It's as if they have decided that the best way to get the most cherries is to chop down the tree" (Sinek, 2019, p. 79).

Effective leaders in the development of a post-COVID, post-GDP, *post-climate change denial* tourism industry will need an inclusive, infinite mindset that focuses upon generations to come, instead of the next quarterly report.

References

Bramwell, B. (2004). Mass tourism, diversification and sustainability in Southern Europe's coastal regions. In B. Bramwell (ed.), *Coastal Mass Tourism: Diversification and Sustainable Development in Southern Europe* (pp. 1–31). Clevedon: Channel View.

Bremmer, I. (2022). *The Power of Crisis*. New York: Simon & Schuster.

Christoff, J. (2020). Survey shows pent-up demand for travel continues to build among Americans. https://www.travelpulse.com/news/features/survey-shows-pent-up-demand-for-travel-continues-to-build-among-americans.

Fallows, J., Wadhwa, V., Iver, P., Potts, R., Beckr, E., Crabtree, J., & de Juniac, A. (2020). Tourism after the corona virus pandemic. *Foreign Policy*. https://foreignpolicy.com/2020/06/13/travel-tourism-coronavirus-pandemic-future.

Godbey, G. C., & Bevins, M. (1987). The life cycle of second home ownership: A case study. *Journal of Travel Research*, 25(3), 18–22.

Holligan, A. (2023). Amsterdam launches stay away ad campaign targeting young British men. *BBC News*, March 29. https:// www .bbc .com/ news/ world -europe -65107405.

MacCannell, D. (1973). Staged authenticity: Arrangements of social space in tourist settings. *American Journal of Sociology*, 79(3), 589–603.

Ng, W. (2019). Four principles for the future of city streets. https:// medium .com/ sidewalk-talk/street-design-principles-fe35106e0f92.

Pilling, D. (2018). *The Growth Delusion: Wealth, Poverty, and the Well-Being of Nations*. New York: Tim Duggan Books.

Pink, D. (2009). *Drive: The Surprising Truth About What Motivates Us*. New York: Riverhead Books.

Pollock, A. (2019). Regenerative tourism: The natural maturation of sustainability. *Activate the Future*. https://medium.com/activate-the-future/regenerative-tourism-the-natural-maturation-of-sustainability-26e6507d0fcb.

Robinson, A. (2020). Future transportation technologies that will change transportation (and the trucking industry) forever. *Cerasis*. https://cerasis.com/transportation-technologies/.

Sinek, S. (2009). *Start with Why*. New York: Portfolio Penguin.

Sinek, S. (2019). *The Infinite Game*. New York: Portfolio Penguin.

Sorkin, A. R. (2020). Deal book/business and policy. *New York Times*, September 15.

Stiglitz, J. E. (2019). *People, Power, and Profits: Progressive Capitalism for an Age of Discontent*. New York: W. W. Norton and Company.

World Tourism Organization (2019). International tourism growth continues to outpace the global economy. http://UNWTO.ORG/.

Index